Alberto Fortis, Anna Riggs Miller

Letters from Italy

Describing the Manners, Customs, Antiquities, Paintings, etc. Vol. 3

Alberto Fortis, Anna Riggs Miller

Letters from Italy
Describing the Manners, Customs, Antiquities, Paintings, etc. Vol. 3

ISBN/EAN: 9783744689243

Printed in Europe, USA, Canada, Australia, Japan

Cover: Foto ©Thomas Meinert / pixelio.de

More available books at www.hansebooks.com

LETTERS

FROM

ITALY,

DESCRIBING THE

Manners, Customs, Antiquities, Paintings,
&c. of that Country,

In the Years MDCCLXX and MDCCLXXI,

TO

A FRIEND residing in FRANCE,

By an ENGLISH WOMAN.

VOL. III.

LONDON:

PRINTED FOR EDWARD AND CHARLES DILLY,
MDCCLXXVI.

LETTER XLI.

Rome, April 4th, 1771.

AT length the functions are finished; and now I may avail myself of the indulgence of finning for three hundred years to come, having been in St. Peter's church every day during the *Santa Setti-mana*; but it is to be apprehended the faint might cavil at a continuance in the error of herefy. However, there is a Bri-tifh lady here, a native of Caledonia, who has renounced her *proteftant errors*, embraced the tenets of the old lady at Rome, and married a Roman marquis. She was fo obliging as to lend the private theatre in her palace to the Englifh, who gave

VOL. III.   B   therein

therein a fine concert and collation; many of the nobility of Rome were prefent, and the Pope would have allowed the Englifh to have danced, but they, from delicacy, as the permiffion extended no farther than to them as ftrangers, would not take advantage of his politenefs. I have ftrayed from the Functions, which ought, in order, to have taken place of this amufement.

Functions. .I fhall begin with thofe of Palm-funday, and proceed to mention the moft remarkable during the *Santa, Settimana.* The ceremonies of Palm-funday commence in the chapel at Monte Cavallo, where the Pope bleffes the palms, and hears mafs. Two forts of cardinals are drawn up on each fide of the altar; who are diftinguifhed by the appellations of cardinal priefts and cardinal deacons; their veftments violet colour, ornamented with ermine and lace. The ecclefiaftics, their train-bearers, are feated at their feet. Juft as the

the Function is about to begin, the cardinals take off their furrs and outward
drapery, and put on other veſtments embroidered with gold, and adorn their heads
with mitres made of ſilver tabby ; then
they riſe and approach his Holineſs, from
whoſe hands they receive the palms; which,
however, are not palm branches; but ſprigs
of box, as there are no palm-trees, to be
had. After ſeveral more ceremonies of riſ-
ing up, ſitting down, bowing, kneeling,
ſtooping, ſtanding, &c. &c. the proceſſion
begins; penitents, prelates, cardinals; &c;
proceed, in due order of march, round the
firſt great falloon of the palace (Monte
Cavallo); then they reaſſume their violet
and furr drapery, and aſſiſt at the maſs
which is ſung. The paſſion is recited by
two eccleſiaſtics ; one narrates the words
and accuſation of Jeſus Chriſt from the
Evangeliſts, and the other anſwers for our
bleſſed Saviour ; the clamours and uproar

of

of the Jews is imitated by the clergy.
—After the cardinal, dean, and others
have been complimented with incenfe, they
embrace and falute each other, in imitation of the Kifs of Charity. A moft curious proceffion makes part of this Function : the ftreets of Rome, through which
it is to pafs, are ftrewed with fand; and
the pontiff, accompanied by the cardinals,
makes a kind of public entry, in imitation
of our Saviour's, into Jerufalem, mounted
on mules, as is his Holinefs; they bear
branches of box-tree in their hands, and
proceed, in the moft ridiculous manner
that can be imagined, to the Pantheon:
Vain were the attempt to defcribe the horfe-
manfhip difplayed upon this occafion :—the
obftinacy of the mules ;—their kicking and
curvetting ;— the embarraffments arifing
from the cardinal's garments, which are
like petticoats, &c. A litter, covered with
crimfon-velvet, is provided for the Pope's
use,

[5]

ufe, in cafe his Holinefs fhould come to
the ground.

The next principal ceremony is the
Tenebræ of the Holy Wednefday, performed
at five o'clock afternoon in the chapel of
St. Paulina in the Vatican. The Pope is
feated under a canopy; cardinals and bi-
fhops form on each fide of him; and fome
cardinals take poft in his front. Behind
thefe, Englifh and other foreign gentlemen are allowed to ftand. About one
third of the chapel is railed off with iron
grates, which divide it into two parts, and
here thofe ladies, foreigners, and Italians,
who have permiffion to be prefent, are
ftationed, to fee the ceremonies through the
iron rails. It is, however, a great favour;
for our names, I mean particularly us
ftrangers, were wrote down, and the door-
keepers held the lift in their hands that
there might be no miftake as to our identity, &c.

Chapel
St. Pauli-
na.

B 3   The

'The *Tenebres* are chanted as in other Roman-catholic churches, but executed with more judgment and by better voices. The *Miferere D'Allegri* concludes this Function, and is performed by vocal muficians only. I own I never heard mufic before. I fuppofed I had formed fome idea of the powers and effects of the human voice; but had I been conveyed blindfold into this chapel, and no intimation given me whence the founds proceeded, I fhould have believed myfelf in Paradife. How then fhall I attempt conveying to your mind the flighteft idea of this celeftial melody by any defcription ? I muft fay no more, than that I have heard enough to make me diffatisfied with the fineft opera and the moft perfect performers that are to be found out of the chapel of St. Paulina.

This chapel appears fmaller than it really is, probably from the juftnefs of its

4   proportions,

proportions. The cieling is vaulted and painted in frefco, as are the walls. The altar-piece and cieling by Michael Angelo : but the fmoke of the lamps has fo blackened his paintings, that the fine ftrokes of this great mafter are no longer difcernible. Other painters have done the reft; who are equal fharers in the general obfcurity. The tabernacle is of rock cryftal; the columns of the altar of fine porphyry; they were taken from the temple of Romulus. I was quite vexed when the charming vocal concert ended, and quitted this Function with regret.

The next day which is Maundy Thurfday, the morning fervice is performed with pomp, in St. Peter's church : the Pope officiated in perfon, and all the cardinals affifted. After the mafs, which is chaunted in a fmall tribune, the facrament is borne under a canopy, in proceffion, to the chapel of St. Paulina. The cardi-

nals,

nals, in magnificent habits, and each
carrying a large wax-taper lighted, come,
two and two; and laft of all, the Pope
bareheaded; his mitre being born before
him on a cufhion of crimfon velvet. The
mitre is made of gold tiffue, and embroidered in a very clofe pattern, with fmall
pearl and a few coloured precious ftones,
but none of great value; they appear
thin and very ill fet. The Pope's guards
are under arms in cafques, and with cuiraffes
beneath their habits.

Juft before the Pope paffed by, I was
defirous to know (as he muft come very
near us) whether or not we ought to curtfey, as is ufual when other Princes proceed
in grand ceremony. I afked one of the
gentlemen of the chamber, or chamber-
lains, an abbe, who was our conductor; he replied, if you make a little
curtfey, the Pope will efteem you well-
bred and polite; but if you have any ob-
jection,

jection, he himself would be sorry you should put the least strain upon your in-. clination. I thought it better to inquire the ceremonial from this gentleman, than to apply to the *Marchesa Massimi,* and four or five Italian ladies, who, with two English and myself, composed the group. I curtseyed to the Pontiff, as we all did, and he seemed well pleased. He has a piercing sensible countenance, which, when brightened by a smile, is full of benignity and complacence. As soon as the procession had passed us, we went to the chapel of St. Paulina, which was finely illuminated. The evening concludes with a *Miserere,*

From a room in the Vatican we were to see the Pope give the benediction. These windows look into one of the great courts of the palace. The Pontiff appears in a balcony in the center of a portico of one of the principal fronts of St. Peter's, which commands this court. He is seated in a

chair,

chair, and borne on the fhoulders of twelve
people; his mitre on his head, and the
cardinals all attending upon him. Immediately upon his Holinefs's appearance at
the door which leads into the balcony, the
full choir unite in a grand chorus—the
foot and horfe guards are all drawn up in
the court—the fpace is filled by the Roman people—the air by their acclamations.
The bells ring out from every church—
the cannon fire inceffantly from the caftle
of St. Angelo. The redoubled ecchos from
the banks of the Tiber, through the Vatican and St. Peter's, refembles a fucceffion
of the loudeft thunder. On a fignal given,
all is inftantly hufhed to filence, and the
Pontiff pronounces the benediction in a clear
and audible voice. This prefent Pope (who
is unqueftionably the beft that Rome could
ever boaft of) has made an extraordinary
reform; for he never denounces the *ana-
thema*, which all his predeceffors have
done before him; but in lieu thereof,
                                    throws

throws down from the balcony, inſtead of curſes ſome indulgences, wrote on ſlips of paper, which are ſcrambled for by the mob. · Then the muſic choir, cannon, acclamations of the people, all recommence, and ceaſe not till the Pope and cardinals quit the balcony, in which they remain but a ſhort time. During this Function we were entertained with an elegant collation, conſiſting of chocolate, ſweetmeats, and *maſpinerie*, in great variety, and the beſt at Rome, which is ſuperlatively famous for theſe ſort of things. We then quitted the room, and I really believe we walked a mile through the apartments of the Vatican, in order to ſee the Pope waſh the pilgrims' feet (as it is expreſſed) and ſerve them at table, *&c.*

At length we reached a tribune faced with gilt lattice, through which we looked into a large ſalloon; in this, upon a bench placed along one of the ſide walls, raiſed a ſtep from the ground, and covered with

carpets,

carpets, are feated thirteen poor priefts of different nations. The prieft who fits in the middle reprefents our Saviour, and the fix on each fide of him his apoftles. An Italian lady of our company fpied one amongft them who had red hair, which occafioned much laughter; all, with one accord, pronouncing him to be Judas. Thefe priefts are dreffed in a kind of wrapper, or *Robe de Chambre* of new white flannel, with a hood lined with white fattin, and caps of flannel like jelly-bags on their heads. They have wide trowfers of the fame materials, tied down midway the leg, and focks of the fame over their naked feet. The Pope enters, and feats himfelf in a purple great chair, elevated two or three feet from the ground. The cardinals bear his train; he himfelf is dreffed more fimply than ufual with a ftole, and a plain white fattin mitre. The falloon is filled with ecclefiaftics of different orders; on one fide is placed a defk and

the

the choir: A priest gives the tone, and then the choiristers chant the chapter in St: Mark which relates to the washing of the disciples' feet. The book of this Evangelist is then brought to the Pope, who kisses it where open. One of the cardinals brings an apron (of old point, with a broad border of Mecklin lace) and ties it with a white ribbon round his Holiness's waist. He then descends from the chair, and approaches the poor priests, beginning with the nearest to him. A cardinal bears a large gold bason, another carries an ewer of the same metal, and a third napkins. The Pope stoops down, and the pretended pilgrim presents one foot (from which he has already drawn off the sock): his Holiness takes the foot in one hand, he who bears the ewer pours water over it, which is received in the gold bason held underneath; the Pope, with his other hand, rubs and washes the foot; he then, with a napkin, wipes it

very

very cautioufly and tenderly, till it is quite
dry; that done, he kiffes the inftep; then
prefents the pilgrim with a *bouquet* and
fome money folded up in a paper: he
proceeds, in order and filence, till he has
wafhed a foot, &c. of each of the thirteen,
who only bow their heads when the *bouquet* is given them, but do not fpeak or
rife during the Function. The Pope, upon
his return to his chair, is prefented with
water in a gold bafon to wafh his hands,
which he does flightly and carelefsly; he
then joins his hands, fhuts his eyes, and
fays a prayer foftly to himfelf. After
which he rifes and goes out, in order to
proceed to the hall where the pilgrims are
to eat; the cardinals, &c. all do the fame.
We women all quitted our tribune, and
were conducted by a different way to another tribune, into which we were locked
up fafe, and through the lattice faw a large
hall, with a long table in the middle, on
which was a furtout of looking-glafs, with

images

Images of clay placed thereon, reprefenting our Saviour and two loaves, with a
ferpent on a table: further, St. Peter and
other faints; the glafs was ornamented
with fweetmeats, olives, anchovies. There
were thirteen filver plates laid, with fpoons
and forks; the napkins curioufly plaited;
and over the table-cloth a lay-over of
clear lawn, pinched fo as to form a very
pretty pattern. I fhould have mentioned
the drefs of the images, which was the
moft taudry imaginable, of red, blue, and
yellow porcelain. The pilgrims, whofe
feet had been wafhed, now made their appearance, and feated themfelves along one
fide of the table; then entered the Pope
and cardinals: a plate of boiled rice covered with cinnamon and fugar, was prefented on the knee to his Holinefs; he
took it, and placed it before the pilgrim
whofe foot he had firft wafhed; then another plate of the fame, and fo on till the
thirteen were ferved. Then came a boiled
herring, garnifhed with fallad, on a plate,
and

and a fucceffion of them till all were ferved
as before. Thefe were fucceeded by plates
of fried fifh, cut to pieces; then plates of
broccoli and cauliflower fricaffeed in oil;
the fame ceremony obferved as at firft, and
the quantity and quality of the viands exactly alike; then, on a magnificent falver,
was brought a decanter of wine, another
of water, and a gold goblet. The Pontiff
filled the goblet almoft full of wine, and,
with an arch fmile, dropped one drop of
water into it, and prefented it to the pilgrims as before. They each of them
drank it off. This done, the Pope leaves
the hall. I hoped thefe poor priefts were
not hungry, for had that been the cafe,
they muft have remained fo; the difhes
being removed from before them the moment after they had been placed there;
but upon inquiry, I found they were all
fet by, and diftributed to them after the
Function was over, in another place and
without fo much ceremony.

During

During this Function, the Pope's guards
ftand in rank and file behind him, to
keep the crowd from incommoding him.
There were prefent a great number of Italian and Englifh gentlemen, befide other
foreigners. We then went to the hall
where the cardinals were to eat. The
figures placed on the glafs were of the
fame materials, and draped in the fame
manner as thofe of the pilgrims' table;
but in the middle was a different reprefentation. A grove of palm-trees, formed
of green paper, furrounded a paper mount,
on which was placed a figure, to reprefent
our Saviour, with a gilt goblet in his
hand, alluding to the paffion. But, to my
great furprife, I perceived each end of the
furtout to be terminated by two centaurs,
of filver, gilt. This abfurdity of mix-
ing paganifm with chriftianity feemed
wonderful; nor could I account for it in
any other manner, than by fuppofing
thefe centaurs might allude to the incon-

gruity and mixture of character of the company for whom the table had been prepared. I could expatiate upon the *Fable* of the centaurs, but that might tranfport me too far into antiquity from the prefent fubject. The cardinal's table was very differently ferved from that of the pilgrims, each having eight or ten covered difhes, brought from his own kitchen, with lamps under them : fo that obferving nothing curious or uncommon in this *Function* of their eminencies, we took our leave and returned home. As to the Pontiff, he always eats alone, and in the moft temperate manner. He has a friend called *Francefco*, who buys his provifions in the market, and not always from the fame people. His conftant dinner, excepting on faft days, confifts of a foup with rice, which is ferved with the fowl that had been boiled in it. Then a fmall *Friture*, with a little *defert* of cheefe and fruit. This is all. And on the maigre and faft

2   days

days his extremely abftemious. His vic-
tuals are dreffed by *Francefco*, in the room
adjoining that in which he eats, and he himfelf brings it in. This caution is probably
the refult of an apprehenfion of poifon.
The only recreation the Pope allows himfelf, is the going after dinner to the *Villa
Patrize fuori di Roma*, where, after taking a few turns in the garden, he plays a
little at billiards in a room of the villa.
Certainly no Pope ever led a more innocent
life. But to return to the Functions;
Good-friday and Eafter-eve there are no
extraordinary ceremonies. The common
Miferare is chaunted; but in the evening
the church of St. Peter is crouded with
people, who walk about and converfe.
This beautiful temple has now an additional ornament, which produces a fine
effect: a large crofs, gently let down
(by cords almoft imperceptible to the eye)
from the top of the dome, remains fufpended during the night, but not near

the

the ground; its diftance from thence appearing to me to be about a third of the
height of the church from the pavement
to the top of the dome; it is compofed of
fmall lamps in ftrait rows, which throw
out fuch a light as illuminates the great ifle,
and appears as if compofed of brilliant
diamonds. It is remarkable that Friday
and Saturday are not efteemed fo facred as
the foregoing days of the holy week, and
that during the faid week no fhops are
fhut; but trade and bufinefs go on juft as
ufual.

Eafter-funday in the morning we went
to St. Peter's, to fee the Pope celebrate the
mafs to a prodigious concourfe of people;
their numbers were fuppofed to be about
ten thoufand. I, as before, accompanied
the Countefs of Maffimi; there were alfo
fome Englifh ladies; chance brought us all
together, and very near his Holinefs;
where we happened to fall into a line precifely before his guards. The gentlemen

of

of our party were, by the accidental crouding, a good way behind us. There is a particular part of the fervice (the moment in which the hoft is elevated) at which all the people are to kneel; I had no time for reflection, but it ftruck me that as a proteftant I ought not to kneel; nor did I, though a lady of my country, clofe to me, * * * * *, dropped upon her knees, and would have perfuaded me to do the like, but I would not. The halberdiers, who were clofe behind us, fell on their knees, and their halberts accidentally came fo near me, that at firft I thought they were about to ufe them to bring me to order, but was miftaken. They faid nothing, nor did they make me any fign to kneel. Whilft ftanding I looked about me, and as far as I could fee, all were on their knees. I turned myfelf towards the Pontiff, and caught his eye, but he did not look four at me, and feemed only to notice the fingularity of my ftanding up; nor was I reprimanded afterward, either

from

from his Holineſs, or any of the Romans.
Some of my own country-people, indeed,
criticiſed my conduct with the aſſiſtance of
the old adage, that "one ſhould, when at
Rome, do as they do at Rome." But as
M—— applauded and highly approved
my conduct (and he, it ſeems, never kneel-
ed either), the opinions of others has not
the leaſt effect upon me.

I ſhould have mentioned before, that
the Pope made his entrance this day in a
triumphant manner, being borne in a chair
on twelve men's ſhoulders into the church,
to a temporary altar placed in the great
iſle; when the chair, being gently ſet
down, he advanced a few ſteps to the altar,
which was much adorned and ornamented,
and thereat celebrated the maſs. The Pontiff laſtly appears at the great door of entrance, aſſiſting at ſome trifling ceremonies
relative to the bleſſing of relics and pilgrims, but theſe were not worth waiting
for; ſo, to avoid the croud, we got into
our

our carriage, and arrived safe at home, while the mob were ftill occupied in crouding the courts of St. Peter's.

Having at length concluded this circumftantial narrative of the Functions of the *Santa Settimana*, I ought to account for my having entered into fo tedious a detail. My reafons were, to give you an idea of the impofitions, rites, and ceremonies, of the Roman Catholic religion, as practifed at the fountain-head of all popery. Had I been writing to another and not to you, I fhould have fatisfied myfelf with faying, after the example of other travellers, " It is needlefs to mention the Functions during the holy week, as they are fo univerfally known, and have been fo often defcribed already," &c.; but I believe both you and myfelf, in our courfe of travel-reading, have not gained much more knowledge upon the fubject, than the univerfal affertion of their having been already *fo often defcribed*. Therefore, doing by you as I

fhould

should like you had done by me, instead
of apologizing for the *length* and *dulness*,
&c. of this letter, I expect your acknowledgments for the infinite pains and trouble I have taken to inform you of what
you could not have a just idea of before,
and to insist upon your believing my assurances, of being so tired with what I have
wrote, that if this letter, by any accident,
should not reach you, you shall ever remain in ignorance of the Functions for
me. For you may depend upon not being
favoured with its second edition. Adieu.

> Your ever affectionate, *&c.*

LETTER XLII.

Rome, April 12, 1771.

THE arrival of your letters, replete
with that warmth of friendship
which disperses every gloomy thought, and
completed with assurances of the blessing
of health which you and * * * * * enjoy,

joy, give me frefh fpirits to continue the daily labours my curiofity incites in thefe regions of oddity and antiquity.

-I will now give you a flight fketch of what we have feen, &c. fince I wrote laft; but firft, cannot forbear mentioning an impediment extremely teazing to ftrangers. Having formed your plan for a morning's progrefs from church to church, from palace to palace, and fo on, you fet out in your carriage with impatience to commence your operations; when, after driving two or three miles, you are nipped in the bud of your expectation, by being told at the firft palace you reach, that it is twelve o'clock, and therefore you cannot fee it, for *all the world are dining:* you reply, you will call again in an hour; the rejoinder is, *every body will then be taking the Siefta* *: you ftare about, and fpy a fhop in a corner; you order your coachman to drive to it: " *The beggar's fhop*

* A nap after dinner.

is

is shut," for all the world are at dinner; and this anfwer is frequently accompanied by a parti-coloured fmile of contempt and pity for *you,* who alone in the *creation* are *not* at dinner. However, notwithftanding fuch teazing delays, we have vifited many a fuperb ruin, where are no diners nor dofers, the ftupendous monuments of paft ages, magnificent churches, and gorgeous palaces. Amongft the firft, the following (that I have as yet feen) are my reigning favourites. In Campo Vaccino, which was the old Forum, are many fine re-

Ruins. Temple of Jupiter Stator. mains of antiquity. The three fuperb columns, the only remnants of the temple of Jupiter *Stator,* attract the admiration of the traveller by the beauty of their proportions and fculpture; and much is it to be regretted, that the greater part of them, at this day, lie fmothered up in

Temple of Vefta. the foil of this foul cow-market.—The Temple of Vefta; where the famous Palladium was guarded by the chief veftal,

who

who along had the honour to look upon it.—The Arc of Septimius Severus, in white marble; one half of the great middle arch is buried in the ground, by which accident it loses the lightnefs its architecture befpeaks.—The ruins of the Temple of Concord; the veftibule remains entire; it is compofed of fix columns of oriental granite, of the Ionic order; they fupport an elegant pediment.—Of the Temple of Peace remain only three vaults, which is but a part of the portico of its veftibule; this temple was ranked among the moft magnificent buildings of Rome when in her glory; it was erected by Vefpafian, after his conqueft of India, and was the repofitory of the rich fpoils he brought from Syria and the temple of Jerufalem, was decorated with ftatues and pictures by the moft famous artifts of that æra, and contained, befides, a large library. One of the columns belonging to this Temple was found by accident, and erected by Pope Paul

the

Arc of Septimius Severus.

Temple of Concord.

Temple of Peace.

the Fifth, 1614, in the piazza before the church of St. *Maria Maggiore*; it is one entire fhaft, and meafures 64 Roman palms in height.—Of the Temple of An-

Temple of Antoninus and Fauftina.

toninus and Fauftina there remains only ten pillars, with a frieze and part of the Corinthian capitals; the proportions are fine, and the ornaments in a good tafte: within fide of thefe columns a modern church has been built, which difgraces as much as poffible this venerable ruin.—Near

Temple of Remus and Romulus.

this place, and in full view, is the Ruin of the Temple of Remus and Romulus, from whence was taken the plan of Rome, which now decorates a ftair-cafe in the capitol, as I have already faid in a former letter. The Ruin is a fmall rotunda, and ferves as a veftibule to a modern church.—The Arch

Arch of Titus.

of Titus terminates one fide of *Campo Vaccino*; its bas reliefs, within fide, are of fine workmanfhip; the drawing is cor-rect; the horfes are particularly well done. —Here are fome remains of the Golden Palace

Palace of Nero; they confift of broken arches
one above the other, but fo imperfect as renders it impoffible to form a judgment of
its plan and diftribution. There is ftill to
be feen a little painting and gilding on
the ornaments within fide, but much de-
faced.—In the center of Campo Vaccino
they fhew a place where is faid to have
been formerly the Gulph into which Curtius leaped;—but I muft reftrain my pen,
nor fay more of the Ruins which are here
all together, or I fhall exceed the limits I
prefcribed to myfelf; therefore I quit
Campo Vaccino, and proceed to the *Coliffeo*,
which I think is the moft grand and ftupendous Ruin in Rome. Twelve thoufand
Jewifh captives were employed by Vefpafian in the building, which they are afferted to have completed within the year.
It has been ftripped of all its magnificent
pillars and ornaments, at various times
and by various enemies. The Goths and
other barbarians began its deftruction,

Golden Palace of Nero.

Gulph of Curtius.

Coliffeo.

popes

popes and cardinals have endeavoured to complete its ruin; the cardinal Farnese, laftly, robbed it of fome fine remains; of its marble cornices, friezes, &c. and, with infinite pains and labour, got away what was practicable of the outfide cafing of marble, which he employed in building the palace of Farnefe. This amphitheatre is faid to have been capable of containing eighty-feven thoufand fpectators feated, and twenty thoufand ftanding; the proportions of this glorious Ruin are fo juft that it does not appear near fo large as it really is. Its architecture is perfectly light, and it muft ever be admired even by thofe who enjoy but a moderate fhare of tafte for the fine arts, were they devoid of love or refpect for antiquity. To others, who really delight in that refined ftudy, it muft fully gratify their great ideas, being a de-finition of the *fublime* in *architecture*. I think this founds fomewhat enthufiaftic; but I don't fear expofing myfelf to you,

who

who am as likely to give into enthufiafm upon this fort of fubject as myfelf. There are ftill to be feen feveral of the dens for the beafts, which remain entire, and the conduits for the water, with a hollow in the ftone for them to drink out of.—In the piazza of the amphitheatre are the remains of an antique fountain for the ufe of the people, which was called *Meta Sudante.* A little farther on is the Arch of Conftantine. The architecture is of the Corinthian order, and executed in a grand and noble ftile. It is beautifully adorned with fluted pillars of *Giallo Antico.* The *bas reliefs, medallions,* &c. are finely fculpted. —The Pantheon anfwered the idea I had formed of it; it is at prefent converted into a modern church, is generally called *La Rotunda* or *Santa Maria ad Martyres,* to whom it is dedicated. It is one of the moft perfect remains of the magnificence of ancient Rome, and the only Roman temple which is ftill entire. Its juftnefs of proportion

Arch of Conftantine.

Pantheon,

La Rotunda.

proportion ftrikes the eye at firft fight. The portico is an example that the noble fimplicity may be ftill preferved, though decorated with the moft ornamental order, the Corinthian. This portico prefents to the view 16 pillars of this order of oriental granite; eight of them fupport the pediment; they are very thick, meafuring from five to fix feet diameter, yet their look is light; they are faid to be thirty-feven feet high, exclufive of their bafes and capitals, which is probable; but we did not take their height; their fhafts are each one entire piece. Having entered the portico, the great door merits attention for its noble and majeftic appearance; the architrave confifts of only three pieces of fine African marble; the door is of brafs and of antique fculpture, but does not feem to have been originally defigned for this place. On entering the temple, which is quite round, you are ftruck with its apparent fmalnefs; but this deception

muft

muſt riſe from its proportions, - being as wide as it is high; it is covered by a dome open in the center; whoſe compartments muſt have made a beautiful appearance, when plated with gilt bronze, but at preſent there is not the ſmalleſt veſtige remaining of any metal. M⸻ ſtepped the pavement, and it meaſured ſixty yards diameter within, from wall to wall. There are no windows; a ſufficiency of light being admitted from the opening in the dome. The pavement would have amuſed me for hours, being compoſed of a great variety of morſels of fine Italian marble, opaque gems, alabaſters, agates, and jaſpers. Theſe have been picked up indiſcriminately from amongſt the ruins, and uſed without the leaſt regard to their quality, in repairing the pavement where wanted. Here are ſome fine pillars of porphyry and *giallo antico*; alſo altars, particularly the chief one, worthy of notice.

A Monument erected in honour of Raffaello, by Carlo Maratti, is not in a good tafte. His bufto appears in a nich, and near to it the following lines by cardinal Benbo ;

Ille hic eſt Raphael, *timuit quo foſpite vinci,*
Rerum magna parens, & *moriente-mori.*

Here is alfo a monument to Annibal Carracci, by Carlo Maratti ; one to the famous Corelli ; and others in honour of different artifts. In general, the decorations are mean and bafe ; bad pictures, votive reprefentations, the weak efforts of fuperftition, every where cover the walls.

Behind the Pantheon appear ruined walls and part of a round building, which is all that remains of Agrippa's baths. What I propofe to add farther in regard to the ruins of Rome I fhall referve for another letter, and proceed now to an account of the evening amufements. There are private affemblies at feveral houfes ; thofe of the Dutchefs of *Brachiano*, of the Dutchefs of
Monte-

Mortalibretti, of the Dutchefs *D'Arce,* of the Princefs *Altieri,* and of cardinal *Bernis,* of the *Cafa Verofpi,* and the *Cafa Carpegna,* are the moft brilliant. The bufinefs of thefe affemblies is cards, and you are continually prefented with all forts of excellent refrefhments. The opera is good; the theatre not indifferent, yet greatly inferior to that of Naples. What difgufts me much is, to fee boys dreffed in women's cloaths, as no female actreffes are permitted. The fcenes are agreeably painted, moft of them reprefenting architecture well done in perfpective, and the point of view being taken from the angles, you have two views at once. The Corfo lies along the main ftreets; where the cattle being frequently killed at the doors of the butchers' fhops during the time of airing, renders this amufement odious to me. The living oxen are witnefs to the murders of their innocent companions; their bellowing, and this barbarous cuftom fhocked me fo, that I am determined

termined

termined to avoid, in future, thefe fcenes of butchery as much as poffible. We have already fome curious articles, which will be fent to England from Civita Vecchia * *
* * * * *

Adieu, &c.

P. S. I fhall add an anecdote of the Pope, that came to my knowledge very lately.——He was fitting at his writing-table which was covered with papers, whilft two confiderable perfons of his court converfed together at a window near him ; his Holinefs had occafion to quit the room fuddenly ; thefe gentlemen were curious —feized the opportunity that offered to infpect fome of the papers ; when the Pope, a very fhort time after, entering, and perceiving inftantly they had meddled with them, thus addreffed them : I know, that you know the contents of thefe papers ;— make me no reply, for this inftant I dif-mifs you my fervice ;—depart from my prefence ;—but if ever I hear the leaft ru-
mour

mour of what thefe papers contain, before the time their contents are to be made public, your heads fhall anfwer for it.

You fee what firmnefs there is in the Pontiff; nobody doubts their keeping the fecret.

LETTER XLIII.

Rome, April 25, 1771.

THE weather is extremely warm; the Englifh complain of the heat; but you know I love the fun, and the hotter he fhines, the more health and fpirits are dealt me. However, this luminary is no friend to the complexion, and I have contrived to make a hat of pafteboard, and trimmed it with blond and pink ribbon, as was the fafhion when we quitted England. I believe I fhall find it extremely convenient in the mornings when we are walking amongft the Ruins; for conftantly going

D 3   out

out in the Roman fashion, with nothing
to shade my face but a black lace hood
hanging down over my eyes, has tanned
me to such a degree, that I know not whether all the strawberry-water in Rome will
be able to whiten me again. I find it more
difficult here to pursue my intention of
being concise than I imagined I should;
there is so much to be seen—so much to
be admired—whole labyrinths of curio-
sities;—my difficulty is, which to choose;
it seems a kind of injustice to omit things
so highly worthy of notice, and was I to
mention them all I should send you folios
instead of letters; but be persuaded my
determination is against folios. Amongst
the Ruins of this once Imperial Mistress
of the world, Caracalla's baths are in high
estimation with all the lovers of antiquity.
We were a whole morning wandering
amongst these superb remains. They appeared to me to occupy as much ground as
a mo-

a moderate fized town; and not only af-
forded conveniencies for three thoufand
perfons to bathe at the fame time, together with fquares and courts for all kinds
of fports and other public fpectacles, but
even fcience found a place here. There
were porticos for philofophers to affemble
in. The whole adorned with a profufion
of ftatues, and the moft precious ornaments
luxury could invent. Now, alas, what
remains! nothing but broken walls and
naked bricks; yet even thefe laft are
fine in their way, as none can be formed
at this day of fo large a fize: they are alfo
of an extraordinary texture and colour.
The pipes which conveyed the water to a
prodigious height into the upper apartments are made of as fine clay as the old
red china, and are equally fmooth. One
part of this immenfe building remains fufficiently entire to ftrike awe into the fpec-
tator; it confifts of a prodigious dome,
which has no fupport but from the wall

whence

whence it fprings, and, like an unfinifhed rainbow, feems fufpended in air. Clofe to thefe baths ftood Caracalla's magnificent palace; but of this there is not the leaft veftige remaining. The Theatre of Marcellus is fo disfigured by time and abufe, that it is impoffible to make out the whole of the plan; but what remains is of beautiful architecture. Part of the entrances may ftill be traced. There are alfo two ranges of arches, one over the other; the lower decorated with the Doric, the upper with the Ionic order; both of them of light and graceful proportions. The remaining friezes, cornices, and mouldings appear plainly, by their fculpture, to have been intended for a near view. This Theatre feems to have had an oval figure; the learned, however, differ in regard to its form; for had it been oval, it had been an amphitheatre, confequently deftined to the tormenting of wild beafts, and the inhuman fports of gladiators; but upon fuppo-fition

Marcellus' Theatre.

fition of its being a theatre, could have been only ufed for the reprefentation of dramatic performances. We cannot help regretting their having built wretched ha-bitations for mechanics between the arches, and confequently filled them up, which difgrace thefe venerable remains extremely.

We have vifited the famous Tarpeian Rock. The precipice is, at this day, no longer terrific; it is filled up with rub-bifh in fuch a manner, that though ftill fufficiently deep to break a limb of who-ever fhould chufe the leap, yet I think they might poffibly efcape too without much damage. The way to it is encumbered with old buildings, and nothing can be more difgufting than the dirt of the inha-bitants of this wretched part of Rome. Mr. Pope's defcription of thofe *of the Al-ley*, in Spenfer's ftyle, amongft his imi-tations of the Englifh poets, will give you a juft idea of the polite neighbourhood of the Tarpeian Rock. The Circus of Cara-calla

Tarpeian Rock.

Circus of Caracalla.

calla is still so entire, that the plan may be easily made out, and is more perfect than any now remaining at Rome. Here are apparent remains of the walls where the seats for the spectators were placed; that part of the Circus, at the greatest distance, terminates in a semicircle. The great gate which the victors passed through to their triumphs is still to be seen. In the middle remains also a line of walling, the extremities of which were the bounds fixed for the chariots to turn at. In one of the sidewalls you discern the places where large empty vases of *terra cota* were inserted, in order to augment the applauses of the people by a reverberation of the ecchos from side to side. Considerable vestiges of three or four large brick towers still remain, which were probably those granted by the emperors to a few of their most considerable favourites, for the convenience of seeing the sports to advantage, and which were hereditary in their families. There is another

square

fquare building, fuppofed to have been a
kind of dreffing-room for the competitors,
and fome remains of two moft refpectable
temples erected to honour and virtue, by
M. Marcellus. This great man conftructed
them in fuch a manner, that the Temple
of Honour could not be entered without
firft *paffing through* that of Virtue. On
the other fide of the Circus are the ruins
of a Temple erected to the *Deo Ridicuolo,*   Deo Ridi-
in the time of the fecond Punic war, when   cuolo,
Hannibal, advancing from Cannæ with   Temple
defign to befiege Rome, retired fuddenly   of.
of his own accord, before he had even
commenced the fiege.—Half a mile from
hence, on the Appian way, is an antique
Monument called *Capo di Bove,* the tomb   Capo di
of Cecilia Metella, wife of Craffus. It is   Bove.
a ruined tower, with a frieze and cornice,
ornamented by ox-heads in *relievo,* and
garlands of cyprefs. The walls are extremely thick. In the pontificate of Paul
the Third an excavation was made in the
tower,

tower, which brought them to a cavity that contained an urn made of Parian marble and fluted. It is now to be feen in the court of the Farnefe palace. The infcription on the frieze of this Monument is, *Cæciliæ Q. Cretici F. Metell. Craffi.*

Maufo-
leum of
Auguftus.

The Maufoleum of Auguftus is fituated behind *S. Carlo al Corfo.* It confifts of a great round tower. There are ftill remaining fome columns and marbles, with which the outfide was decorated. As the roof or covering is entirely deftroyed, they have filled up the infide with earth, and made a pretty odd garden within the tower. A terras, formed by the thicknefs of the walls, furrounds all. There are *Souterrains*, or rooms where the afhes of the Auguftan family were depofited.

Pyramid
of Caius
Ceftius.

The Pyramid of Caius Ceftius is the only entire tomb remaining. It is near Porto S. Paolo. The outfide is formed of large blocks of white marble. This monument has a fine effect when viewed at

a proper

a proper diftance; being, I fuppofe, about 40 feet in perpendicular height.

There are many veftiges of tombs to be feen in the environs of Rome, and is it not a cuftom that might be productive of happy confequences if practifed at this day in Chriftian countries, were great and good men, who have ferved their country effentially, to be interred by the fides of the high roads leading to the capital, with proper infcriptions on their tombs (which might be alfo extremely ornamental), reminding their fucceffors and others of the noble examples they had fet them, and exciting in their minds a laudable ambition for the like honours? it would perpetuate the memories of our national benefactors, in my mind, more effectually than all the monuments that can be erected to them in Weftminfter Abbey—which few think of vifiting after the tour made in their childhood—of the lions in the Tower, St. Paul's, the wax-work, and Weftminfter Abbey.

I fuppofe

I fuppofe there is no city in the world fo provided with excellent water and beautiful Fountains as Rome. That of Termini, of Trevi, of the Piazza Navone, and many others, are worthy the atttention of travellers. I dare not enter into the infpection of them, nor even venture to mention the obelifks and fingle columns which you find in every quarter of the town. The only Fountain you fhall hear of at prefent is antique, that of the nymph *Egeria*, which is not in modern Rome, but at a little diftance from the town, or to fpeak with the Romans, *Fuori di Roma.* Here it was that Numa is faid to have had his rendezvous with that nymph. Its prefent appearance is that of a pretty large roomy vault. There are few remains of its antique marble ornaments. A mutilated ftatue of the Nymph, and niches where the mufes were placed, are ftill to be feen. It affords plenty of excellent water, of which you may be fure we drank; alfo

Marginal notes:

Fountains.

That of Egeria.

4

several aquatic plants that spring spontane-
ously from these streams, and hang down
over the entrance in many a fantastic garland. It is woody and gloomy all around,
and, in my opinion, a most charming romantic spot, where one might indulge in
contemplation

Of forests and inchantments drear,
Where more is meant than meets the ear.

Happily for you I have not visited all
the churches at Rome. Indeed I have seen
but a few of them ; so do not be alarmed,
for I shall mention yet fewer than I have
seen. *S. Giovanni di Latterano* is a fine
church, decorated with columns, *&c.* antique and modern, of the most precious
marbles. Several statues of saints and
apostles ; the best, is that of St. Bar-
tolomeo. Round the altar are four very
curious antique pillars of bronze fluted,
which were found where the famous temple of Jupiter Capitolinus stood. The relics

Churches.
St. Gio-
vanni di
Lattera-
no.

lics conferved in the churches of Rome are too abfurd to mention. This once only, by which you may judge of the others, I fhall inform you, that they here boaft the inheritance of a piece of Mofes's rod and a morfel of Aaron's, a ftick of the ark of the covenant, the table on which our Saviour eat the paffover with his difciples, and the napkin which he made ufe of to wipe their feet.

Relics.

The Church of St. *Maria Magiore* is efteemed the moft noble and grand of all thofe dedicated to the Virgin. It is built on the fpot where ftood a temple confecrated to Juno. The plan of this church was, we were told, miraculoufly traced out by a cloud which fell from heaven. The architecture is much admired; the infide of the church ftrikes the eye with a noble fimplicity; the view of a great number of lofty pillars, of the Ionic order, of white marble, have a fine effect; the altar is formed by a beautiful antique urn of porphyry.

St. Maria Magiore.

phyry. The fineſt chapel belonging to this church is that of *Borgheſe*. Here is a profuſion of rich marbles, *lapis lazuli*, the opaque precious ſtones, ſome paintings and freſcos by Guido, and many very valuable ornaments. Amongſt others, an image of the Virgin (attributed to St. Luke), ſurrounded with precious ſtones. I had determined not to tire you with more relics, but here I cannot help announcing to you the manger in which our Saviour was laid, the ſwaddling clothes he wore, and ſome ſtraw on which he was placed.

S. Paolo fuori di Roma alle tre fontane. This Church is built upon the ſpot where St. Paul was beheaded. The pillar to which he was bound, and where he ſuffered martyrdom, is near the firſt of the three fountains. Theſe ſprung up, as you will believe, miraculouſly from the three bounds his head made when ſtruck off. The Church, however, is extremely well worth ſeeing; it is adorned on the inſide

S. Paolo fuori di Roma Church.

VOL. III.　　　E　　　　　with

with very curious antique columns *, particularly two of black porphyry; there are no such to be seen anywhere else. Antiquarians are at a lofs to determine whence they were brought, but the moft probable conjecture is, that they were the productions of Ethiopia, where quarries of *Ba-falte* are common.

St. Urbano Church. The Church of St. Urbano alla Caffarella was a temple of Bacchus, and graceful, indeed, are its remains. It is built of brick, with ftrength and folidity. The Mofaic in the arched roof and between the double row of pillars is finely done. Here are reprefentations of the vintage through all its progrefs : the wine-prefs is particularly worth obferving. The different figures of birds, large as life, are elegantly executed; and the pheafants fuperior to the others. The diameter of the ground-plan, between the inner row of pillars, meafures about forty-five feet English, and

* Some of which meafure twenty-two feet in circumference.

3   ninety

ninety feet between the walls, or from one
fide to the other. The farcophagus of
Bacchus is of one entire morfel of porphyry, nine feet long, fix broad, and four
deep; the fhell nine inches; the lid or
cover twenty inches thick. It is fculpted
in baffo relievo, reprefenting the Infant
Bacchus, feftoons of vine leaves, grapes,
&c.

S. *Sebaftiano alle Catacombe*, fituated on
the Appian way, was founded by Conftantine the Great, in honour of this faint;
who is reprefented lying in his tomb,
pierced with arrows. The fculpture by
Giorgetti. The portico of this church is
fupported by fix antique columns of a very
rare fpecies; two of them of white granite, and two of green, with uncommon
fpots in them.

The catacombs are the vafteft, and the
moft noted in the neighbourhood of Rome.
We explored them accompanied by a
ragged ill-looking fellow, whofe bufinefs

is

is to fweep the church, and fhew thefe
filent manfions of the dead. One of our
footmen was fent of a meffage, the other
followed us. We were provided with little
wax candles, and defcended the ftair-cafe,
each carrying a lighted *Bougie*; the others
were for provifion, left any of thofe already
lighted fhould burn out or extinguifh.
Having, at length, reached the bottom,
after no very agreeable defcent, we found
ourfelves in a labyrinth of very narrow paffages, turning and winding inceffantly; moft of thefe are upon the flope,
and, I believe, go down into the earth to
a confiderable depth. They are not wider
than to admit one perfon at a time, but
branch out various ways like the veins in
the human body; they are alfo extremely
damp, being practifed in the earth, and
caufed our candles to burn blue. In the fide-
niches are depofited the bodies (as they fay)
of more than feventy-four thoufand martyrs. Thefe niches are moftly clofed by an
upright

upright flab of marble, which bears an infcription defcriptive of their contents. Several are alfo buried under thefe paffages,
whofe graves are fecured by iron grates.
We followed our tattered guide for a confiderable time through the paffages; at
laft he ftopt, and told M—— if he would
go with him to a certain *Souterrain* juft by,
he would fhew him a remarkable catacomb. At that moment I was ftaring
about at the infcriptions, and took it for
granted that M—— was really very near,
but after fome moments I afked the foot-
man who was ftanding at the entrance if
he faw his mafter; he replied in the nega-
tive, nor did he hear any voice: this
alarmed me; I bid him go forward a little
way, and that I would wait where I was,
for I feared lofing myfelf in this labyrinth
in attempting to get out, not knowing
which way they had turned. I waited a
little time, and finding the fervant did not
return, called out as loud as I could, but,

to

to my great disappointment, perceived that
I scarce made any noise; the sound of my
voice, from the dampness of the air, or
the lowness of the passages, remaining (as
it were) with me. I trembled all over, and
perceived that my *Bougie* was near its
end; I lighted another with some difficulty, from the shaking of my hands, and
determined to go in search of M—— myself, at any hazard; but figure to yourself
the horror that seized me, when, upon attempting to move, I perceived myself
forcibly held by my clothes from behind,
and all the efforts I made to free myself
proved ineffectual. My heart, I believe,
ceased to beat for a moment, and it was as
much as I could do to sustain myself from
falling down upon the ground in a swoon.
However, I summoned all my resolution
to my aid, and ventured to look behind
me, but saw nothing. I then again at-
tempted to move, but found it impractica-
ble. Just God, said I, perhaps M—— is
assassinated,

affaffinated, and the fervant joined with the guide in the perpetration of the murder, and I am miraculoufly held faft by the dead, and fhall never leave thefe graves. Notwithftanding fuch dreadful reprefenta- tions that my frighted imagination pictured to me, I made more violent efforts, and in ftruggling, at laft difcovered, that there was an iron grate, like a trap-door, a little open behind me, one of the pointed bars of which had pierced through my gown, and held me in the manner I have related. I foon extricated myfelf, and walking for- ward, luckily in the right path, found M—— who was quietly copying an in- fcription, the guide lighting him, and the fervant returning towards me with the moft unconcerned afpect imaginable. I had the difcretion to conceal my fright as much as I was able, and only expreffed, with fome impatience, my defire of returning into the open air. M——, who is ever complai- fant to my wifhes, inftantly complied; and as we were retiring, the poor guide, whom my imagination had reprefented as an affaffin, told us, that there was a pit amongft the Catacombs of which the bottom could never be difcovered; and he had been told, that formerly a great many people had been abufed, robbed, and flung into it. I thanked God, inwardly, that he had not told me this ftory earlier.--Having entered the carriage, I determined within myfelf that this vifit to the Catacombs fhould be my laft. That you may not dwell longer upon the adventure, I fhall return to Rome, and conclude my letter with a flight defcription of the Vatican.

The fuperb palace called the Vatican is attached to St. Peter's church, and was, for many years, the refidence of the Pontiffs. But they have of late preferred *Monte Cavallo,* as a drier and healthier fituation. The dimenfions and elaborate defcriptions of this palace have been given by feveral Italian and other authors. According to
M. Venuti

M. Venuti it contains eleven thoufand and five hundred rooms; but according to *Bo-nanni* thirteen thoufand, including the *Sou-terrains* and cellars. It is afferted by fome, to have been built on the ruins of Nero's palace; others fay, on the fpot where that Emperor's gardens commenced. The principal objects that merit the attention of a traveller are, the library, the paintings of Raffaello, and the antique ftatues. After having paffed through two great courts, you afcend a ftair-cafe called *La Scala Regia*, defigned by Bernini, which is really magnificent. You then enter a vaft falloon called *Sala Regia*, painted in *frefco*, by various artifts; the fubjects moftly allegorical and hiftorical. Many of them have been much injured by the painters who were employed, owing to their rivality and private enmities to each other; blurring over and malicioufly fpoiling the labours of their brethren from motives of envy and revenge. You are then fhewn the Chapel of of Sextus the Fourth. Michael Angelo painted the vaulted cieling. The plan of this Chapel is an oblong square. Over the tapeſtry are twelve pictures repreſenting different hiſtories from the Old and New Teſtament, by Pietro Perugino. The heads of the figures are finely executed, but their drapery is quite abſurd, being, for the moſt part, attired in gold and ſilver. Over the door, a picture repreſenting St. Michael fighting with devils for the body of Moſes, is executed, in what the Italians call, *Une Maniere Terribile*, by Matteo Dalecio. The famous picture, by Michael Angelo, of the laſt judgment, occupies the whole end of the Chapel. It is painted in freſco. The group in the middle repreſents Jeſus Chriſt; on his right hand the elect; on his left, the condemned ſouls; at the top, two groups of angels, who bear the attributes of the paſſion. The ſaints, ſpectators of the laſt judgment, are ranged on each ſide of two groups which ſurround

our

Michael Angelo.

Pietro Perugino.

Matteo Dalecio.
Michael Angelo.

our Saviour. There are also choirs of angels who sound the trumpets, some conduct the blessed into heaven, and others thrust the damned into hell. At the bottom of the picture is Charon in his boat; and in the corner of hell stands a man with serpents twisting round him, being the portrait of a person to whom Michael had a particular aversion. This vast piece of painting is more surprising than pleasing; the confusion such crowds of figures produce—the variety and strength of design—the powers of imagination, and all the whims of fancy, are here united. The back ground, representing an azure sky, all of one tint, gives no *relief*; and, upon the whole, there is a poverty of colouring, joined to a great correctness in the drawing.

I shall here omit the chapel Paulina, having mentioned it already. In a grand apartment called that of Borgia are many fine morsels of painting by Raffaello, Giulio

ulio Romano, Pierino del Vaga, Pelegrino da Modena, and others. The celebrated *Salloni di Raffaello* confifts of a long *fuite* of rooms, painted in frefco by that great mafter. The firft falloon contains all the virtues, charities, &c. under fymbolical figures; the fecond, the twelve apoftles, &c.; the third, called that of Conftantine, fhews the miracle of his converfion; the aërian crofs is borne by two angels. In another, the battle and victory of Conftantine, gained over the tyrant Maxencius, at Ponte Mole. In this laft is a remarkable figure of an old foldier who lifts his fon, juft expiring, from the ground; the expreffion in the father is truly affecting. This falloon is completely covered with reprefentations of different events in the hiftory of Conftantine. The next falloon prefents hiftories from the book of the Maccabees; here is a compliment to Pope Julius the Second, who would be introduced as borne into the temple where

Onias

Onias the high prieſt is invoking heaveń.
His meaning was, that, after the example, of Onias, he had delivered the eccleſiaſtical ſtate from many uſurpations and
diſorders which had affected the patri-
mony of St. Peter. Alſo a famous picture,
and finely done indeed; it is called the
Maſs, and repreſents a miracle which happened at Bolſenna: A prieſt, who doubted
of the real preſence in the Euchariſt being
at the moment of conſecrating the wafer,
blood dropped from it. The different effects of ſurpriſe and aſtoniſhment amongſt
the people is repreſented in the moſt lively
and natural manner.

The ſubject of another piece which merits attention is Atilla, who ſees St. Peter
and St. Paul coming in the clouds to give
him battle. Here Pope Leo the Tenth
appears alſo mounted on his mule, with
the whole cavalcade of cardinals prancing
on various nags. Raffaello has alſo introduced

duced his mafter Pietro Perugino as mace-
bearer, curvetting before his Holinefs.

School of Athens.

In the fifth falloon are fome of his moft
efteemed paintings. The School of Athens
is a picture remarkable for invention,
grouping, juft perfpective, and colouring.
It reprefents a place decorated with fine
architecture. About the center appear
Plato and Ariftotle, who feem engaged in
philofophical difcuffions, furrounded by
their difciples. Socrates is reprefented
fpeaking earneftly to a young and beautiful hero in armour, by which figure is
meant Alcibiades. In another place, Py-
thagoras is graving mufical concords upon
a-tablet, held by a youth clothed in white,
who reprefents *Francefco Maria di Rovero
Duim d'Urbino*, and nephew to Pope Julius the Second. At a diftance is Dio-
genes, reclined on a ftep of the architecture; he has a book in his hand, and a
fmall bowl near him. Raffaello has placed
a relation

a relation of his own in another part of this picture. One Bramanti, who was a famous architect at that time; he is reprefented as Archimedes, tracing an hexagonal figure. Near him appears a young man, who puts one knee to the ground, and pointing to him expreffes great refpect and veneration; by this young man is meant Ferdinand the Second, Duke of Milan. Zoroafter makes a capital figure; he is draped in cloth of gold, and holds a globe; by him ftands Raffaello himfelf, with a black bonnet on his head and the moft filly face imaginable under it; he has placed his mafter Perugino by him. The *coup-d'œil* of this picture is very ftriking, and it demands fome time to examine it properly. Oppofite the School of Athens is a large painting, the fubject a difpute about the facrament, fo replete with fymbolical, typical, and allegorical reprefentations, that we did not contemplate it long.

Mount

Mount Parnaffus is another efteemed picture. Raffaello has introduced here all the moft celebrated poets of Italy, and placed himfelf between Virgil and Homer. Apollo plays on a violin; a great abfurdity. The moft capital figure is Sappho; her head, in particular, is finely done. Several other paintings merit obfervation, but you will excufe my paffing them over.

The cieling of the fixth room is painted by Perugino. Its beft picture reprefents the fire of *Bergo S. Spirito*, efteemed a *chef-d'œuvre*. The tumult, the confternation of the people, the 'effect of the wind upon the flames, and the different epifodes introduced, render this piece extremely curious.— The feventh room is called that of the Confiftory: the fubjects of the paintings are, St. Leon purfuing the Saracens, and Charlemagne crowned emperor. The two laft chambers exhibit fome fine perfpectives, by Baltazer Peruzzi. In the apartment of the Countefs
Matilda

Perugino.

Baltazer
Peruzzi.

Matilda are elegant frefcos by Romanelli. Roma-
nelli. There are many other apartments, chapels, and galleries, finely decorated with paintings, by famous mafters, which I fhall pafs over, and proceed directly to the Belvidere, Belvidere. or the *Torre di tutti gli Venti.* It has a communication with the Vatican by means of an open gallery or terras, and is called *Belvidere,* on account of the glorious profpect feen from it; which I fear would lofe by any defcription I fhould attempt. The apartments of the Belvidere have been inhabited by feveral Popes, though but fimply furnifhed. Here are fome curious morfels of antique mofaic ; one, in particular, reprefents an Egyptian dance.—A Model of Model of
St. Peter's
Church. St. Peter's Church opens in the middle fo as to fhew the fections, and, by means of a void left in the center, you may fhut yourfelf into it, and fee all the ifles, chapels, &c. at one view. In order to go to the court of the Antique Statues, you muft pafs along the great corridor of

Vol. III.   F   the

the Belvidere, which is in length 1692 feet, or about the third of a mile. Half-way is an iron-gate which conducts you to the Vatican library. We returned back to the library, after vifiting the Antique Statues. At the end of this gallery is the famous Statue of the dying Cleopatra. She is reprefented in a fupine pofture, with a ferpent twifted round her arm. I am forry to be obliged to confefs to you, that not-withftanding fhe is fo much admired, we were not ftruck as with a perfect piece of fculpture. Very improperly, from the pe-deftal or bafe of this Statue proceeds a fheet of water, which falls into a bafon on your left hand as you enter the above-mentioned Court. It is afferted to be the moft fuperb affemblage of the fineft Greek Statues in the whole world; there are eight in all. The Laocoon, the Apollo, the Antinous, and the famous *Torfe*, are thofe I fhall particularly mention; the other four being, in my opinion, unworthy of their fituation

Antique Statues.

Court of the An-tique Sta-tues.

2   here,

here, though they might possibly appear
to some advantage in another place. This
Antinous is esteemed of more beautiful *Antinous.*
proportions than that in the Capitol. He
is a model for grace; his limbs are elegant, and there is a lightnefs and eafe in
his whole figure, which is rarely found in
the moft beautiful nature; his attitude is
more genteel than noble; he expreffes
more penfivenefs than joy; yet we rather
prefer the face of the Antinous of the Capitol to this of the Belvidere.—The Lao- *Laocoon.*
coon aftonifhes and terrifies; the fubject is
fo horrible, and the expreffion fo juft, that
I could not contemplate it for any time together, but returned to it frequently; my
imagination almoft caufed me to fancy I heard
the piercing fhrieks of the fons *, proceeding from the agonizing pain expreffed in
their diftorted yet beautiful features, and
from the cruel folds of the ferpents that

---

* Thefe are in fhut-up niches to preferve them from being
injured by the weather.

confine

confine and twift round their delicate limbs. The old man's diftrefs is of another fpecies, and equally horrible. I believe Michael Angelo may be juftified when he pronounced the *Laocoon Il portento d'ell Arte*. This Statue was found in the baths of Titus. I fhould have added alfo that the Antinous was taken from a place called *Adrianello*, near the church of *S. Martino di Monte*.

When the folding doors were thrown open of the nich which conceals the Statue

Apollo.

of Apollo, I ftarted back with furprife. Never did I fee any fculpture come fo near the life, nor animation exprefs fo much majefty and dignity. I was ftruck with awe. The beautiful proportions of the limbs, the grandeur and noble air diffufed over the whole figure, his commanding afpect blended with angelic fweetnefs, joined to the moft perfect features, made me almoft fancy he breathed, and was about to fpeak: at length, coming out of

my

my firſt ſurpriſe, I ſaid to myſelf, it is but
marble that I ſee.—This Statue was found
at *Nettuno* *.

As to the famous Torſe I cannot pretend
to ſay that I am knowing enough to be
fenſible of its beauties. A headleſs trunk,
without arms or legs, appeared to me a
frightful object ; but I make not the leaſt
doubt of its poſſeſſing all the beauties and
perfections attributed to it by antiquaries
and connoiſſeurs. The muſcles are ſo
ſtrongly marked, that I ſhould think it
muſt have been a ſtatue of Hercules; and
what makes this conjecture very probable
is, that it is placed or reſts upon a lion's
ſkin.

From hence we adjourned to the Library.
I ſhall paſs over the garden, which is very
large, and laid out in the old-faſhioned taſte:
it is remarkable for little elſe than a great

The Torſe.

Library.

* Nettuno is a maritime town of the eccleſiaſtical ſtate,
fituated near Capo d'Anzo, the ancient port of Antium, a
town originally belonging to the Volſci, and where Coriola-
nus was killed.

number

number of concealed water-works, or rather *water-traps*, intended to fprinkle the
unwary. Here are alfo more *confiderable*
fountains.

This Library is fo conftructed as to afford a very agreeable *coup d'œil* at your
entrance; but the books being inclofed in
preffes which are painted, deprives it entirely of the appearance of a library. The
paintings are by various mafters, and the
fubjects taken from facred hiftory, or the
hiftory of the early ages of the church of
Rome. Some good antiques ferve to adorn
it; fine Etrufcan vafes, and amongft other
curiofities, a remarkable column of oriental alabafter, white and tranfparent; it is
folid, and beautifully fluted. Oppofite to
this pillar is a tomb of white marble, and
in it a winding fheet made of a linen which
readily catches fire, but does not confume
thereby. This linen is fecured by iron-
work, and in order to prove that it ftands
the fire, our Ciceroni pulled one end of it
out

out through the iron, and set fire to it with a lighted *Bougie*. It burnt fast, and presently extinguished of its own accord. The corner which had endured the flame appeared rather cleaner and whiter than the rest of the sheet, which was all the effect the fire produced. I pulled it as hard as I could, with design to have torn and brought off a rag of it with me, but in vain; and I believe the *Ciceroni* suspected me, for he thrust it into its place, and so secured it from any further attempts. It is probably formed of the *asbestus*, or, what is called in the Royal Cabinet of natural history at Paris, *Le lin Fossile*. Here is also a great collection of medals, which we had not time to examine. They told us the presses contained seventy thousand printed volumes and forty thousand manuscripts; several curious antique Bibles, in Hebrew, Syriac, Arabic, &c.; a very pretty Greek manuscript of the Acts of the Apostles in gold letters, given by Pope Innocent the

F 4 Eighth

Eighth to Charlotte Queen of Cyprus;
feveral manufcripts, with curious and
high-finifhed miniatures. Amongft thefe
is a Pliny, with the pictures of all the animals; a Virgil of the fifth century, all
wrote in capital letters, with the figures of
the Trojans and Latins, in their proper
habits; a beautiful manufcript of Taffo,
and a Dante, with miniatures at the top of
each page defcriptive of the fubjects. The
Original Letters of Harry the Eighth to
Ann Boleyn, and a Treatife on the Seven
Sacraments, compofed by himfelf: he fent
it as a prefent to Leo the Tenth, with thefe
lines, written with his own hand;

Anglorum Rex Henricus, Leo Decimo *mittit,*
Hoc opus, & *fidei teftem* & *amicitiæ.*

Here are many other curiofities of leffer
note, which our time did not permit us to
fcrutinize.

The Arfenal is a long falloon, faid to
contain arms for eighteen thoufand men.

Adieu.

Adieu. You fhall hear from me again
as foon as I have fufficient materials for as
long a letter as the prefent. Believe me
as ever, &c.

LETTER XLIV.

Rome, May 1, 1771.

IT is impoffible to feel *ennuié* at Rome,
though not a place of gaiety. This
city is the moft agreeable retreat in the
world (if a capital can be fo called) for all
thofe who love the fine arts, and have a
real pleafure in the ftudy of antiquity;
which yet rather inclines one to melancholy than cheerfulnefs. We propofe,
however, quitting it in a few days; but it
will be with fome regret, as we feel ourfelves fettled very much to our liking in
every refpect. Even the ceremonial of returning and receiving vifits is not exacted
here from us Englifh, as it would be in our
own country : one reafon is, we are fuppofed

poſed to come here to *ſee*, and to inform
ourſelves; another, becauſe whatever an
Engliſhman does, *is right*. Such is the flat-
tering idea the Italians, in general, entertain of our nation. This is a ſubject we
muſt not enlarge upon, left it ſhould increaſe
our vanity. The very recollection of all
the civilities and friendly ideas our Roman
friends have impreſſed upon us, are difficult
to combat; ſo predominant is ſelf-love.
Therefore I ſhall ſay no more on this head,
but proceed to a deſcription of what we have
ſeen ſince I wrote laſt. The Palace Borgheſe
is a magnificent building, decorated with all
the orders of architecture. The arcades of
the court are ſupported by an hundred columns of granite. The whole ornamented
with antique ſtatues. Thoſe of Julia, Fauſtina, and an Amazon, are amongſt the
beſt. The apartment of the *rez-de-chauſſée*
(lower-floor, over the under-ground apartments) conſiſts of eleven noble rooms or
ſalloons, all *en ſuite*, as full of fine paintings

Palace
Borgheſe.

ings as their walls can bear. We were told this Palace contains seventeen hundred original pictures. Do not imagine I am about to give you a description of them all; I shall confine myself to a very few, as I have so many palaces to mention. A Picture, by Dominichino; the subject, the sports of Diana and her nymphs; the Goddess is represented giving the reward to one of them, who has had the good fortune to gain the prize. This beautiful scene passes at a river's side: the Nymphs are in various attitudes; one, in particular, the most admired, is undressing herself for the bath. Two fine portraits of Cardinal Borgia and Machiavel, by *Raffaello*. The three Graces blindfolding a Cupid, by *Tiziano*. In a gallery highly ornamented and covered with looking-glasses and gilding, the Paintings that conceal the joinings of the glasses are extremely pretty; they represent Cupids, little River-gods, &c. in many elegant attitudes; the works

Domini-chino.

of

of *Ciroferi*. A fine Drawing, by Giulio Romano; the fubject Adonis dead in the arms of the Graces; a weeping Cupid and an afflicted Venus; two fwans offer to carefs her; and in another part of the picture are Cupids mounted on the back of a wild boar, and piercing him with arrows. There are charming Fountains in the middle of many of the rooms, which play conftantly, and fall into beautiful antique marble bafons. In this Palace is a great curiofity amongft the collection of marbles; it confifts of three antique flabs of white marble, found at *Monte Dragone* at *Frafcati*; they are above three feet long, and about an inch thick, yet fo pliable, you may bend them with little force; and when they lean againft a wall, placed on their edge, they bend of themfelves, fo as to form a curve of above an inch.

Palace Corfini.

The *Palazzo Corfini* is efteemed one of the fineft in Rome; it was the refidence of Chriftina Queen of Sweden, whilft in this capital.

capital,; Her apartment is neither large
nor magnificent, nor does it contain any
thing curious or remarkable. From refpect to her memory,. they have not
changed or removed the furniture, &c.
which is now much faded and worn. Near
her bed-fide are fome pictures, &c. of the
fort often found as furniture to bed-cham-
bers in Roman-catholic countries, *emblems
of fuperflition*. The exterior architecture of
the Palace is not much efteemed, but the
interior plan is indeed very fine ; the apartments noble and well contrived, as are the
ftair-cafes which lead to them. Here is
a vaft collection of pictures. I fhall mention the following, as they feemed to us
to be amongft the beft. But where one
fees fuch numbers, and does not return to
them again, I cannot, with the fame cer-
tainty, decide upon their merits, as though
I had had an opportunity of confidering
them a fecond time.

A Saint

Pictures.
Guercino.
Tenieres.

Wover-
mans.

Bourgig-
none.
Guido.

Rofa.

Statues.

Library.

A Saint Girolimo, by Guercino, in a great ftyle.—A Butcher's-fhop, by Tenieres; horribly natural, particularly in *a hot day.*— A fine Wovermans reprefents a fportfman on horfeback, leading another horfe; the fubject is coarfe; the moment the painter has taken is a vulgar German, or Dutch *joke.*—A fine Picture of a Field of Battle, by Bourgignone.—— A beautiful Piece, by Guido; the fubject Herodias, with the head of St. John: the girl's head is extremely graceful, and the whole highly and elegantly finifhed.

A Prometheus; the vulture dragging out and feeding upon his bowels. All the horrors attendant on fuch a fcene are reprefented to the life, by Salvator Rofa.— Amongft the Antique Statues with which this Palace abounds, there are two Buftos of admirable workmanfhip, one a Veftal; the other Seneca; and a beautiful Statue of a Woman, finely draped. There is alfo here a very great Library, confifting

ing of feven rooms contiguous to each
other; the books contained in them are
faid to treat of feven different fubjects;
a fubject to each room; and that all that
can be faid upon *each* by different authors
is collected here. They contain alfo fome
curious manufcripts, and a large collection
of prints and drawings. The gardens belonging to this Palace are pretty, in an old
ftyle; a great deal of fhade and regular
arbours; alfo a Sylvan amphitheatre with a
fountain in the middle, being frequently
the place of meeting for the academy of
Quirini, at which the cardinal *Neri Corfini* prefides, and where many curious and
interefting fubjects are difcuffed, particularly fuch as relate to the antiquities of
Rome. The public are allowed to walk
in thefe gardens; a very great convenience, and an inftance, amongft others, of
the Italian hofpitality.

The *Palazzo Barberini* refembles two or
three palaces joined together, and contigu-

Palace
Barberini.

ous

ous to it is a very large garden, ornamented with fountains, ſtatues, &c. The cieling of the grand ſalloon was painted by Pietro da Cortona, and is eſteemed a *chef-d'œuvre*; its ſubject allegorical, and relates to the Barberini family. This Palace contains a prodigious collection of fine pictures, antiques, and other curioſities. As I have had frequent opportunities of examining its contents at my leiſure, from the intimacy of our acquaintance with the family, I may be more accurate in my deſcription, than in regard to ſome of the others that I have only ſeen by walking once through the apartments. I ſhall

Pictures. begin with the Pictures : A Sleeping In-

Guido. fant, by Guido; the colouring delicate and tranſparent, the drawing correct, the figure of the moſt amiable character, and ſleeps as if *rocked by the Graces.*

Raffaello. A Portrait, by Raffaello, of his favourite Miſtreſs, for whom he died. She is of a brown complexion, and if at all handſome, fome, to my mind one of the moft difagreeable beauties I ever faw. Her face is of a vulgar *contour*; a fharp chin, ftrong lines, with features lean and hard; her countenance ftupid and infenfible. She has a bracelet above her elbow in the antique fafhion, on which is engraved Raffaello.

A Holy Family, by Parmefan. Hagar in the Defart, by Mola; finely coloured; the head of Hagar is beautiful. A very pleafing Picture, by *Pietro da Cortona*; its fubject the reconciliation of Jacob and Laban. A Magdalen, by Guido, in high eftimation with all the Virtuofi, which I muft confefs I' do not like. She fails in character. The figure is, no doubt, beautiful, but it might be taken for any other perfon. Repentance, remorfe, devotion, fhould be ftrongly expreffed in a Magdalen, and, to my eyes, none of thefe are here to be found. There are feveral fine Portraits by Tiziano, and one of Raffaello by himfelf.

Parmefan.
Mola.
Pietro da Cortona.
Guido.
Tiziano.
Raffaello.

VOL. III.   G   Amongft

Antiques. Amongſt the Antiques are two famous Buſtos of Marius and Sylla; a beautiful Head of Jupiter; a fine Head of Alexander the Great, and another of Antigonus. A Diana; her body of oriental agate. A ſmall Statue of Diana of Epheſus. A Head of Julius Cæſar, of Egyptian pebble. A Scipio Africanus, of *giallo antico*. A Coloſſal Buſto of Adrian; the head of bronze, the cuiraſſes and faſh of marble, with curious red veins. An Antique Moſaic, very well done; its ſubject the rape of Europa. A beautiful Antique Lion, in white marble. A fine Statue, in a nich, of a young Man, who holds in one hand a kind of ſtick, and in the other a *patera*; this Statue is perfectly well proportioned and of very antique ſculpture. A Sleeping Faun, which is a Greek ſtatue, and deſerves to be held in the higheſt eſtimation for its admirable workmanſhip. Two triangular Altars, and one round; in *baſſo relievo* appear Egia Goddeſs of Health, Iſis holding

the

the flower Lotus, and Mars. The *baſſo relievos* on the other altar are, Jupiter, Juno,
and a young Man, who, with one hand,
is leading along a ram for ſacrifice, and in
the other holds a cup. A Modern Statue,
by Bernini, of a ſick Satyr lying on his Bernini,
back: there is admirable expreſſion of pain
and ſuffering in this figure. A Statue, in
terra cotta, of Pope Urbino the Eighth,
made by a blind man, and ſaid to be extremely like. It bears this inſcription;
Giovanni Gambaſio cieco fecit.

Here is a fine Library, conſiſting of Library,
above ſixty thouſand volumes, beſide a
great collection of valuable manuſcripts,
medals, antique gems, cameos, intaglios,
and bronzes. One of the moſt curious
things in this Cabinet of Antiques, is an
ancient inſcription which bears a treaty of
peace between Rome and Tivoli. The
apartment inhabited by the Dutcheſs of
Montelibretti is nobly furniſhed in the Italian ſtyle. Some of the fineſt Pictures in

the

the collection are its decorations; but the
rooms are not crowded with them, as is
frequently the cafe in Italian palaces. Her
bed-chamber is extremely pretty; it is
hung with a Lyons filk, brocaded with fmall
flowers, and ftriped with filver, which has
an exceeding good effect: the chairs, curtains, &c. are all covered with the fame
materials. The jewels of this family (as
is the cuftom with all the great and princely
families in Italy) are kept in a large cabinet, and form a kind of *regalia*. They are
fhewn to ftrangers, and an houfehold officer
has the care of them, who is anfwerable for
his truft. Quantities of precious ftones
and pearl to amaze one; the jewels the
Dutchefs wears are magnificent; the diamonds of a much larger fize than any I
have feen in England, excepting thofe belonging to the crown, and a vaft number
of large pearl of the fineft water and moft
exact formation. The apartment of the
Princefs Paleftrine is furnifhed in a graver

ftyle

[85]

ftyle than that of her daughter-in-law; and contains feveral curious cabinets, china, and fmall pictures in oil, fome of which are very well done.

Pallazzo Farnefe. This magnificent edifice was, for the moft part, built by Michael Angelo. The *Collifeo* and the theatre of Marcellus were, by facrilegious hands, ftripped of their marble ornaments to adorn this Palace, as I have already mentioned in a former letter; and the memory of Pope Farnefe, Paul the Third, is held in execration at Rome for this illiberal action. It is a noble pile, but not without faults in the architecture; many of the members, by their fculpture, ornaments, &c. have too folid and weighty an appearance; and the confequence of enriching the fronts has been the throwing a gloom over the apartments. The grand court is a fquare, decorated with the three orders; under the arcades which environ it are placed certain famous antique ftatues. The

G 3 Hercules,

Hercules, called the Farnefian, (to diftinguifh it from the other Hercules) is efteemed a *chef-d'œuvre*, and was fculpted by one Gliton an Athenian, as the infcription upon it fets forth. It may be very beautiful, and the moft perfect model of a man in the world; but I am infenfible enough to its charms to own, that if all mankind were fo proportioned, I fhould think them very difagreeable and odious. The mufcles of this Hercules (allowing for the manner of fpeaking) are like craggy rocks compared with the Belvideran Apollo. Here is placed, alfo, the large urn wherein were depofited the afhes of Cecilia Mitella, taken out of her Maufoleum called Capo di Bove on the Appian way, as I told you before; but left you fhould have forgot it, I mention it to you again. The Flora is a fine Statue; her arms and feet have been replaced, and but indifferently; but the antique part has great merit; the drapery is glorioufly done. Having afcended the great ftair-cafe, the

Statues

Statues of two Slaves make a ftriking appearance, and are worthy the attention of
the curious. In the interior part of the
Palace are a numerous affemblage of buftos,
ftatues, &c. all antique. The vault of the
great gallery is painted in frefco by Annibal Caracci, and is efteemed one of the no-
bleft efforts of this mafter. The fubjects
are; in the center, the Triumph of Bacchus and Ariadne; the proceffion is comic,
and old Silenus on his afs makes a capital
figure; at one end of this piece appears the
God Pan, offering a fleece to Diana; at
the other, the Judgment of Paris. The
whole is admirably well done. Between
the center, and the extremities are the following: Triton on the Sea, with Galatea;
the Rape of Cephalus, by Aurora; the
epifode here introduced of Morpheus afleep
has a very fine effect. Polypheme endeavouring to charm Galatea with mufic, and
then hurling a fragment of a rock at Acis,
are finifhed with great fpirit. Other com-

partments

partments reprefent Jupiter inviting Juno
to his nuptial bed. Juno, graced with the
Ceftus, entertaining Jupiter. Diana careff-
ing Endimion ; the love expreffed here is
worthy of fo chafte a Goddefs. Hercules
and Iole ; they have exchanged dreffes,
and he is trying to amufe her by playing
on the *tambour de Bafque*. Anchifes taking off the Bufkin of Venus. There are
many more events of the fabulous hiftory
here reprefented, and which take up a
great deal of time to examine, as they are
all worthy of the clofeft notice. At the ends of
the gallery are two fine Paintings in frefco ;
one reprefents Andromeda chained to the
Rock; the other, Perfeus converting into
Stone, by the view of the Medufa's head,
Phineus and his companions; but I think
the picture we faw at Genoa on the fame
fubject better done. This gallery is painted
with various fubjects, all taken from the
heathen mythology, and decorated with
curious antique buftos ; many very fine are

in

in a *Gabinetto*, particularly the famous representation of Hercules between Vice and Virtue (by Annibal Caracci), in which the figure of Vice is out of all comparison more charming than that of Virtue.

Annibal,

A great number, in every Room, of antique statues and buftos of the firft clafs, and each merit a particular defcription. That of Caracalla is unqueftionably the fineft yet found. The defcription of the contents of this Palace would eafily furnifh matter for a folio. The famous Group of Dirce, the Bull, and the two Men, can never be fufficiently admired. This enormous compofition is of one block of marble, as white and as frefh as if newly executed; it would take me half a quire of paper to enter into a detail of its merits: let it fuffice, that it is one of the moft ftupendous efforts of fculpture that has as yet been difcovered, and that I am fure we fpent at leaft two hours in gazing upon it. It is kept under a fhed in a court contiguous to the Palace.

A fine

A fine *Basso Relievo*, representing an *Orgie* of Bacchus broke into three pieces: A Second represents Trimalcion leaning upon a Fawn, whilst another odd creature pulls off his sandals; a troop of comedians follow him. There are several Antiques in this place that are extremely curious.

Pallazzo Spada.

Near the *Pallazzo Farnese* is that of *Spada*, an inferior palace at Rome, but which, however, is worth seeing. The most remarkable Antiques and Pictures are; of the former, a Pompey, about fourteen feet high, and finely proportioned. Paris, Venus, and a Gladiator. A beautiful Statue of a Greek Philosopher. A Ceres, finely draped. Eight very large Tables of Marble, wrought in *basso relievo*. Amongst the Pictures, the Rape of Helen, by Guido. A repose in Egypt, by Carravagio. The Sacred Fire supplied by the Vestals, a fine sketch, by Ciroferri. A large Portrait of Cardinal Spada. A View of the Market at Naples during the usurpation of the famous

Guido.

Carravagio.

Ciroferri.

mous Maffenello the *lazzarone*. In a small
court is a pretty deception in perspective;
it is a little gallery or arched vault, sus-
tained by Doric pillars, which lessen according to the rules of perspective; the
plan on which they are built drawing towards the point of view in which the reality would have appeared to the eye. The
plan is only twelve feet in front, and con-
tracts gradually, being but six feet at the
end. It is built upon a slope, is eighteen
feet high at the entrance, and but nine at
the opposite extremity. A Statue of a
Fluter is placed at the end of the little
Court, which, when seen through this arch,
appears to be full five feet high, but is,
in reality, no more than three. This little
piece of architecture might be easily imitated, and would have a very pleasing effect in a London garden.

The *Palazzo Colonna* is a vast edifice, Palazzo
with a garden in proportion, and a prodi- Colonna.
gious collection of antiques and pictures.
The

The grand apartment is nobly furnished. Amongst the Pictures I observed the following in particular: A St. Margaret and Dragon, by Guido; a beautiful sketch. A Cephalus, and Procris endeavouring to dissuade him from the dangers of the chace; this is by Titian and extremely interesting. The Rape of Ganimede by the Eagle of Jupiter; by the same artist and very fine, though the colouring has suffered a little. The Gallery is superb, and of a prodigious length; it is furnished with fine paintings: A St. Francis, by Guido. A Flight into Egypt, by the same. St. John preaching in the Defart, by Salvator Rofa. A fine Picture, by Guercino; the subject David bearing Goliah's head; the daughters of Ifrael following, dancing and beating little kettle-drums; altogether ridiculous in the composition, though deservedly admired in other respects. A Man drinking out of a Glafs, by Tiziano: what is curious in this Picture is the nose, lips, &c. of

the

Guido,

Titian.

Guido,

Tiziano.

the Man forefhortened, as feen through
the Glafs. A moft admirable grotefque
Picture of a Peafant eating beans, by Tin- Tintoret.
toret. The Gardens are in a bad tafte,
having too many parterres formed of box
edgings and coloured ftucco, which are
dignified by the name of Englifh Flower
Gardens.

The *Pallazzo Bracciano*; rich in valuable Pallazzo
antique marbles, and many good pictures. Bracci-
On the ftair-cafe is a fine Bufto of Antoni- ano.
nus Pius, and in the firft falloon a rare
Statue of Caligula. Amongft the Pictures
that decorate the apartment, is the Woman
taken in Adultery, by Tiziano. The Hif- Tiziano.
tory of Cyrus, in five Pictures, by Rubens; Rubens.
and feveral other originals, by great Mafters. The Dutchefs of *Bracciana* told me,
that the beft Pictures in the *Palais Roy-*
ale at Paris, and all thofe, in particular,
which are hung in the Lanthorn-Room
there, were part of the *Bracciano* collection.
She is a near relation of the Duke of Or-
leans.

leans. I am not fure that I did not mention this circumftance in my firft letters
from Rome, where I had occafion to fpeak
particularly of this noble Lady, who is as
much diftinguifhed at Rome for her fenfe
and accomplifhments as for her high rank
and great connexions.

Cabinet of Curio-fities.
The Cabinet of Curiofities belonging to
this family contains a fuperb collection of
medals. They belonged formerly to Chriftina Queen of Sweden. Amongft the Antique Gems is a Cameo in oriental agate;
its fize exceeds fix inches by four; it reprefents the Profiles of Alexander the
Great, and his Mother Olympia.

Pallazzo Altieri.
Pallazzo Altieri. This Palace ftands
alone upon a great deal of ground. The
grand apartments are highly ornamented
with paintings and gilt ftucco, embellifhed
Claude Lorrain.
in a very good tafte. There are two Claude
Lorrains in them, efteemed the beft productions of that famous landfcape painter.
One is a View of the Sea; the other, to
which

which the preference is generally given, reprefents a beautiful Landfcape, in which is introduced the Temple of the Sibyl at Tivoli. If, I might venture to criticife this great artift, I fhould fay that his landfcapes would have been better, was there not an air of ftiffnefs in all his objects;—his trees too trim and of too fine a green, failing in that contraft that withered branches and fantaftic old roots and trunks of trees often produce in a reprefentation after Nature. At the fame time it is juft to obferve, that his paintings are highly finifhed, the glowing warmth of his fkies are inimitable, and never to be found in the landfcapes of any other painter.

Two Philofophers, by Salvator Rofa; and two Landfcapes of fine Rocks and Water, by the fame. A Virgin, by Corregio. A Lucretia, by Guido. A Roman Charity, by Guercino: this fubject is curioufly treated; the fcene prefents the outfide of a dungeon; the Daughter looks

Salvator Rofa.

Corregio.

Guido.

Guercino.

through

through the grated window and calls to her
Father, who is very conspicuous in the
interior of the dungeon, but from his age
and defect of hearing, he turns his head
and looks behind him, in order to difcover
from whence the voice proceeds. His
error produces great expreffion of anxiety
in the countenance of the Daughter.

Pallazzo
Chigi.

The *Pallazzo Chigi* contains fome good
paintings, a curious collection of. original
fketches and drawings of the greateft mafters, with fome antiques. An Adoration

Carlo
Marratti.

of the Shepherds, by Carlo Marratti. Some

Claude
Lorrain.

fine Landfcapes, by Claude Lorrain: one,
in particular, which prefents a beautiful
View of the Sea: on the fore-ground, the
Rape of Europa. A pretty Landfcape, by

Salvator
Rofa.

Salvator Rofa; in which he has introduced
Mercury piping to Argus in order to make
him fleep, and the beautiful Cow *Io* wateh-
ing the event. A Satyr carrying a bafket
of Fruit; by his fide a *Bacchante*: this

Rubens.

Picture is finely coloured; it is by Rubens.

An

An extravagant Picture, by Carravagio; Carrava-
gio. the fubject Mars whipping Cupid in the prefence of Venus.

Here is alfo a very good Library, con- Library. taining many curious manufcripts, enriched with fine miniatures. A Miffel of Pope Boniface the Eighth, bound in filver, inftead of leather.

The Chapel is pretty and richly ornamented.

Pallazzo Giuftiniano has not a very bril- Pallazzo
Giuftini-
ano. liant appearance. The Interior wants new furnifhing, but it contains a vaft collection of Statues and Paintings, which are not protected and kept as they ought to be. There are feveral valuable Antique Statues in the Court. The Grand Apartment is decorated with antique columns of green porphyry and green marble, ftatues, frefcopaintings, and pictures. Amongft the latter is a very fine Flemifh Picture, by the famous Handftorft of Utrecht, known in Italy by the nick-name of *Gerardo della* Gerardo
della
Notte. *Notte;*

Notte; for how can a foft Italian mouth pronounce fuch a hoarfe rumbling word as that
of *Hundftorft*. The fubject of this Picture
is Pilate on the Judgment Seat. The effect of the candle-light fhews wonderfully.
A Picture reprefenting St. Peter, who the
executioners are undreffing, in order to
prepare for his martyrdom on the crofs:
the colouring and the expreffion are great;

Saltarelli. it is by Saltarelli a Genoefe.

A Portrait of a Widow to whom Cupid

Paul Ve-
ronefe. prefents a looking-glafs, by Paul Veronefe.

St. Anthony and St. Paul, a fine picture,

Guido. by Guido. Socrates in Prifon, to whom
they are about to prefent the poifoned
bowl; and oppofite to it, Seneca, with his
veins opened and bleeding to death. Both
thefe tragic fcenes arc reprefented at night;
the lights of the flambeaux and lamps are

Gerardo
della
Notte. finely thrown by the Utrecht painter I
mentioned before.

In the Chamber of the Madonnas are
various reprefentations of the Bleffed Virgin,

gih, by Raffaello, Leonardo da Vinci, Pe- *Raffaello.*
rugino, Parmefan, and Andrea del Sarto. *Leonardo da Vinci.*
The Gallery holds a crowd of Sta- *Perugino. Parmefan.*
tues. The beft amongft them, an an- *Andrea del Sarto.*
tique .Goat, lying down. An antique
Marble Vafe, with beautiful rowled han-
dles. A Minerva. A Veftal. A Fawn,
with his hand full of grapes. A Head of
Homer. A Head of Vitellius. A Bufto
of Serapis. A Diana of Ephefus; and feveral Buftos of Emperors. Meffalina fitting. . The greater number of ftatues and
other antique marbles depofited in this Palace were dug up, in finking for its foundations, amongft the Ruins of Nero's Baths.

Pallazzo Rofpigliofi. This Palace be- *Palace Rofpigliofi.*
longed formerly to the Borghefe family.
Here are feveral pictures highly worthy
particular attention ; but I muft reftrain
myfelf in their defcription for want of
time, and proceed to the antiques. In the
Gallery is a remarkably large round Bafon
of *Verd antique*, fupported by a pedeftal of

H 2   porphyry.

porphyry. An antique Piece of Frefco-
painting, reprefenting a landfcape, with
a houfe in the middle, and palm-trees
about it, in the Chinefe tafte. Four fmall
Frefco-paintings, antique, found in the
Ruins of Conftantine's Baths; the fubjeéts
chiefly Bacchanalian, but one, in particular, is extremely pretty; it reprefents a
Cupid on a Branch of Flowers, holding a
ladder. In the Garden is a well-propor-
tioned little building, which contains the
beft paintings in the colleétion. On the
cieling of its falloon or veftibule is the famous painting in frefco, by Guido, known
by the name of the *Aurora*, and reprefents
the bringing on of the Day. Phœbus, in
a triumphal chariot, is drawn by four fiery
courfers a-breaft; the hours, under the
figures of beautiful nymphs, dance around
him; he is preceded by a Cupid, holding
a torch, and Aurora, who ftrews the earth
beneath with flowers. The figures here
reprefented may ferve as models for grace;
the

the folds of the draperies are light, natural,
and fimple; and the clouds finely rendered.
It is much to be regretted that the falloon,
the repofitory of this fine piece of frefco,
is damp, by which it has fuffered confiderably, as well as by negleét. Here are alfo
two fine Friezes painted in frefco, by Tem-
pefta. I fhall now have done with Palaces,
left you fhould be furfeited with them, as
you were with Churches at Paris, and mean
to conclude this voluminous letter with a
defcription of the Jefuits College. You
fhould here afk, How it was poffible for me
to have feen the Jefuits College? I fhall
inform you; for, to be fure, no female has
ever entered it, (at leaft, by public permiffion) fave the Emprefs Queen, Chriftina
Queen of Sweden, and your moft humble
fervant. Know then, that I, not devoid
of that curiofity natural to us all, had
learned that this fame *Sanctum Sanctorum* of
a feminary for learning was poffeffed of a
moft rare collection of antique marbles,

H 3   gems,

gems, pictures, natural hiflory, and what
not, and was confequently defirous of in-
fpecting this pure and holy edifice, but
found that females were never permitted to
enter, fave only the before-mentioned royal
perfonages, who had, as a great grace and
favour, obtained permiffion, to that effect,
from the fovereign Pontiff; and that, in
fhort, it was impoffible for me to gain ad-
mittance, unlefs by an order from the Pope,
I ftill perfifted in wifhing to fee it, and frequently expreffed my conjectures in regard
to its contents in prefence of a dignified
ecclefiaftic who was in his Holinefs's good
graces, and who being tired, I fuppofe,
with conftantly hearing the fame fubject
harped upon, undertook to afk the favour.
The Pope had the goodnefs to grant it,
and an order was accordingly given upon
ftamped paper, addreffed in the form of a
letter to the general of the Jefuits, with
our names mentioned and thofe of *****,
this gentleman and lady having much
wifhed

wifhed to accompany us, and we fucceeded
in procuring this additional gratification.
The paper was figned in all form, firft by
his Holinefs himfelf, then by *Monfigniore
Pallavicini*, fecretary of ftate, the general
of the Jefuits, and this paper empowered
us to vifit the College and every part of it
at any hour, and as often as we pleafed.
We accordingly went thither, and were received by the general and the chiefs of that
fociety with the utmoft politenefs. They
were fo obliging as to give themfelves the
trouble of conducting us about, and fhewed
us all the interior of the building, with its
curiofities. It is a vaft edifice ; contains **J-fuits College.**
excellent apartments, well fitted up and
moft commodioufly difpofed. A Mufeum
that would employ an antiquary many
months to give a proper defcription of its
rare antiques and other contents. Part of
this fuperb collection is compofed of the
famous cabinet of Father Kircher, that of
the *Marchefe Gregorio Copponi*, and a col-

lection

lection of gems given by Auguſtus King of Poland. Here are beautiful antique vaſes of agate and cornelian, cups of egiade, jaſper and onyx, fine cameos and intaglios, antique ear-rings ; the drops in various ſhapes ; ſome repreſent little Cupids ſuſpended, others vaſes, &c. Gold chains for the neck, of exquiſite neatneſs. A ſeries of medals, and, amongſt them, ſeveral of gold, and extremely rare. Antique marbles, ſuch as ſtatues, *baſſo relievos*, altars. Inſtruments of ſacrifice very antique and of beautiful workmanſhip. Inſcriptions, &c. beſides weights, meaſures, and various other articles in bronze. An antique Sun-dial, found at Tuſculum, eſteemed a very great curioſity : by this Dial it appears that the Romans reckoned twelve hours to the day, including one hour of twilight. A prodigious ſeries of natural hiſtory, including the whole ſcience, animal, foſſil, mineral, vegetable, &c. nothing excepted. All the ſciences are taught here,

here, and there are profeffors appointed to
inftruct youth. Almoft every neceffary
and ufeful article is made within their own
walls. Here are buildings for the taylors,
fhoe-makers, carpenters, &c. who are
folely employed for the College.

A very fine Library; alfo fome excellent pictures. Amongft thefe I particularly remarked the following. A beautiful
one of the Woman of Samaria; it is, I
think, the beft I ever faw on this fubject;
fhe is charming, and her figure graceful in
the higheft degree. Our Saviour's figure
is not quite equal to hers, but has great
expreffion. The copper bucket which fhe
has juft drawn out of the well appears wet,
and chilled with the coldnefs of the water.
The whole of the picture is as highly
finifhed as poffible, not the flighteft circumftance omitted; even the cord faftened
to the bucket is as natural as if really there.
It is a fmall picture, the joint work of Livia
Fontana and Dominichino, and cannot be
too

Livia
Fontana,
and Do-
minichi-
no.

Carravagio. too much admired. A St. Jerome, by Carravagio. A young Chrift among the doc-
Vandyke. tors. A Refurrection, by Vandyke. A
Corregio. holy Family, by Corregio. A Nativity, by
Calvert. Calvert, Dominichini's mafter. The Difci-
Jacopo Baffano. ples at Emaus, a fine picture, by Jacopo
Guercino. Baffano. St. Gregorio, by Guercino. All thefe are perfect, and in the higheft confervation. There is a fine terras at the top of the building, from whence you have a beautiful view of all Rome and the country adjacent. Amongft the many conveniencies attached to this College, I had almoft forgot to mention a botanic garden, with a laboratory, where are all forts of chymical utenfils, the fineft drugs (I fuppofe) in the world, and many curious preparations for different branches of phyfic. In the garden is a fountain that pleafed me much by its fimplicity. Suppofe a moderately large arched nich in a wall, and rocks piled up within the nich, fo as to form half a protuberant or convex pyramid. Thefe

I rocks

rocks are overgrown with various moffes,
over which the water gently ftreams, and
falls into the bafon below. In the fpace
between this fmall pyramid of rocks and
the nich has grown a quantity of maiden
hair, which hangs down to a great length,
and makes a graceful appearance. We
then adjourned to the Church of St. *Igna-* Church of
zio, which belongs to the College. The St. Igna-
riches of this edifice are immenfe. A profufion of the fineft marbles adorn the infide. The chapels are beautiful, and the
cleanlinefs and neat order in which it is
kept moft ftriking. Here are fome good
pictures, but that which moft caught my
eye was, the Portrait of St. *Ignazio*, done
by a brother of the order. It is the reprefentation of a beautiful young man, with
an innocence and fweetnefs of countenance
that charms you. It might very well pafs
for a reprefentation of that glorious faint
St. Stephen, at the moment of his martyrdom, when he faw heaven open to him.

My

My partiality to the portrait of St. Ignazio was extremely grateful to the
holy fathers, who conceived an excellent
opinion of my *taste* and *discernment*, and
made me many compliments thereupon.
At length we took leave, highly satisfied
with the obliging deportment and hospita-
ble reception we had met with. We were
offered all kinds of excellent refreshments,
and the professor of botany having observed
me examining some drugs I saw in the laboratory, insisted upon my accepting some
Venice treacle and some Arabian gums, the
best I ever saw. I ventured to slip a sequin
into an empty crucible which was near me,
in hopes the lad who was at work might
find it, but was perceived by one of the
fathers, who returned it to me with some
resentment. Nor would they suffer us to
leave any perquisite for their servants. ....

I do not wonder this society is so numerous. The advantages they have over
others are conspicuous. A Jesuit may indulge

dulge himfelf in every inclination. If hè
loves the *Belles Lettres*, he will find an
ample fociety to improve and inftruct him
in that purfuit. If his difpofition prompt
him to a rigorous devotion and hard ftudy,
he may purfue it without interruption.
Does his tafte lead him to travelling? No
people travel more. It is, no doubt, by
the permiffion of the general of the order,
or by his commands; but he is furnifhed
with every convenience for the occafion.
If he prefer lazinefs and idlenefs, the pleafures of the table and fenfual delights, he
will not find himfelf deftitute of companions or opportunity. Has he his own
notions of religious matters, or no religion
at all? there are of the holy brotherhood
who would only wonder he was not worfe,
and bid him be thankful that a creature
born prone to all evil and averfe to all
good, fhould be capable of the flighteft
virtue, in any refpect. But I muft expatiate no longer on this artfully contrived
religious

religious fociety, or my letter would never finifh. So adieu, &c.

P. S. I fhall write once more before we quit Rome.

LETTER XLV.

Rome, May 14, 1771.

THIS is the laft letter you will receive from hence, as we propofe leaving Rome to-morrow or next day, and purfuing our *route* to Loretto with all poffible expedition.

As the weather is extremely hot, I think it will be more agreeable to you to make your ideal excurfion to Frefcati, Tivoli, and fome of the villas, than to be detained by a view of the *Cloaca Maffima*, in which we paffed fome time admiring its curious conftruction, being built of large blocks of ftone, which unite fo clofely, that no cement or mortar was neceffary. But, as I

Cloaca Maffima.

fufpect

suspect you would choose to breathe a purer
air, I shall immediately conduct you, first
to *Castel Gondolfo*, and then to *Albano*, Castel
Gondolfo.
where we lay one night. *Castel Gondolfo*
is a small town, or rather a village, built on
the borders of a lake called *Lago Castello*,
from a house or sort of castle where the
Pope generally passes the autumnal season,
called by the Italians *la Villagiatura*, an-
swering to the season for the *Vandanges* in
France, when all the great people are at
their villas and country-houses. There is
nothing remarkable in *Castel Gondolfo*; it
is a plain, strong-looking, old-fashioned
house. The road from hence to Albano
lies along the borders of the lake, which
renders it delightful. The prospect is very
beautiful, the lake being fringed round Lago
Castello.
with fine trees, and the grounds lying
wildly scattered in a variety of shapes. The
reflection produced by the different tints of
greens, &c. with the sky, forms a fantastic appearance in the lake, which is about

seven

seven or eight miles in circumference, and seems a great round mirror, fixed in a prodigious concave frame. Near Castel Gon-

Villa Barbarini Gardens. Ruins.

dolfo, in the gardens of the Villa Barbarini, are the Ruins of a Country Palace of Domitian. The remains are considerable, though detached from each other. Here are to be seen vaulted chambers; a wall, with niches in it, supposed to have been a gallery; an arched way, about fifteen yards wide, as many high, and above two hundred and fifty long, stuccoed in compartments, exactly resembling those of the interior part of the Arch of Septimius Severus. Some of the gilding on these compartments is still distinctly visible; therefore, it is probable this place was never intended for a reservoir of water, which the *Grande Virtuosi* here assert it to have been. On the border of the Lake D'Albano or Lago Castello are two Grottos

Grottos of the Nymphs.

(which were discovered by the famous *Piranese*); they are practised in the mountain

on

on the fide of the Lake; one is of a regular form, about the fize of a moderately
large church, in which are niches appa-
rently defigned for ftatues, and two or
three fmall chambers detached. The other
a cavern of about forty yards long, and
fifteen wide; it has neither nich nor
other ornament. Thefe *Souterrains* are
called the Grottos of the Nymphs, and
probably were ufed as baths; for there are
remains of feats to repofe upon, and the
center of the grotto is hollowed out as
though it had been a receptacle for water.
The Canal which proceeds from the lake is
of great antiquity. It is a fubterranean aqueduct, made by the Romans three hundred
and ninety-eight years before the Chriftian
æra; when this lake having fwelled to an
amazing height, it was apprehended that,
fhould it overflow, Rome might be in danger from the inundation; the Delphic
oracle was hereupon confulted, and the
Pythian god replied, that the Romans

Canal.

fhould poffefs the town of Veia, which
they were then befieging, when they fhould
have found a vent to carry off the fuper-
abundant water of the lake, and not before. They were ftill farther encouraged
in this undertaking by the prophecies of
a foldier to the like effect. They begun
the work and completed it in one year,
penetrating through the mountain, and
forming an aqueduct of three miles long,
near four feet wide, and between nine and
ten in height. The work was finifhed
with fuch folidity, that it has never wanted
repairing fince, and ftill ferves the fame
purpofe as it then did, carrying off the
wafte waters that rife above a certain level.
A few years paft, a man undertook to walk
through this aqueduct. He entered, but
was never more heard of. The water
paffes freely through it, and fpreads itfelf
over a plain on the other fide of the mountain whence it comes out. Piranefe, in
his *Antichita d'Albano*, &c. has given a
moft

moſt curious account of this work, with
very ingenious conjectures of the manner
in which it was carried on, &c. In this
famous mouñtain of Albano are frequently
found marble pillars, cornices, &c. of beautiful ſculpture. It is alſo curious to ob-
ſerve, that the ſoil bears the moſt evident
marks of former volcanos and irruptions, like
thoſe of mount Veſuvius, it being incor-
porated with burnt ſubſtances, ſuch as black
talc, a ſort of cinders, and ſhining vitrified
particles like that mixed with the lava;
alſo ſcoria, or droſs of metallic ſubſtances.
Juſt before we entered the town of Albano,
we ſaw the ruins of a Mauſoleum, which
the people here call the Tomb of Aſcanius,
the ſon of Æneas. Near the other entrance
of Albano is a great Mauſoleum. This
ſtructure is of coarſe and rude architecture. Five round broken pyramids ſpring
from a large ſquare baſe; it is here called
the Monument of the Horatii and Curatii; Monu-
but the learned antiquarians differ much in ment of
the Hora-
I 2   this tii and
Curatii.

this point, fome believing it to be a monument of Pompey the Great. To you I may venture to add my opinion, and own I fhould think it of earlier antiquity. One of our poftillions inquiring the road to this Ruin, of a gardener upon the road, received for anfwer, that the *Antica Roba Inglefe* he afked for, was about half a mile from the town. This idea of its being an Englifh antiquity muft have arifen from the numbers of Englifh who inquire for and vifit it. The town of Albano is a fmall inconfiderable place, yet contains fome pretty clean-looking modern-built houfes, where people lodge for the benefit of the air, when the heats of fummer become incommodious at Rome. We lay at a little Albergo or inn, were pretty well lodged and ferved, and returned to Rome the next morning. Our excurfion to Tivoli took us up the greater part of a day, though we fet out between three and four in the morning, as we ftopped frequently upon our

road

Albano.

Tivoli.

road thither, and faw the cafcades, &c. quite
at our leifure. From Rome to Tivoli is fixteen miles. The road very good. We
croffed the river Teverone, or the antique Antique
Anio, twice. It would confume too much Anio.
of my time, fhould I particularife the antique bridges which ftill remain upon this
river. At about fourteen miles from Rome,
we came to the *Aqua Zolfa*. It is a kind Aqua
of canal, about five or fix feet wide, and Zolfa.
as many deep. Its water of a deep blue
colour, ftinks horribly of fulphur and rotten eggs, and is of fo penetrating a quality
as to have undermined a great part of the
plain through which it runs. This Canal
was cut by a cardinal of Efte, and takes
its fource from the *Solfatara*, a fmall lake Lake.
above a mile out of the road, of a very
muddy yellowifh caft, and ftinks as
much as the canal. This is covered
with little floating iflands, or rather large Floating
tufts of grafs and rufhes growing in Iflands.
a foil from one to about three feet thick.

Some

Some are as large as a moderate-fized
ferry-boat, others not larger than a card-
table. You may pull thefe latter towards
the fhore, and the children of fome of the
poor people who live near the lake jump
on them, and fail about by the help óf a
ftick, with which they paddle. Several
kinds of weeds grow on thefe iflands, and
flourifh along with the grafs, which is remarkably green, though the water of the
lake is fo impregnated with fulphur, that
one would think no plant could vegetate
in its vapour. On throwing pebbles in,
the water boils up and bubbles ftrongly for
fome time after, nor do they fink as foon
as in common water. The poor people
who live near this lake told us it was un-
fathomable toward the middle; but we
had no time to make the experiment ourfelves, nor were we properly provided for the
Incrufta- purpofe. This water forms incruftations,
tions. which at length become ftone, and retain
a ftrong fulphureous fmell. All about this
country

country are remains of antique country-
houfes. 'Among others, that of Regulus, Houfe of Regulus.
which had magnificent porticos (as men-
tioned by Pliny). Near the *Ponte Lucano* Ponte Lucano.
are the remains of the Tomb of the family Tomb of the Plau-
of Plautius, which had fome little refem- tius.
blance to that of *Capo di Bove.* At prefent
it makes no other appearance than that of a
round tower. Near it are the fhafts of fix
columns. Two infcriptions ftill remain on
flabs of marble, one of which is very le-
gible; it runs thus :

M. Plautius m. f. an. Silvanus cof. VII. *vir.* Infcrip-tion.
Epulon. huic Senatus triumphalia ornamen-
ta decrevit ob res in Illyrico bene geftas.
Lartia gn. f. uxor A. Plautius M. F. Vir-
gulanius. vixit an. IX.

Having paffed Ponte Lucano, we turned
off to the right, in order to vifit the Ruins
of Adrian's Villa, which is two miles from Ruin.
that bridge, and the fame diftance from Adrian's Villa.
Tivoli. Thefe Remains cover a large piece

of

of ground. Several country-houfes have been built upon them, and the greater number of the fineft antiques in the Roman collections have been found here. Various authors agree, that this Villa was in length three miles, and in breadth a fifth of that fpace. Two theatres, of femicircular plans, terminate thefe Ruins. An exterior portico belonging to one of them, with chambers for the actors, ftill remains; with fix ftair-cafes, to afcend to different parts of the theatre. One of the fide-entrances to the profcenium and the orcheftra are yet difcernible.

Ranging along a terras are a great number of rooms, which let into each other. They are all vaulted, and of ftrong architecture. Thefe are called the *Cento Camerelli*, and are faid to have been the lodging-rooms of the Prætorian guards. Alfo edifices for baths (fome fupplied by the *Anio*, others by the *Aqua Martia*), and a variety of buildings, with various-fized apartments,

ments, fome very fmall, others large and well proportioned; in many of which are ftill difcernible the ornaments of the cielings in ftucco, and painted in arabefque. Amongft many other ruined ftructures, one is very remarkable: it is called *Canopus*, and forms a great bafon, fuppofed to have been ufed for *Naumachias*. The front of this edifice is fallen, and a temple belonging to it (that is, in any degree, perfect) only remains. It was dedicated to Neptune, who was worfhipped by the Egyptians under the name of *Canopus*. There have been feveral fine antique ftatues found in this place. A Sea Horfe, confecrated to *Canopus*. An *Ifis*, *Ofiris*, *Ibis*, with hieroglyphic infcriptions. Here are alfo the remains of a beautiful grotto, confifting of feveral apartments, ornamented with niches for cafcades of water, with contrivances to let in the light to great advantage. The cielings of thefe grottos are painted in compartments of various colours.

On

On part of thefe gardens is built a religious
houfe for the Jefuits; they are faid to have
been laid out formerly in the moft beautiful reprefentation of the Elyfian fields,
contrafted with the regions of Pluto; even
the rivers *Lethe, Cocytus,* and *Flegeton*
were introduced, and the moft exquifite
efforts of art contributed to heighten the
delufion. Here ftill remains veftiges of co-
lonades, temples, aqueducts, &c.; and in
another part are porticos, fupported with
marble columns of great beauty. Much
more may be faid of this Villa, even in its
prefent ruined ftate; but what it has been,
is ftill to be gathered from a variety of ancient authors. Suffice it to fay, that the
utmoft efforts of the arts and fciences were
exhaufted in its improvement, with all the
refinements luxury could invent, *riches*
and *defpotic power* beftow, upon a fpot
kind and beautiful by Nature. A wet and
marfhy piece of ground, which was partly
under water, and had been an immenfe
bafon

bafon in the front of this Villa, is rented by a Mr. Hamilton, a very ingenious English artift, who keeps a great number of men at work upon it, and has fucceeded fo far as he has gone, in draining it; with great expence and labour. He very fenfibly fixed on this fpot, concluding that many valuable antiques might have been thrown into the water, to preferve them from the barbarous fury of thofe who demolifhed this fuperb edifice. He has already found a great number of curious articles, which will, I believe, by their fale, yield him an ample indemnification. The work is continued with vigour, and I do not doubt but that in time you will fee in England very fine morfels of antique fculpture, refcued from oblivion by this induftrious artift.

In continuing our rout to Tivoli, we paffed by the fpot where once ftood the Villa of Caffius, and where the confpira- Villa of tors met. Tivoli is fituated on a hill; the Caffius. town

town itfelf is a wretched place, and made more difagreeable by a number. of forges : it was founded fifteen hundred years before the Chriftian æra; was famous for its oracle, as mentioned in Virgil, and for the falubrity of its air. Horace, Cicero, and many other claffic authors have celebrated it highly. The former had, unqueftionably, a houfe there, or in its neighbourhood : at prefent it is an epifcopal town. The cathedral is built upon the Ruins of the Temple of Hercules ; but the moft re-

Temple of the Sybil.

markable antiquity here is the Temple of the Sybil : the beautiful architecture and fine proportions of this fmall edifice ftrike you at the firft view : its form is moft elegant, its fculpture perfect and peculiarly graceful. The lines fo infifted upon by Hogarth in his Analyfis of Beauty, are to be traced in all the ornaments of this building. Its fituation is on the brow of a hill; on one fide appears the town, and in front the great cafcade. This Temple has been

fo

fo accurately defcribed with the plan, mea-
furements, &c. by various architects, and
particularly by Palladio, Vitruvius, and
others, that I am furprifed it has not been
copied in fome of the fine gardens of England, where there might eafily be found
fituations proper for fuch an ornamental
building. The Englifh unqueftionably fur-
pafs all the nations of the world in their
gardens. That free people take the beauties of Nature *captive*; they then prefent
Art to her acquaintance, who flatters,
adorns, and dreffes her, till, forgetting fhe
is imprifoned within the limits of concealed
walls or invifible *ha-ha's*, fhe willingly
confents to difplay her native charms in all
their luftre, and fubmits to the rules Art
has enjoined her, in purfuit of *elegance*,
utility, convenience, and *liberal neatnefs.*
But I muft not let the gardens of England
confume my time; Italian only fhall at
prefent engrofs my thoughts, as I am foon
to conduct you to the Villas near Rome.

At

Cafcade of Tivoli.

At prefent we are at the great Cafcade of Tivoli; it is formed by the Teverone or antique *Anio*. This river following its natural courfe till it comes near and above Tivoli, is there confined within a narrow valley, between two mountains, and precipitates itfelf down a high and pointed rock, which oppofes its paffage, into another fteep valley. The dafhing of this torrent is re-ecchoed back from the inmoft receffes of the fhades of Tivoli, and the fpray of the water fo fills the air, as to produce a very broad and beautiful rainbow, compofed of a greater variety and of more glowing tints than that of the Heavens. The *Cafcatella*, which I think a much finer cataract, is a little way out of the town. This is compofed of one great fheet and three leffer falls, which at length all unite. In their defcent they tumble down amongft rocks, and, by the force of their fall and the refiftance they meet, are thrown up with fuch violence as to form new cafcades.

Amongft

Amongſt the rocks grow trees in the moſt fantaſtic ſhapes. The ſpray cauſes rain-bows as in the great caſcade, and the whole landſcape forms the moſt romantic and pic-tureſque view imaginable. The rude brawl-ings of the water, daſhing from rock to rock, is finely contraſted by the ſtillneſs that reigns in the adjacent paſtures, covered with ſheep, feeding and repoſing in the utmoſt tranquillity.

Here are remains of the houſe of Mæ-cenas, at leaſt they are ſhewn for ſuch. They chiefly conſiſt of ruined arcades and detached morſels, but it is very doubtful whether theſe were not rather ruins of baths, that might poſſibly have belonged to Mæcenas's villa. Returning to Tivoli by a ſteep hill (another way) we had a fine view : the dome of St. Peter's is quite vi-ſible ; the country which forms the nearer proſpect preſents the moſt agreeable variety of ground : Tivoli loſes its defects by the diſtance, though it is but ſhort, and forms

7   a moſt

a moſt beautiful amphitheatre; the Tem=
ple of the Sybil appears much larger, and
feems to overlook the whole view; the ſky
behind it is extremely advantageous, and ⸱
there is fomething fo lively and agreeable
in the difpofition and affemblage of all the
objeds, as muſt enliven the dulleſt imagination. The Cafcades of Tivoli have a particular effed on the morfels of broken rock
upon which they fall, grinding, and as it
were, poliſhing them in fuch a manner as
to give them exadly the appearance of the
fineſt and whiteſt fugar-plums of various
ſhapes, but particularly thofe of almonds
and barberries, and are fo corredly fa-
ſhioned, that they would deceive the niceſt
eye. Thefe little ſtones are to be had of
the cottagers whofe habitations are near
the cafcades, and who difpofe of them to
travellers as a natural curiofity.

Villa
Eſtenfe.
The Villa Eſtenfe is built on one of the
heights of Tivoli; it was a very fine thing
in its day. The cardinal d'Eſte, fon of
Alphonfo

C

Alphonſo Duke of Ferrara, and Lucretia Borgia, built it in the year 1544. The ground is laid out in hanging gardens and terraſſes, fountains, baſons, parterres, labyrinths, &c.; it is decorated with ſtatues, and appears altogether pretty enough in a very old-faſhioned way. At the top of a caſcade is a grotto; it formerly contained a water-organ, which is at preſent out of repair. There are ſome pretty water-works in the gardens; one ſet, in particular, which play from the beaks of eagles, and are placed ſo as to form the coats of arms of the houſe of Eſt. I believe I forgot to mention, that in the road to Tivoli a conſiderable part of the plain is covered with incruſtations, produced by the quality of the water or river; they are, when newly formed, extremely brittle, but, after ſome time, grow hard; they take the forms of herbs and blades of graſs, or whatever other ſubſtance the inundations of the river

VOL. III.　　　　　K　　　　　have

have flowed over, and would be extremely ornamental in grotto-work.

Having, I think, been sufficiently particular in regard to Tivoli and its environs, I shall now proceed to the villas near Rome. That of cardinal Albani is the most esteemed: it is rather a small palace than a villa, but the Italians give this modest name to all the fine buildings in the environs of their capital cities. The portico of this elegant edifice is supported by columns of Egyptian granite, and ornamented with antique statues of the emperors, and some very curious *basso relievos*, which serve them for pedestals. Amongst the statues of the emperors, the most remarkable is that of Domitian, being the only one of him that has as yet been found quite entire. Here are two beautiful vases of *alabastro fiorito*; they measure above seven feet in diameter. Through the vestibule, which is also filled with antique marbles,

Villa
Albani.

3

bles,

bles, you enter the Chapel, where is a profufion of precious marbles and ornaments of gold. The altar is a farcophagus of red granite, which contains the body of a faint and martyr. The wings or fide-colonades are formed by pillars of granite, between which are placed, on one fide, the buftos of the 'moft celebrated conquerors in antiquity, and on the other fide the moft famous philofophers, orators, and poets. Amongft many other very curious antiques, an Etrufcan altar, in particular, here claims our attention: it is fquare, and is fculpted in *baffo relievo* on three of its fides; thefe reprefent Mercury conducting a Nymph, preceded by Bacchus; the fecond fide Ceres, Neptune, and Juno: on the third appears a Divinity, holding a bird on the top of a ftaff, and two Nymphs, who follow each other, bearing ftaffs; the hinder holds her that precedes by part of her drapery. Thefe figures are correct in their defign, and perfectly graceful.

K 2 Here

Here are also two beautiful Urns of a
very large fize, of yellow tranfparent antique *Alabaftro:* they were found in a
vineyard belonging to the *Marchefe Pa-
liotti,* who prefented them to his eminence
the prefent Cardinal *Albani.* The *Sala,* or
principal *Stanza* above ftairs, contains two
beautiful columns of *Giallo Antico.* In the
gallery is a fine collection of rare antiques,
columns, mofaicks, *baffo relievos,* &c.
Two ftatues are particularly admired; one
a Pallas, the other an Ino with the infant
Bacchus in her arms. Here is a very fine
portrait of *Antinous* in *baffo relievo,* efteemed by the *Virtuofi* at Rome, a moft rare
and curious morfel.--All the apartments are
elegantly decorated with antique bronzes,
vafes, fine pieces of mofaic formed of
real marbles, and opaque gems inftead of
compofition; very large looking glaffes,
gilding, old japan, &c. The ceilings
are painted; one in particular reprefents Apollo and the Mufes : thefe perfonages

fonages, are all of them portraits. * *
* *r* * * * * * What charm-
ed me much in this villa, is the elegant
order in which all is kept, joined to the
moft exquifite and univerfal cleanlinefs.
The gardens are large for Italy, and laid
out in the old tafte of parterres, terraffes,
and formal walks. Some very curious
antique ftatues, fountains, and bafons, con-
tribute not a little to their decorations.
The Egyptian ftatues are more curious than
beautiful: one is of Theban alabafter, the
others bafalte. In the middle of a large
parterre you fee an antique fountain and
bafon of granite, fupported by four old
crouching fawns, of good workmanfhip,
in the Etrufcan ftyle. Here are arcades
and arbours formed of trees planted regularly, and a building called the Temple of
Jupiter; confifting of a vaulted room fupported by two large columns, one of which
is of an entire piece of *alabaftro fiorito*.

The

The villa Aldrobrandini is near that of
Albani: this is worth feeing only on account of certain antique fragments, and a
famous painting in *frefco*, found in the
baths of Titus, which reprefents a wedding; fome of the female attendants are
graceful; the bridegroom feems not very
far from his *grand* climacterick, the bride
is young and looks *forrowful*. Altogether,
the perfonages reprefented might well pafs
for affiftants at a funeral feaft, fo little appearance is there of mirth or gaiety. The
colours have fuffered much by the under-
ground damps, and the tints are univerfally inclined to a brick colour caft.

The villa Pamfili, or *Belrefpiro*, a country
palace belonging to prince Doria, ftands in
a park and gardens about fix miles round:
thefe gardens are fuppofed to occupy the
fame fpot with thofe of the emperor Gal-
ba, on the Aurelian way. The architecture of this villa has been much criticifed;
however, its appearance at firft fight pleafes
the

the eye. A kind of square tower rising from the middle of the building, agreeably breaks the too great length and formality occasioned by the linear uniformity of the elevation. Here are some good antique marbles and some pictures worthy of notice.—In one of the rooms is a fine antique statue of a Vestal; there is great dignity and expreffion in her face and figure; the drapery is elegant, and the plaits easy and natural. In another room is a Claudius in woman's clothes; his expreffion of countenance is admirable. In one of the lower rooms are the portraits of two remarkable persons, Pamfilio Pamfili, brother to Pope Innocent the Tenth, and his wife Olympia Maidalchini, who is said to have had the power of a queen in Rome, during the pontificate of her brother-in-law, with whom she was believed to have been too intimate: this pontiff flourished about the middle of the last century. Above stairs, is a Venus and sleeping Cupid painted on

K 4   wood,

wood, by *Tiziano*; a Cupid and Pfyche,
by Guido. — In the tower before mentioned at the top of the houfe, is a round
room, which contains feveral curious articles, pretty morfels of fculpture in coral
and amber, gold and, cryftal difhes curioufly wrought; a whole fervice in gold
fet with turquoifes, and one beautiful fruit
difh of the fame metal pierced and richly
ornamented with turquoifes; alfo a great
number of cups, faucers, bowls, vafes, cruets,
and ewers, of ferpentine ftone.—Antique
vafes, and a few Etrufcan.—A great collection of very fine old china, and various articles of natural hiftory. In other apartments
are fome fine verd antique columns, with a
ftatue of an hermaphrodite much admired
by the virtuofi : groups of children by
Alguardi extremely well fculpted.

The garden is laid out in very bad tafte;
the parterres contain no flowers, nor were
they intended for that purpofe : they defcribe a formal and very ugly pattern, filled

up

up with coloured plaſter, and edged with ragged box *ſtruggling in vain* to grow. The walks are ſtraight, fenced in on each ſide by ever-green hedges clipped to the quick; alſo a labyrinth not very unlike in appearance to ſome of Euclid's problems: lines interſect-ing each other, and forming various ſharp angles. Here are alſo terraſſes ſurmounted with baluſtrades, a ſemicircular court orna-mented with fret-work, and ſome indifferent ſtatues and buſtos. However, in the mid-dle of this court is a receſs, and a very fine water-organ concealed behind the ſtatue of a fawn, *&c.* This receſs is an agree-able retreat from the heat of the ſun, for when the organ plays, a very fine breeze proceeds from it: the water alone occaſions the wind, and at the ſame time turns a wheel ſhaped like a cylinder. In ſhort, I can explain this no better to you than by ſaying, there is *a wheel within a wheel.* To one of theſe belong keys or hammers, which the water cauſes to riſe and fall; the

the effect of this piece of machinery is
really delightful; the organ plays feveral
airs in exceeding good time; birds fing as
if in great numbers, accompanied by falls
of water: at the end of each ftrain, the
birds repeat the two or three clofing
bars, which are finely returned to you
again by an echo, and the found of diftant falls of water gradually dying away,
concludes the mufic.—They told us the
machine was not fubject to be out of order,
nor could I difcover that the expence attending the making fuch an organ, exceeded one hundred pounds fterling.

The Park contains a few deer; but do
not imagine it laid out and planted like
an Englifh park.

Villa Bar-
berini.

The villa Barberini is built in the fame
place where Nero had a houfe, from whence
he could fee the fports in the *Circus Caïus*;
and where he repaired to glut himfelf with
the fpectacle of the cruel deaths he gave
the Chriftian martyrs in that place.

This

This villa is extremely habitable and agreeable; the gardens, tho' not as well laid out
as they might be, are neverthelefs in a good
old fashioned ftyle : the trees are fine and
not much tortured ; the walks well kept,
and there is a great abundance of flowers.—In the garden is a houfe, here called an Englifh Coffee-houfe, to which
however it bears not the moft diftant refemblance. It is an elegant, well built com-
pact houfe, on one of the prettieft plans I ever
faw ; fuch a one would be efteemed a beautiful villa near London. The curious contrivance of the ftaircafe is worthy the attention of good architects, and I am forry
we did not procure the plan and exact dimenfions of this Englifh Coffee-houfe.
There are exceeding good rooms in it, the
proportions of which have hit moft luckily.
In the gardens are fome very pretty perfpective views well painted which terminate the walks, and produce an exceeding
good effect : alfo feveral fountains with
very

fine bafons of earthen ware, painted by Raffaello; large vafes of alabafter, and fome veftiges of antique baths. To this villa the duke and dutchefs of *Monteli-bretti* often repair and pafs their evenings: there is a very good billiard-room where they and a fmall party of their friends a-mufe themfelves part of the evening in walking in the gardens. In the Englifh Coffee-houfe they are ferved with all forts of refrefhments. La Farnefina, a beautiful country palace fituated on the banks of the Tiber, is a large edifice compofed of three parts ; that which forms the center is the moft confiderable, the others confift of two pavillions: the front of the centrical building is ornamented with the two orders Doric and Ionic well executed. An arcade below conducts to a *Sala*, decorated by the paintings of Raffaello and his pupils: they reprefent the council of the gods; the marriage of Cupid and Pfyche ; groupes of figures occupy large angles between the windows,

La Farne-fina.

Raffaello.

windows, and various ornaments of feſtoons
of fruits, flowers, Cupids, &c. with curtains
drawn up in large folds well expreſſed; all
theſe are painted on the wall and are extremely fine, though they have ſuffered
much by the air at the time the arcades were
open; which are now glazed, though too
late. They have alſo received much injury
from being retouched by Carlo Maratti,
who heightened ſome of the back grounds
with a kind of blue colouring, which has
taken from the figures their proper keeping.
The wiles and pranks of a great number
of little Cupids are here delineated, in a very
ingenious allegorical ſeries, with various
repreſentations of the loves of Cupid and
Pſyche; that diviſion which repreſents him
ſhewing her to the Graces for their approbation is extremely pretty: the gods and
goddeſſes are finely done, their attitudes
noble and characteriſtic; and the wedding banquet particularly well ordered and
grouped. I muſt not venture into a detail

of

of the various reprefentations on the ceilings and walls of the other apartments
decorated by this great mafter, though they
have all very great merit.—Here are alfo
fome antiqueftatues extremely fine. Amongft
the beft is the celebrated Venus, called by
the Italians *Venere Callipighe*; the head
and hands are modern. Two crouching
Venufes. A Coloffal Head of Cæfar, and
fome other antiques that are very good.
The *Villa Mattei*, formerly a fine houfe
with gardens, is now much neglected and
out of repair: it is fituated upon *Monte
Celio*; and here you find fome very curious
remains of antiquity. A long grafs walk
in the garden pleafed me much, on account of feveral antique *ccnnerurias* (fmall
tombs containing the afhes of the dead)
ranged along the fides. What a fine evening's walk would not this have been for our
famous Doctor Young! What a fcene for
his contemplations, what moral reflections
would

Villa Mat-
tei.

would not have rifen to him out of thefe tombs.

Oppofite to one of the fronts of the houfe, upon a piece of turf furrounded with trees ; a monument is placed, which, though not very good in itfelf, produces a fine effect from its point of view. In thefe gardens is a Coloffal Head of Auguftus, fo wonderfully executed, as to have the appearance of that of a *giant's petrified*, you will make allowance for the extravagance of this idea of mine. Here are fome pretty grottos, fountains, antique infcriptions, *&c.* and the garden, upon the whole, muft be better at prefent than when it was kept, the trees having grown out of the tortured fhapes into which they were forced by the mercilefs fhears of the Roman gardeners. The plan of thefe gardens is not bad, and fhould an Englifhman take a fancy to purchafe the villa (which is now to be fold), he might, at a very eafy expence, give a model to the Romans for

their

their imitation in gardening. I fay any of
our country men, for I flatter myfelf, that I do
not know one void of, and many who poffefs, a very great fhare of tafte; and I pre-
fume as well of thofe with whom I have
no acquaintance. Amongft the antique
ftatues in the villa, are the following which
are very good, and deferve to be particularly
noticed : an Amazon fhooting with a bow
and arrow; her drapery appears to be of
fine lawn, through which her limbs and
mufcles, though very delicate, are extremely confpicuous. A horfe fleaed in
bronze, the anatomy very fine. An Altar,
fmall but elegantly decorated with feftoons
of flowers faftened to the ears of fawns.
A fmall baffo relievo of Etrufcan fculpture;
it reprefents two Women and a Dog; one
feems employed in teaching the animal to
dance, fhe holds him by one of his fore-
feet. A beautiful table of green porphyry; this kind of marble is very rare, and
greatly efteemed at Rome. A little ftatue
of

of Ceres, of the moſt delicate ſculpture in every reſpect, and highly finiſhed. A Fauſtina draped after the ſtatue of Modeſty; her drapery is very fine. A Diana of Greek ſculpture: a Satyr lying down, whilſt a Fawn extracts a thorn out of his foot; the expreſſion is very good in both theſe queer creatures, and the effect of the charitable aſſiſtance ſeems to be nearly completed.

The Villa Borgheſe, or Pinciana, is fa- Villa Borgheſe. mous among the villas near Rome. Here is an aſſemblage of Antiques, that merit Antiques. much attention: many fine *baſſo relievos* are inſerted in the walls on the outſide of the building, which is highly decorated; it would conſume much of my time and patience, to enter into a particular detail of the various ſtatues, buſtoes, *&c.* all of which preſent themſelves before you enter the palace; ſo I ſhall paſs over theſe, and be as conciſe as poſſible in regard to the interior collection. In the firſt *ſtanza*, you are ſhewn a capital repreſentation of

Seneca dying in the bath, in touchstone
or black marble; the eyes enamelled,
and round his waist is a fash of yellow
marble: this ftatue is amazingly well executed, the anatomy is rendered with a
variety truly admirable; the effect of the
great lofs of blood appears on the furface of
the veins, and in the mufcles, particularly of the feet and legs; and the progrefs of
diffolution in the whole figure is very affecting: the expreffion of his countenance is in
conformity with the exalted fentiments of
that martyred philofopher. This ftatue is
placed in a grey marble bafon, lined with red
porphyry at the bottom, to appear like blood.
In the fame room, is a very fine wolf, of
red Egyptian marble, fuckling the founders
of Rome. The famous hermaphrodite,
eftimated at Rome greatly fuperior to that
at Florence, is ranked in the fame clafs
with the Seneca, as a *chef d'œuvre* of the
powers of antique fculpture in their different ftyles. A Juno, her head and arms

5   of

of white marble, her drapery finely done in porphyry to imitate the purple; her countenance is noble and majestic; her arms are modern, and not as well done as they might have been.—A group, by Bernini, of elegant modern sculpture in one entire morsel, to the full as large as life: it is the finest thing I ever saw of his doing.—The subject is the metamorphosis of Daphne into a laurel-tree; the moment the sculptor has taken, is the commencement of her transformation; Apollo pursues and has not quite come up with her; he appears out of breath, and astonished at the approaching change; her figure is perfectly beautiful! she is stopped in her flight by the quick growth of the bark and branches; young sprigs of laurel spring from her toes, and her feet and ancles are taking root, while the increasing bark makes a rapid progress to inclose her delicate limbs. She lifts up her extended arms, and from the ends of her stiffened

Modern Bernini.

L 2 fingers

fingers fprouts the budding laurel : her hair,
which falls from her fhoulders in beautiful
ringlets, is partly blown by the wind, and
begins to thicken into wreathing bays:
her face is beautiful, and the fculptor has
expreffed in it a furprifing mixture of agi-
tating paffions; it is plain fhe fears Apollo,
but the effect of her prayers being granted,
frightens her ftill more, fo that regret,
terror, and horror at the quick progrefs of
the growing rind, is plainly to be perceived in her countenance and action. On
the pedeftal are the following lines, written by Pope Urbano the Eighth, when he
was a young man;

Quifquis amans fequitur fugitivæ gaudia formæ,
Fronde manus implet, baccas vel carpit amaras.

There are here two other groups of this
famous ftatuary, by no means equal to this.
They reprefent Æneas and Anchifes, and a
David throwing the ftone at Goliah : the
David is too old, but it feems Bernini
meant to reprefent himfelf under that character.

racter. A modern piece of sculpture in *baffo relievo,* by François Flamand; it was François Flamand. prefented by the king of France to the Borghefe family: the figures are in touch-ftone, upon a ground of *lapis lazuli,* they reprefent Bachanalian children.

A beautiful Diana antique; her body is Antique. one piece of agate. A Hercules Aventi-nus, with the bull's head under his club. A group of Fauftina and her lover Carinus the gladiator, whom fhe loved to diftrac-tion. A moft beautiful bufto of Lucius Verus, the famous gladiator. I do not think I can convey to you a competent idea of the merits of this piece of fculpture: his attitude is that of rufhing upon his adverfary, fired with rage and ambitious of victory, every nerve and finew fhew ftrained to the utmoft; his features are beautiful, his countenance haughty, fierce, and impatient; the fymmetry of his limbs is wonderful, and you every moment ex-pect the onfet: fuch is the movement

L 3 and

and violent action expressed in this marble; it is antique, and was sculpted by Agathias of Ephesus. A small group in bronze, the subject Dejanira bore away by the Centaur Nessus: it is finely done, particularly Dejanira, who struggles violently, and endeavours to leap off his back, on which she is forcibly held by one of his arms, whilst he gallops away with her at full speed. Another Centaur in marble; a Cupid riding and breaking him as a horse, who strikes him with his fists, and kicks him with all his might: this is a most animated group. A Fawn, dandling an infant Bacchus; a beautiful and highly esteemed antique. A Cameo, large as life, the face is antique and finely done; it represents the busto of Alexander the Great, in different coloured marbles: Michael Angelo has restored the casque and plume. The antique Fluter, is a Fawn about twelve years old, his attitude is elegant, and his air bespeaks

Agathias of Ephesus.

befpeaks a correct ear and mafterly per-
formance.

A modern Morpheus, by Algardi; this Modern
Algardi.
god of fleep is here reprefented under the
figure of a beautiful child, fleeping on his
back; in one hand he holds a bunch of
poppies in a negligent manner: by him
lies a toy, the Italians term a *giro*; the
foftnefs and fleepy look in his limbs and
flefh, are furprifingly natural; he even
feems to perfpire: this ftatue is in black
marble or touch-ftone.

An antique *baffo relievo*, reprefenting Antique.
the young Telephus found by the Nymphs;
one is fitting, the others ftanding; they
are well done, and exprefs great admiration and joy on the difcovery of this beautiful child. The goat that fuckled him
is repofing; but what is very remarkable
in this piece of antique fculpture is, that
Telephus appears to be in fwadling clothes,
fwathed round in the fame manner as now
univerfally practifed through Italy; and

differing

differing very little from the method of
treating some children in England: the
linen being rolled round and round them,
till by close straining, a total deprivation
of liberty is effected, to the great gratification of the vulgar nurses. In one of the
rooms, is the oddest and ugliest bed I ever
saw; it is carved in brown wood partly
gilt, and is the clumsiest, awkwardest
piece of lumber, that ever crowded a house;
but it is of the sculpture of Michael Angelo, and was made for Pope Paul the
Fifth, who bespoke and always lay in it.
In another room is a chair with springs,
being a trap to whoever sits down in it, for
they are held fast and so confined, as to
have no use of their limbs. I am obliged
to omit mentioning a great number of fine
antique statues and pictures, by famous
masters; this villa is so filled with rare
articles of every kind. The garden is by
no means beautiful; is laid out in a bad
taste; the trees chiefly consist of yew,

box,

box, and bay, and other evergreens, looking black and ragged. The flower garden
is small and very formal, but this kind of
garden admits of more formality than any
other. - There are two pretty aviaries in it,
shaped something like bells and well la-
ticed; here they keep turtles and some
other birds. Amongſt the flowers which are
very fine, I was much ſurpriſed at the carnations; ſome were brown with yellow,
others deep yellow with dark brown edgings; and ſome of a ſky blue all over,
extremely double, but of the burſting ſort;
they were well dreſſed on pieces of gilt
paſte-board, and ſo large, as to cover a ſau-
cer or ſmall deſert plate : had I not ſeen
theſe blue carnations, ſmelt, and touched
them, I ſhould have eſteemed myſelf credu-
lous for believing from books, or from or-
dinary report, that ſuch really exiſted. I
ſhould have procured ſome of the ſeed, had
not the gardener aſſured me it was not to
be depended upon for producing the ſame
                                         ſort;

fort; and that it frequently happened, that among a great number of feedlings, perhaps not above one has proved blue; they therefore, to fecure the kind, propagate them by layers; I might have had fome of thefe, but I confidered they would be very troublefome to carry with us, and difficult to preferve through the reft of our tour; particularly over the *Appenines* and the *Mount Cenis*, where the colds and viciffitudes of weather muft have infallibly deftroyed them.

I forgot to mention, that there are ftatues and antique *baffo relievos* in the gardens, fome of the latter *Etrufcan*, and very curious. Here is an odd idea (but not antique), a coloffal mafque; the eyebrows and beard formed of petrified water, the teeth are of ftucco, a cafcade of water falls from the mouth, which is of fo ample a breadth, as to fhew a confiderable part of the garden through

its

its jaws, like a landfcape feen through an arch. The park is fine, and with a few alterations, would be efteemed fuch in England; the verdure lively, and the trees old and well grown; there are fome deer in it. To this park the Englifh are permitted, by the Borghefe family, to repair twice a week, and play at cricket and football: we women go fometimes and fee the fport, as do the Roman ladies and their fine *Abbatis*, who form a brilliant body of fpectators, * * * * * * * * * I muft haften to give you a defcription of Frafcati, when I fhall conclude this long letter, which had I not the art of fcribbling away very faft, I muft have finifhed at Loretto: but I know you can read any writing of mine, and are not fcandalized at interlineations, abridgments of words, neglects of ftops, &c.

Frafcati or ancient Tufculum is about twelve miles from Rome, fituated in *La-*
tium

Frafcati.

tium or *La Campagna di Roma*; it is a bifhop's fee, now filled by the Cardinal of
York. Tufculum is often marked in ancient hiftory, as the fcene of many memor-
able events; it was the birth-place of
Cato the Cenfor, the great grand-father of
Cato of Utica; it was rendered illuftrious by
the celebrated villa of Cicero, to which he
frequently retired, where he compofed thofe
philofophical differtations fo juftly admired
in our times: Frafcati boafts, with juftice,
the giving birth to Metaftafio, who is unqueftionably the firft poet of modern Italy.
The prefent town of Frafcati is agreeably
fituated; it is not ancient: in the year 1550,
there were no other remains than fome
veftiges of the ruins of Tufculum, overgrown with brambles and thorns; from
this circumftance, the new town took its
name of *Frafcati*. It is built on the fide of
a hill, and commands a fine view of the
country below, and of the many villas and
gardens,

gardens, which clothe and beautify the brow of the mountain.

The principal Villas at Frascati.

The Villa Aldrobrandini is very remarkable for its architecture, and decorations,
and the gardens for their curious water-
works. The approach is by avenues,
which conduct to a fountain; near which
are two flights of steps leading you to a
terras, and from thence you mount to
another terras on which the villa is built;
it contains few marbles, and fewer good
pictures, but here are some ceilings tolerably painted; one reprefents David and
Abigail, by Giufeppe d'Arpino; another
Judith and Holofernes, and a third David
and Goliah, all by the fame mafter. They
have contrived to introduce air into their
apartments, by means of pipes operated
upon by water, which alfo caufes a found
refembling that of thunder; from the terrafes is a fine and very extenfive view. The
gardens furprife and aftonifh by the water-

Villa Al-drobran-dini.

Giufeppe d'Arpino.

works,

works, and being formed upon falling grounds, they confift chiefly of terrafes, rifing one above the other. A building is conftructed againft the fide of the moun- tain, (to caufe the cafcades to fall regularly from ftep to ftep) decorated with pilafters of the Ionic and Corinthian orders. Here are feveral ftatues made mufical, by the means of water organs ; a Centaur founds a horn, the blaft of which may be heard (as they affert) at the diftance of four miles; Pan plays various airs upon his paftoral flute of feveral tubes. A Lion and Tiger appear fighting, the water fpurts to a confiderable height from their mouths and noftrils ; from the tiger proceeds a hiffing and fnarling found, which is faid to refemble the noife that animal makes when enraged : think what the melody muft be, produced by this *trio*; I never heard any thing fo difagreeably curious.— At the top of the water-building, appears the mountain covered with trees, and from

its

its fummit, a river precipitates itfelf down,
forming a beautiful cafcade, which fupplies
a fine fountain in a grotto, practifed in
one of the terrafes and encrufted with petrified water: it then falls down the fteps
of the water-building, paffes under a brafs
-globe, which fpurts water on every fide;
this is fuftained by an Atlas, affifted by a
Hercules, and accompanied by various
allegorical ftatues, forms *jets d'eaus*, and
at length breaks away over rocks and is loft.
Amongft the ftatues that adorn this water-
work, is a Silenus of antique Greek fculpture in marble of Paros, a much efteemed
figure. In a large *fala* near the grand cafcade, is a reprefentation of mount Parnaffus, with Apollo, the nine Mufes, and
Pegafus; they perform a concert, by means
of a water organ concealed behind. The
walls of the *fala* are painted in frefco, by
Domenichino, and reprefent all the hiftory
and adventures of Apollo. One of the
beft, is that of the flaying of Marfyas, in

Domeni-
chino.

the

the prefence of three women and a fatyr. This laft figure implores Apollo on his knees, in behalf of Marfyas : his attitude, uplifted hands, and poor diftreffed countenance, is extremely affecting, the painter having blended the moving expreffion of a human creature, with the dumb pleadings of a beaft for mercy. The fala is paved in mofaic, and in the center is a hole, over which a light ball is kept continually dancing in the air, through the action of a ftrong guft of wind, forced up the hole by the water underneath. In thefe gardens is a wildernefs, feveral fine fhady walks, very few ever-greens, but a confiderable number of large and well grown plane-trees; the effect is, that this garden appears much more natural and agreeable, than do in general thofe of Italy.

Villa Conti.

The Villa Conti is worth feeing, upon account of its gardens and water-works, and particularly for the ancient remains of

eighteen

eighteen vaulted buildings, faid to have
been part of the *menagerie* of Lucullus.

The Villa Taverna belongs to the Borghefe family; it is very large, well built,
habitable, and elegantly furnifhed; contains
fome good pictures, and feveral curiofities;
amongft which, the following are the moft
remarkable; a fmall wooden crucifix, carved by a blind man. The victory of the
arch-angel Michael over the dragon; this
animal is reprefented with a woman's head,
the face a portrait, and the countenance
expreffive of the moft infamous and vile
character, by Perugino. A St. Pietro, by
Spagnoletto. Several animals, by Pioli.
The portraits of the unfortunate Mother
and Daughter, of the family of *Cenci*;
the daughter is beautiful; I faw another
portrait of her taken juft before fhe was
led out to execution; I think it was in the
Pallazzo Colonna, and I fuppofe I mentioned her ftory in one of my letters, fo will
not hazard the troubling you with a repe-

Vol. III.　　　　M　　　　　tition

tition of fo fhocking a tragedy.—The view from the villa is beautiful; the gardens are of great extent, and through them you mount up to the *Villa Dragone*, built in a much more elevated fituation, which alfo belongs to the Borghefe family. In thefe two villas, this noble family receive and entertain a great concourfe of company, during the autumn feafon *per villagiature*. I have before mentioned this cuftom in Italy. This is a large palace, they told us they could reckon 364 windows in it; I did not difpute it, left they fhould count them, and we had not time to fpare for fuch minutenefs. The architecture is not very remarkable, the portico by Vignola has a good effect, being built of *pietra di perone*, which is of a fine brown colour. The building is rather too heavy; fome paintings in this villa are tolerable; one at the end of the grand gallery, reprefents Solomon furrounded by his concubines facrificing to idols, by Paulo Veronefe.

Here

Villa Dragone.

Veronefe.

Here is an antique coloffal head of Fauftina, wife to Marcus Aurelius. A coloffal
bufto of Antoninus, and fome other antiques
not of the firft clafs.

From the terras is a moft beautiful view
of Rome, and the country adjacent, till
the fea bounds the profpect on that fide ;
villages, ruins, and the *Lago Cafiglione*
with mountains, form another beautiful
profpect; the whole is truly admirable,
uniting all the advantages of a near, to all
the grandeur of an extenfive profpect.

The Villa *Bracchiano*, formerly *Mon-*
talto, is a very pretty country houfe, neatly and elegantly furnifhed : here is a ceiling painted by fome of the fcholars of
Dominichino ; the fubject is the fun's
courfe. The gardens, nothing remarkable ; they confift principally of long walks
regularly planted, where I obferved a great
number of cherry laurel amongft other
evergreens.

The

Villas Lu-
doviciand
Falconi-
eri. The Villas Ludovici and Falconieri are
worth feeing, principally for their water-
works and gardens. In the villa Falco-
Carlo Ma-
ratti. nieri, is a ceiling painted by Carlo Maratti.
The fubject, the birth of Venus: a Neptune in the fea, prefents her with all the
treafures of his element, while the Graces
upon the fhore attend with impatience to
crown her with flowers; it is well compofed, and the figures graceful. The other
ceilings, painted by Ciro Ferri, reprefent
the Seafons.

The ruins of the ancient town of Tufculum, are to be traced above a villa
Villa La
Rufinella. belonging to the Jefuits, called La Rufinella: here they fhew what are called the
grottos of Cicero; but it is by no means
certain, that thefe veftiges, made part of
his villa.

I muft now take leave of you, and of
Rome, and fhall write to you, when we
fhall have reached Loretto.

I am

I am very forry for an event, which has juft happened here; to the univerfal regret of her family, her friends, her acquaintance, and the public in general: the amiable daughter of the dutchefs of Bracchiano (the princefs Chigi), died yefterday in childbed! She expired in the arms of her mother, perfectly refigned to her fate: amiable fhe was indeed, in mind, and in perfon, therefore univerfally beloved, efteemed, and lamented!—Should an opportunity offer to write to you on the road, I fhall not neglect it. Adieu, and wifh me a happy pilgrimage *a la fantiffima Madona,*

I am as ever, &c.

P. S. I promifed to mention fome of the principal artifts now at Rome; but am fo preffed in time, that I cannot enlarge on their different manners and genius as they deferve; I fhall therefore be as concife as poffible. Battoni, is I believe with juftice, efteemed the beft portrait painter in the world. Pickler father and fon are

admired

admired by every body of tafte and judgment, for their great abilities in the en-
graving on gems; they execute *cameos*
and *intaglios* in a great ftyle for correction
of defign, elegance, and finifh: I believe
no modern artift can be compared with
them; they are reafonable in their prices,
in their dealings act with an honourable
honefty, and defervedly meet with that
encouragement, both from Italians and
foreigners, that their excellent characters
as artifts, and their reputation as men of
probity, fo juftly entitle them to. As for
Piranefe, his prints are fufficiently known
to rank him amongft the firft of engravers
on copper. He fometimes is carried by
his tafte, into romance: as a fculptor, he
can do almoft what he pleafes; when he
is in good humour, he is very ufeful, in-
forming, and agreeable to ftrangers; he is
what in England would be called a humo-
rift, confequently uncertain and capricious.
To deal with him, it is neceffary to know

before

before-hand, his peculiarities.—A miniature painter, of the name of Giorgio,
paints the beft pictures I have feen in that
way: his colouring is glowing his defign
correct, his finifhing high, and his paintings will bear the ftricteft examination and
comparifon with the beft miniatures of
thefe times, and even of thofe of former
days. The beft miniature portrait painter,
efteemed for taking likeneffes at a moderate
price, is one Marfigli; he is a diligent attentive artift, and I make no doubt capable of great improvement. There are feveral young men, who are fent by their families and friends to Rome, in order to ftudy painting, fculpture, &c. many of whom
promife to attain to a great degree of ex-
cellence in thofe arts: it is a pity they are
fo frequently reduced to very difagreeable
ftraits, by the ill-judged parfimony of their
friends in England. The Englifh gentlemen
upon their travels have indeed often gene-
roufly fupplied their wants, but as they can-

not

not always enjoy fuch advantages, and this
refource muft, from its nature, be more or
lefs precarious, it is felf-evident a young
perfon has little encouragement to ftudy
the beauties of painting, fculpture, &c.
&c. whilft in want of fuch neceffaries, as
makes the body fuffer great inconvenience,
and the mind a total want of eafe. As
for fuch Englifh artifts, who are already in
affluent circumftances in England, and who
travel into Italy to improve their tafte and
gratify their curiofity; the Italian artifts
are continually mentioning them with great
encomiums on their genius, works, &c.
Amongft thefe, no man holds a higher
place than Mr. Strange, who has taken
copies, and engraved prints, after the moft
capital original pictures in Italy; and executed them in fo liberal a manner, as to
give the beholder the true image and
fpirit of the original; not a hard and fervile copy ever came from his hands. I
muft obferve here, that I think bafe and

laborious

laborious copyifts do infinite injury to the world of artifts. They excite falfe ideas, prejudice the minds of people who, not having feen the works of the great mafters, difguifed by their copies, are apt to fuppofe fome glaring fault in the original; when, alas! moft probably the defect may be found only in the felf-fufficience and conceit of the young artift; who flattered himfelf, perhaps, with improving upon a Tizziano, a Corregio, or a Raffaello.

The poft-horfes are waiting, the baggage faftened on to the carriage, fo I muft feal this letter and fend it immediately to the poft-office. Adieu...

LETTER

LETTER XLVI.

Narni, the 25th May, 1771.

Road from Rome to Narni.

WE are well and safely arrived here without any accident, and might have reached Terni, though we set out late, had it not been for the warmth of the weather, which obliged us to lie by in the heat of the day; are therefore obliged to sleep here to-night. The face of the country the firſt three poſts from Rome, is diſgracefully uncultivated; no villages, no habitations (except poſt-houſes), nothing but a dreary diſmal waſte, without track of man or beaſt to be ſeen. Having paſſed Rignano, the fourth poſt, the country begins to improve a little to Soreſte, and then to Civetta-Caſtellana (the ancient Veia), and ſo on to Borgetto, Otricoli, and Narni, is a moſt beautiful country. Near Rignano

Flaminian way.

our road lay over part of the Flaminian way; it is extremely firm and good, com-

poſed

poſed of very large blocks of ſtone, ſo
nicely fitted and put together, and withal
ſo ſmooth, that the horſes could with difficulty keep their footing. Civetta Caſtel- Civetta
laæt is ſituated in the ancient country of no.
the Sabines : it is built on a rocky elevation, and appears like a ſmall iſland;
three ſides of it being incloſed by as many
little rivers, which falling into the valley
below, and uniting together, at length
empty themſelves into the Tiber. On the
other ſide of the town is the citadel, behind which, the mountain immediately
riſes. Three ſides of Caſtellano is inac-
ceſſible, on account of the perpendicula-
rity of the rock on which it ſtands; and
the fortreſs defends it ſo well from behind,
as to render it (I ſhould imagine) capable
of ſuſtaining a long ſiege. Some antiquarians have diſputed the ancient Veia's being ſituated on this ſpot, but the greater
number are of opinion, that it certainly
was.

Having

Having paffed through Borghetto, we came to a fine bridge built by Pope Sixtus the Fifth, over the Tiber; it is called *Pontefelice*. The next poft is Otricoli, near which place are remarkable hills, formed of what the Italians call *brefcia*, round pebbles, which feem to have acquired that form from having been in the fea. The profpect from Rignano to Narni confifts of hills, fome clothed with woods, others with vines, and fome crowned with villages: ruined fortifications and old towers appear amongft the trees; and frequent remains of Roman antiquities, as fragments of temples, maufoleums, &c. The valleys are narrow, fertile, and moft *pittorefque*; imagination cannot feaft upon a more variegated and beautiful affemblage of objects; but this variety of ground produces a moft fatiguing effect to travellers, as you are repeatedly afcending or defcending fteep and rapid hills.

Pontefelice.

Narni

Narni is a fmall town, fifty-five miles Narni.
from Rome; it is fituated on the fide of a
hill, and forms an amphitheatre. At the
foot of the town runs the Nera; here is a
fine aquedu&t of fifteen miles long, which
conveys water through a mountain to the
town, where it fupplies feveral fountains.
Our inn is tolerable, and we have not as yet
met with infolent poftillions, or extortion-
ing poft-mafters, I hope a good omen for
the remainder of our journey. I had
made provifion at Rome againft our *eating
cares,* of a piece of cold boiled beef, falt-
ed the Englifh way, and fome dozens of
lemons; as we generally drink nothing
but lemonade on our journey, on account
of the heat of the weather, and the ftrong
wines of this country being rather inflam-
matory, we have found our provifion very
neceffary, the inn affording us nothing
but eggs not entirely rotten; no butter,
very ftale and coarfe bread, and no meat
of any kind excepting goat's flefh, which
I could

I could not eat unlefs near ftarving; the rank odour fills all the rooms in the houfe, and I have an unfortunate averfion to the fmell of thofe animals *living* or *dead:* our hoft, it is true, offered us fome half-ftarved old fowls, that were importunately cackling and demanding food at the door, and which he would have executed upon the fpot if permitted, but we preferred our cold beef, to the fruits of fuch affaffination, and have dined extremely well upon it.

To-morrow morning, M— goes to fee the ruins of the famous bridge built by Auguftus; it is only half a mile from the town, but the way is difagreeable; and there is a defcent juft before you arrive at it, which they tell us is extremely rapid; I do not think I fhall accompany him, for fear of the heat and fatigue, dreading the flighteft indifpofition upon the road, as Italian inns are by no means commodious quarters for the fick.

I fhall

I fhall keep this letter open, and write in it occafionally, till I have an opportunity of fending it by the poft, which is fo uncertain and fo ill regulated, that I do not know when I may have it in my power. Good night for the prefent.

May the 16th.—We are juft arrived at the next poft, Terni. M— went this Terni. morning to fee the bridge: he fays the way to it is much worfe than was reprefented, the defcent exceedingly rapid, and muft be walked down, as it is covered with heaps of large round ftones, over which he ftumbled every moment, many of them rolling down after him, of fize fufficient to break the legs, if you are not quick and cautious to avoid them; I am convinced this walk would not have fuited me. When he came to the bridge, he found it had been built in the common manner, with mortar and cramped with iron: fo little can the authors be depended upon, who all affert the contrary, and

4   rank

rank it as a wonder of the world; nor did
it in any manner anfwer the idea he had
formed of it, from what he had heard.
Notwithftanding that, it is a fine remain of
antiquity, and would furprife, and pleafe
much more, was it not fo much over-rated.
Five miles from hence, is the famous cafcade, but I cannot fee this neither, for the
mountain is fo fteep, that there is no afcending it but upon a mule's back, or on a
very fure footed horfe; and in order to fee
it well, there are fuch ugly fteps to pafs,
that I fear I may break my neck, and M—
wifhes me ardently not to attempt it; at the
fame time, that he is forry to perceive my difappointment; it is a great mortification to
me to be fure. He is juft fetting out, for
he will fee it; and I have been recom-
mending ftrongly to him to walk, if he
fhould find the road very fteep. The inn
here is tolerable, and the people a little
humanized. Above Narni appears a town
Cefi. called Cefi, fituated at the foot of ponde-
rous

rous Rocks, which feem to threaten its deftruction every moment. The common
people affert, that the town is faftened
with adamantine chains (which they grant
are invifible) to the neighbouring mountain; but it is certain that their law for-
bids, on pain of death, the felling any of
the trees that grow amongft the rocks on
the mountain above the town; by which
it feems the rocks are fuppofed to be fupported, and prevented from falling, by the
roots of the trees being interlaced with
them.

On the right, a little before we came to
Terni, appears the village Collicipoli (the
ancient Collis Scipionis), and on a height
Torre Majore, a kind of obfervatory, where
the learned father Bofcovick had geome-
trical inftruments, in order to take the
heights of the lands between Rome and
Rimini, &c. For this purpofe he had
poles fixed in the ground in proper places
for meafuring the angles, &c. and the

Collis Sci-
pionis.

VOL. III.   N   ftupidity

ftupidity and folly of the peafants imped-
ed this learned man as much as poffible
in his ingenious labours, by moving his
marks, fuppofing them placed with defign
to aid him in the magic art, which they
believed he ftudied.

In this country the peafants have a
contrivance for catching pigeons. They
tame a certain number, which they call
Mandarini, who, flying before the wild
ones, decoy them into trees, where the
peafants remain concealed and catch great
numbers of them. From Narny to this
town, Terni, the road is very good; it
lies through a fertile valley, feven miles
long; the eye is conveyed over a wide extended country; the river Nera, like a great
filver ferpent, winding along in volumes
through thefe plains, forms peninfulas,
which, in fome points of view, appear like
iflands of various fhapes; fome prefent you
with rich meadows, others ftately groves
of oak, others are covered with corn and
planted

planted with regular rows of mulberry
trees, which fuftain the luxuriant branches
of the vine, whofe arms embrace the mulberry-trees from fide to fide; little hills of
different heights and forms interfect each
other; fome of thefe are clothed with
wood, and top'd with ruined towers and
fortreffes, and at the foot of them lie the
humble villages, which, being very irregu-
lar, appear the more picturefque in profpect. This view extends itfelf wide of the
road, and is the commencement of the
plain of Rieta, compared by Cicero to the
valley of Tempe.

Terni is juft fixty-two miles from Rome, Terni
a city famous in antiquity; Tacitus the
hiftorian was born here, and feveral other
remarkable perfonages. Here are ftill to
be feen fome fmall veftiges of antiquities;
in the bifhop's garden, is a fragment of an
amphitheatre and fome *fouteraines :* in the
church of S. Salvadoro, are fome fmall remains of a temple of the Sun, and part of

a temple

a temple to Hercules in the cellars belonging to the Jefuits. M— is returned and quite charmed with the cafcade; it is called *Caduta delle Marmora*, and is formed by the river Velino, which falls above two hundred feet in height into the Nera. This prodigious fall of water defcends in three cafcades; its fpray forms curious incruftations, fome of which he brought me in his pocket. He fays, the colours feen in the drops of water, which by being violently dafhed up in the air fall again in fhowers, are equal in beauty to the glowing tints in prifms; he believes there cannot be any cafcade in the world more extraordinary and more romantically beautiful than this. He placed himfelf in different parts of the mountain, to view it in all its glory, and the variety of its appearances exceeded his expectations; at the fame time he affured me, I never fhould have been able, on a mule or on foot, to have clambered up and down the frightful precipices

4   that

that he did, for he was obliged to walk a confiderable way, it not being poffible in fome defcents for his mule to keep her feet, or avoid being in the utmoft danger of falling down the declivities, even without a rider; I dare fay you a revery glad I did not go. Adieu, our carriage waits.

(In continuation.) We have reached Spoletto, where we fleep to-night, though only twenty-one miles from Terni; but as we did not fet out early, and met with fome impediments in the way, which occafioned much lofs of time, we are determined not to prefs on, but to remain here quietly till to-morrow morning. Having quitted Terni, the road was tolerable till we came to a ftupendous Appenine called the *Somma*, about fix miles before we reached Spoletto. The road by which we afcended is a prodigious work, cut out of the living rock; it winds along the fide of the Appenine; is but juft broad enough for a carriage; is as hard as marble, and almoft as

Somma Appenine.

N 3   fmooth,

fmooth, but not an inch allowed for the confequences of the ftarting or waywardnefs of
a horfe, or the fmalleft inattention on the
part of the drivers. The mountain rifes to
the clouds perpendicularly ftraight on one
fide, with a precipice aftonifhingly deep, and
almoft as rapid on the other fide, without
any wall, hedge, pail, or fence of any kind.
At the bottom of the precipice runs a
river like a torrent, which feen from the
road appears no broader than a fkeyne of
filk. We whirled along the edge of this
mountain in a conftant gallop, drawn by
four of the ftrongeft, largeft, and moft
furious black horfes I ever faw; the poftillions making the moft frightful fhouts to
encourage their pace, and urging them on
by whipping them inceffantly, the horfes
fqueaking the whole time. This method
of driving, it feems, is your beft fecurity,
for if the horfes were fuffered to recollect
themfelves, or even to flacken their pace,
they would be fubject to ftart, or might

fear

fear the precipice, and from apprehenfion
grow reftive, which would be certain deftruction to themfelves and thofe they conveyed; but by being kept conftantly attentive to their mafters, and obliged to exert
all their ftrength, we happily attained the
fummit of the Appenine, without any accident. A carriage had need to be ftrong
and well put together that goes this road,
for fhould any article of it give way, the
confequences could not fail of being difagreeable, if not fatal. We ftopped at a houfe
on the top of the mountain, for refreshment;
where we had a high regale: the velocity of
our motion and the freshnefs of the air had
gained us an appetite, and we fared delici-
oufly, in our carriages, on wild boar ham,
broiled for us in thin flices, accompanied
with plates of fliced truffles, which they
heated over the fire in a moment, and
proved an excellent ragout. Having eat
heartily, and forgot the fright I had fuffered from the precipice, I was curious to

know

know the method of conferving and dref-, fing thefe truffles; fo I called for the mif- trefs of the houfe (for there is a woman in this inn), and fhe told me, that when they are quite frefh, they muft be wafhed extremely clean, in water juft warm, then in cold wine, and left to fteep in this lat- ter for about a quarter of an hour; after which they are cut in flices, then hung up in bafkets to dry in the air under cover, fo as to protect them from the fun, rain, and dew: when crifp, they are put into paper bags and kept in a dry place; they are dreffed in pewter or filver plates, over a lamp or charcoal, putting to them fome oil, an anchovy, and muftard: for thofe who do not like oil, they fubftitute butter, which you may believe the Englifh *Forreftieri* generally prefer. I purchafed fome bags of her truffles, and a very fine ham of the wild boar, difcreetly providing againft our neceffities, in cafe we fhould not on our journey meet with equally good provifion.

provifion. Having defcended the Appenines, the road lying amongft the nether
mountains, very narrow and fteep in feveral places, we were overtaken by a
dreadful ftorm of thunder and lightning;
the claps were loud as cannon, and feemed
quite clofe to us; the lightning flafhed
and darted along the ground; the air was
poifoned with the fmell of fulphur; it pour-
ed cafcades inftead of rain, as if all the
clouds in the heavens had burft over our
heads: we preffed on to reach Spoletto,
the ftorm augmenting, the horfes fcream-
ing and ftarting every moment; however,
we arrived fafe, and without the leaft accident. The ftorm continued, and increaf-
ed; the claps of thunder redoubling, fo
that there was not half a minute's ceffation
between: the lightning fell twice into the
ground amongft the mountains, but did no
hurt. This ftorm lafted full three hours
from its commencement, without ceffation,
and concluded with two amazing claps of
thunder,

thunder, re-echoed from the mountains, like what I fhould fuppofe might be the explofion at the fpringing of a mine.

Spoletto. Spoletto is a confiderable town, eighty-eight miles from Rome, fituated on the top of a mountain. One of the antique *Antique gate.* gates of this city is ftill nearly perfe&; it is called *Porta Fuga*; on it you read this infcription, indicating the caufe of its appellation.

Annibal cæfis ad Trafyminum Romanis, urbem Romam infenfo agmine petens, Spoleto magna fuorum clade repulfus, infigni fugâ portæ nomen fecit.

Cathedral. The Cathedral is almoft entirely built of marble; they fhew an image of the Virgin, pretended to have been made by St. *Guercino.* Luke. A picture, by Guercino, reprefenting St. Cecilia and two monks, praying to the Virgin, who appears in a glory, which is infinitely more valuable; its colouring is good, but the aërian perfpe&ive

is

is not well preferved in the glory. The
Church of St. *Filipo di Neri* contains a good picture of this faint, who is invok- Church.
ing the Virgin; the painter's name not
known. There are fome palaces here
alfo, and feveral other churches, but we
are too much fatigued to vifit them.
They told us, there are antique remains of
a temple of Jupiter, in the convent of St.
Andrea; and of a temple of Mars, in the
church of St. *Ifacco*, but we have not feen
them. There is a wonderful aqueduct to
be feen to-morrow morning, before we
purfue our route; it is about two miles
from hence. We are tolerably well lodged
in our inn; and as it is fummer, do not
fuffer much by the want of curtains to the
beds. Our fare confifts of pigeons, ftrongly refembling crows, and plenty of fried
liver and brains, very bad foup, with giz-
zards of various birds fwimming therein;
in fhort, the ham and truffles are by no
means indifferent to us. Good night.

LETTER XLVII.

Serravalle, 17th of May.

Serravalle.

THIS morning M— went on horfe-back from Spoletto, to fee the famous aqueduct two miles from thence; it conveys, from one hill to another over a deep valley, two confiderable bodies of water, which flow upon arches built like bridges; the center is a double arch, one being built over the other, the height about two hundred and fifty feet; the other arches gradually decline in height, as they fpring from the floping fides of two mountains, the water being thus conveyed to the town of Spoletto.

When we had completed the firft poft from Spoletto, to a place called Vene, we turned off a few paces from the road, to fee the ruins of a beautiful little temple, built near the fource of the once famous river Clitumnus;

Clitumnus; it is called the Temple of Clitumnus, fuppofed to have been dedicated
to that river god. The plan is an oblong
fquare, it has four columns, and two Corinthian pilafters, the portico is vaulted
within; on the frizes are *baffo relievos*,
reprefenting olive branches, grapes, and
leaves finely executed. The two center pillars of the four are fculpted from top to
bottom, defcribing laurel leaves, placed in
alternate rows, the other two are fluted in
fpiral lines; the pediment they fupport
is beautifully proportioned. Its two entrances, which were at each end, are quite
in ruins. The little room in the interior
of the temple, meafures only ten feet by
eight: this fmall edifice is built of an iron
grey marble, which appears to have been
highly polifhed.

The river Clitumnus, at this time but
a fhallow brook, runs at its foot: its
banks were formerly famous for feeding
white

white cattle*, which Pliny attributes to
the effects of the water; be that as it may,
the white were fought for facrifice, in preference to every other colour, as the moſt
acceptable to the gods; which when not
to be eaſily had, the victims were rubbed over with chalk. We, obſerved many
oxen, and other white horned cattle, upon
its banks, which I was determined to believe the defcendants of the antique breed.
From ſome poor people who were fiſhing
here, I bought a very fine trout, and a
large ſilver eel; on the former we dined
well at Foligno, and have juſt ſupped on
the latter; for Foligno or Seravelle afford

---

* ——On the cheerful greèn
The grazing flocks and lowing herds are ſeen,
The warrior horſe here bred, is taught to train,
There flows Clitumnus thro' the flow'ry plain;
Whoſe waves for triumphs after profp'rous war,
The victim ox, and ſnowy ſheep prepare.——

DRYDEN's Tranflation of VIRGIL,
Book. II. of the Georgics.

but

but live pigeons, and wretched fowls
alive alfo, whofe exiftence we refolved not
to fhorten, to gratify the luxury of dining
or fupping. But to return to our route
from Vene; we had a very good road to
Foligno, which is twelve miles from Spoletto, and one hundred from Rome. On
each fide of the road, our view was of a
rich country, clofely planted with white
mulberries, fycamores, elms, and vines.
The corn grows between the rows of trees,
and here the peafant's toil is rewarded with
four rich harvefts; mulberry leaves for the
filk-worms, the mulberry fruit, grapes,
and corn. Foligno is a large town, but
contains nothing curious except a convent,
called *La Comteffa*, where are fome very
fine pictures : a capital one by Raffaello, Raffaello,
befpoke of that great mafter by *Segif-
mondo di Comitibus*, who was fecretary to
the Pope, and who prefented it to his
niece, then in this convent; it reprefents
the

7

the Virgin in a glory feated on a cloud, fupported by the rainbow, holding the Infant Jefus in the midft of cherubims; below appears St. John, St. Francis on his knees, a cardinal in the fame attitude, and admirably well done; a St. Jerome ftanding behind him; a little angel in the center, who holds with both hands a tablet, but without any infcription. I could expatiate for an hour on the different beauties of this picture; the Virgin anfwers precifely the idea I have formed of her; a noble fimplicity, blended with perfect innocence, and piety, dwell upon her face; grace, dignity, and complacence, are diffufed over her whole perfon. The infant appears in the attitude of ftruggling to get away from his mother, in order to grant the prayers of the faints below; his figure is animated, and his benign countenance feems to breathe forth divine love. The St. John is finely done; he appears with all the cha-

characteristicks of his foreft education,
and a noble firmnefs of mind in his
countenance; the colouring. is rich and
glowing, and in my opinion this picture
fhould be claffed amongft the *chef d'œu-*
vres of *Raffaello.* Our fine road now
ended, and we again afcended and defcended the Appenines, the way being extremely
rough and rapid in many places; near
Seravella the mountains feemed clofing
upon us, fhooting one above the other,
till they rofe far above the clouds, and the
road extremely narrow and winding, when
all at once the little fky we could fee,
grew black, the thunder rolled, and the
lightning and ftench exceeded that of yefterday; the whole artillery of Heaven
feemed now pointed upon this narrow valley: with much difficulty the poftillions
kept the horfes to their draught, the rain
and wind beating ftrong againft their faces.
In about an hour or lefs we reached this
moft wretched of all villages; the ftorm

continued with the utmost violence between five and fix hours; though in this
inn, I cannot fay we were in shelter, the
storm and rain beating through and through
the house; I laid myself down upon the
staircase, which is of very rough stones,
and expected every moment the house to
come level with the ground: what induced
me to chuse the staircase was, that the
wall was arched in a vault over head, which
made me think it the most secure place. The
stench of the sulphur was such, and the
closeness of the air, that it made me extremely sick, and I apprehended the being
suffocated at every instant. M— never left
me for a moment, but kindly endeavoured
to console me, by assuring me these storms
must be common amongst the Appenines;
that the people of the house did not appear
much terrified, &c. &c. but I very frequently could not hear what he said, so
loud was the noise of the thunder: the
lightning mean-time darting all about us,

of

of a livid blue and white; the post-horses never ceased screaming and kicking in the stables; at length it ceased. ... ... When I had recovered from my fright and sickness, our host came and was ardent to know what we would have for supper; and not being able to get rid of his importunity, I recollected our Clitumnus eel, which I ordered to be dressed, and to send up whatever he had in the house, which upon inquiry proved to be nothing but *bread* and *eggs*, not *newly* laid. I mentioned to you before, that we spared the lives of the old fowls. Our bed-chamber has casements to it; the walls are white-washed, and adorned with bad pictures of *la Santa Casa* and *Nostra Dama di Loretto*; the beds are not quite so bad as many we have already experienced, and I expect to sleep profoundly; but first I must mention one circumstance, which is, that though it generally thunders every day during the summer amongst these Appenines, yet this storm was fo uncommonly violent, that a young woman, the wife of one of the helpers in the ftable, and who had been born and bred in this village, was fo terrified, that fhe ran along the ftreet in the midft of the ftorm to her mother's cottage; thinking in her fright fhe fhould be more fecure if with her old mama.—This miferable vîl-lage is in a manner fhut in amongft Appe-nines heaped on Appenines, fo that the fun's beams are rarely vifitants here; but clouds and fogs ever hover over the moun-tains, feldom yielding more than a kind of doubtful light : this fo much furpaffes a romantic fituation, that one may pronounce it, a long and narrow pit, big with horror. M— calls it a thunder-cup.

. Loretto, May the 19th. Here we fafely arrived yefterday in the evening, having paffed over nothing but mountains, and traced the brinks of dreadful precipices, whofe perpendicular fides were furnifhed with vaft craggy rocks, whilft mountain

torrents

torrents roar loudly at their feet: this fort
of road continued more or lefs alarming,
till a little before we reached Loretto.
Near Tolentino, part of our carriage broke,
and we were detained above an hour to
have it mended: through the kind provi-
dence of the almighty God we received
no hurt; and happy was it for us, that
we were fo near a town when this accident
happened. Tolentino is thirty miles from
Loretto; there is nothing remarkable to be
feen there. Macerata, which is twelve
miles from thence, is built on the fummit
of a mountain, from whence the Adriatic is plainly difcernible. About two
miles and a half from Macerata, after having paffed over a very long wooden bridge,
which croffes the river Potenza, are fome
veftiges of the ruined town of Recina: Recina.
fome remains of a theatre are here faid to
be difcernible, but we did not ftop to fee
them. From Macerata to San Buchetto, the
face of the country improved upon us very

much,

much, is well cultivated, and planted with mulberry trees, &c. From San Buchetto, to Loretto, which is the laſt poſt, there is a great deal of aſcent and deſcent, but more of the former than the latter; the road is tolerable, and very near Loretto is perfectly good. From Foligno to this town is about fifty-five miles, ſo that Loretto is nearly an hundred and fifty miles from Rome. When within two or three miles of this town, the road is infeſted by ſturdy boys and girls half naked, who purſue travellers begging, ſinging, dancing, running and tumbling over and over; their numbers and clamour increaſe, till happily gaining the town they diſperſe. It is but juſt to confeſs at the ſame time, that they are the moſt complimental beggars in the world; for when tumbling fails to excite your charity, they proſtrate themſelves, and kiſs the ground you are about to paſs over, invoking your beneficence, and giving you all the titles of dignity they ever

heard

heard of; and if those fail, then they give you some of their own invention, as for example to M— *Felice sposo della Madonna*; to me *Eccellentissima Madonna*. On the road coming into Loretto, we overtook two pilgrims; one was dressed in a pilgrim's habit of pale olive green lutestring, ornamented with scollop shells; he was a young stout looking man, with red hair tied behind in a ribbon; he appears to me to be a Scotch gentleman: he endeavoured to conceal himself as much as possible from our observation, and was particularly anxious to prevent our seeing his face. The other pilgrim was a poor old priest, who was employed in dragging along a very large wooden cross; however there was a little wheel fastened to the end of it, to lighten the draft; these two personages were not in company with each other.

Loretto is situated on a plain at the top Loretto. of a mountain; it has a clean, deserted, and bleak look; the houses make but a

O 4   very

very mean appearance; the principal ſtreet
conſiſts for the moſt part of ſmall ſhops, in
which are ſold little elſe beſides beads for
roſaries, gold and ſilver ornaments for the
ſame, worked in fillagree, ſmall braſs bells,
much bought by the country people, as
preſervatives againſt thunder and lightning,
brown paper caps to cure the head-ach,
and broad ribbons with the effigies of
Noſtra Dama di Loretto, painted on them,
to be worn by women in child-birth.

The inn is very indifferent and dirty;
they ſerved us in the dirtieſt pewter-plates
I ever ſaw, and greaſy trenchers. The
proviſions conſiſted of very ſtale fiſh, ragoued in oil and highly ſeaſoned with gar-
lic; peas ragoued alſo, and cabbage; but
all was ſo diſguſting, that we were obliged
to feed upon ſome very bad cheeſe, and
the bread, it being a faſt day, was plenti-
fully ſeaſoned with coriander and anniſe-
ſeed, which to me is very diſagreeable.
Our beds were tolerable, and we ſlept well.

We

We have employed this morning in viewing
the *Santa Cafa, &c.* The church, which
contains the Holy Houfe, is very large; the piazza before it not yet nearly finifhed;
the architecture of the church is neither
beautiful nor remarkable; the door of entrance is of bronze, fculpted in *baffo relievo*; the fubject relates to Adam and Eve,
Cain and Abel, *&c.* and are not ill executed. Towards the further end of the church
is found *la Santiffima Cafa*, built of a kind
of ftone which exactly refembles brick;
the outfide is incrufted with marble, as a
cafe for it; this cafing is loaded with various ornaments of fculpture, all heavy and
ill done. They tell you, that the ftones
with which this houfe is built never wear,
although rubbed and fcraped continually by the pilgrims; yet the marble
pavement which is modern, is extremely
worn by their knees, continually trailing
themfelves round and round it, one after
the other. As I was looking up at the
architec-

Holy
Houfe.

architecture, and not attending to my footing, I made a *faux pas* and ftumbling,
tumbled over a fturdy female pilgrim, who
was proceeding on her knees, faying her
prayers, and in a great heat and fweat; I
could not help laughing, and I begged her
pardon with the beft grace I could, the
other pilgrims laughed alfo, at the oddity
of the accident; the woman was furprifed,
but not angry. The *Santa Cafa* is furrounded with a great number of filver
lamps (very thin), which burn conftantly.
In the interiour is placed the miraculous
image, with the infant Jefus: the Virgin
is made of cedar, but having been in a
fire, from which it was miraculofly preferved, is as black as a coal. She is dreffed in a very bad tafte, with a farthingale,
or old fafhioned hoop-petticoat: the outfide garment is gold or filver ftuff, I am
not clear which; fhe is in fuch a cloud of
fmoke proceeding from the lamps, that I
could not be certain; you are not permitted

ted to touch her. She had feveral *crochets* of diamonds, reaching from the top of her ftomacher down to the hem of her petti-coat, but they appeared to me to be com-pofed of a great mixture of ftones, none of any great value, and many very indif-ferent; I faw none fo fine, or fo large, as fome belonging to the dutchefs of *Monti-libretti* at Rome: fhe wears a triple crown fet with jewels, and a black gauze veil; fhe has new clothes every year, and her veil when fhe puts it off is cut into fmall pieces, and fold or given to devout perfons and genteel pilgrims, as a charm againft witchcraft. As to the coloured precious ftones they are by no means good, being for the moft part clouded and ftreaky, and many of them no better than the root of emerald, amethyft, ruby, *&c.* Here are fome lamps of fine gold, but extremely thin. Several votive gifts, prefented by various princes and great people, decorate the image; fuch as hearts, chains of gold

fet

fet with precious ftones, crucifixes, &c.;
in particular a ftatue of an angel, fhewn
for gold, but which appears to me to be
filver gilt; he is in a kneeling pofture to
the Virgin, and offers a gold or gilt heart,
fet with diamonds, rubies, and pearls.
This ftatue was prefented to the Virgin, by
James the Second's Queen of England,
who was of the houfe of Efte, in order
that the Virgin in return might give her
in exchange a fon; her gift was *accepted*,
her requeft was *granted*, and fhe produced the *Pretender*. On the other fide of
the Virgin is a like ftatue; this is of filver,
was prefented at the fame time, and offers
a heart in the like manner; the gift of
Laura, widow of Alphonfus the Fourth,
duke of Modena, and mother of James
the Second's Queen. Here is alfo another
filver angel, prefenting Louis the Four-
teenth (who is made of gold) upon a cufhion: they told us, this golden infant
was made exactly of the fame weight with

the

the living infant when juſt born.- The
nich in which the Virgin is placed, is lined
with ſilver and ornamented with gold ; but
I ſuſpeċt many of the plates that appear to
be gold, to be no more than ſilver gilt.
The door-caſe and architraves of the window are ornamented with plates of the
ſame metal : it was by this window, that
the angel Gabriel entered to ſalute the Virgin. There is a fine altar at her feet, and
before it a ſilver baluſtrade, which ſepa-
rates this *Sanctum Sanctorum* from the reſt
of the houſe, which in ſize is no more
than thirty feet by thirteen, and about
eighteen high. The canons who ſhew this
place, were extremely polite and obliging
to us ; they admitted us behind the ſanc-
tuary to the holy chimney or hearth, which
is exactly beneath the nich wherein the
Virgin ſtands, and in which fire-place or
hearth is a trunk that belonged to her:
here they ſhewed us the *Santiſſima Scodella*
or porringer, which is of coarſe blackiſh

earthen-

earthen-ware, broke in two or three places
and ftuck together with maftic; this they
affert to be the fame in which the pap
was made for the infant Jefus; the canon
permitted me to take it in my hand, which
was a prodigious favour, and I defired
him to fhake about in it fome rofaries,
chaplets, &c. which I had purchafed to
prefent to fome Roman Catholic friends in
France, and I begged him to do every thing
by them, which fhould render them, *ex-
traordinarily efficacious;* fo they have been
fhook about in the porringer, rubbed to
the holy walls, and to the image and all;
he could not help fmiling at my requeft,
There are but eight canons, they are the
only gentlemen that inhabit this city; here
alfo is a widow lady, a marchionefs, * *
* * * * * * *' *; the other citizens are all common and poor people.

  We were much difappointed at the fight
of the treafury; the treafures they keep
fhut up in preffes, and are by no means very
valuable:

valuable : here you find a few indifferent cameos; the gems in general, and in particular, are but a paltry collection. The famous pearl appears to be formed of three or four grown together; it is a misfhapen mafs not fine, though they have helped it here and there with fome colouring, - in order to induce *the faithful* to *fancy* they difcover a rude reprefentation of the Virgin feated upon a cloud.

Her fcarlet camlet gown which fhe wore when the angel Gabriel appeared to her, is inclofed with great care in a glafs-cafe.

The pictures are all very indifferent, excepting two; one of which is by Annibal Carrachi, and reprefents the nativity of the Virgin. The other, is attributed to Raffaello; the figure of the Virgin is faulty, her head not being well placed on her fhoulders, but the infant is fo well done and fo natural, that at the firft view it appears like a living child; the keeping and clair obfcure being admirably conducted.

Annibal Carrachi.

Raffaello.

ed. They told us, that lord Exeter would have given them fixteen hundred pounds fterling for this picture. We were offered a fight of the cellars, which they faid contained one hundred and forty very large tons of wine; out of one of the tons may be drawn three forts of wine from the fame fpicket, but we declined vifiting them. Here is, a *Speziale* or apothecary's fhop, where all forts of common drugs, particularly *ointments, Venice treacle, plafters, &c.* are provided for the ufe of the pilgrims *gratis:* here is alfo a great number of large gally-pots of fine earthen-ware, painted by Raffaello and Giulio Romano, well worth the attention of the curious. The prieft who fhewed us the Santa Cafa was fo obliging, as to prefent me with fome morfels of *Noftra Dama*'s black veil of laft year ftuck upon a paper, figned and fealed, *&c.* as indubitable atteftations of the identity of the faid veil, *&c.* The great reputation of the Santa Cafa, has much declined within thefe

Raffaello. GiulioRo-mano.

few

few years, from a lack of devotion in mankind; our conductor and some other holy men we converfed with, owned the Virgin had not received a gift of value from any prince or crowned head, for thefe fixty years paft; and that few pilgrims came now, compared with the numbers that ufed to vifit Loretto fome years paft: it is remarkable that this day, one of the firft in the year for the arrival of pilgrims, we faw no more than twelve of them enter Loretto. About ten pilgrims on an average yearly arrive from England, where the people of Loretto believe thofe of the Roman Catholic religion ftick up more ftrictly to the principles of their faith, than do thofe of France or Italy; and I join them in opinion. They affured us, that for many years paft, fcarce any great people had performed the journey; and added, *their pilgrimage need not be confidered by them as very painful, as they*

Vol. III.   P   *might*

might perform it in a poſt-chaiſe or otherwiſe,
provided they walk but a little, when the
weather proved favourable. Pilgrims are
fed and lodged *gratis* on the road, and
during their ſtay in the town. Thoſe we
ſaw were all common people, ſturdy lazy
vagabonds, who preferring ſloth and idle-
neſs to labour and induſtry, ſet out on what
they call a pilgrimage, as it coſts them
nothing; and I make no doubt, fail not to
pilfer what they can on their route: I
ſhould be as much afraid to meet a *poſſé* of
theſe pilgrims, as to encounter a band of
robbers in a lonely place. The Adriatic Sea
is but one mile from the city, and were not
the Turks perſuaded the treaſures of Loretto
would not ſufficiently reward their trouble,
it ſeems probable they might land and take
the town, *porringer, ſanta caſa,* treaſury,
and all its trumpery, with the greateſt eaſe.

To-morrow morning we depart for Bologna; our journey from Rome has hitherto

.5

therto been to me a painful pilgrimage, I assure you; and my expectation here thoroughly disappointed.

P. S. If you should be still curious in regard to the Santa Casa, I have provided myself with a book, containing various views of it, its treasures, its journey through the clouds, its conveyance by angels, its nightly flights from region to region, which you shall study at your leisure, *if you chuse it.* The annual landed revenue of the holy house amounts to fifteen thousand pounds sterling; no bad *broth* for their *porringer*.

Enclosed you have a letter from father Gillibrand, an English jesuit at Loretto, to M—, to satisfy his inquiries in regard to the holy house.'

Dear

" Dear Sir,

" I Tried feveral methods to tranfcribe
" the fhort hiftory you defired; but
" finding it impoffible, on account of fome
" oil fpilt upon the ftone, was obliged to
" fend you a tranflation of it from the
" Latin, found in an ancient MS. of the
" Auguftinian library at Rome, and con-
" fronted with one of Taremani; bearing
" date 1460. The accuracy of mine, you
" will find, upon comparing it with the
" French, to be met with in a fmall French
" book I gave to Mr. Fullarton, to whom
" my grateful refpects, as alfo to Mr.—
" lady, family, &c. yea to all the Eng-
" •lifh there."

*A fuccinct Account of the miraculous Con-
veyance of the Bleffed Virgin Mary's
houfe, from Nazareth to Loretto.*

" The chapel of Loretto was the houfe
" of the Bleffed Virgin Mary, mother of
" our

" our Lord Jefus Chrift, and ftood in a
" city of Galilee, called Nazareth, in which
" the Bleffed Virgin herfelf was born,
" brought up, and faluted by the angel;
" in which alfo fhe bred her fon Jefus
" Chrift, unto the age of twelve years.
" After Chrift's afcenfion, the apoftles and
" difciples, reflecting on the many divine
" myfteries wrought in the faid houfe, de-
" creed by common confent to confecrate
" it into a chapel, and dedicate it in ho-
" nour and memory of the Bleffed Virgin
" Mary, which they accordingly did, and
" in it had divine fervice. St. Luke the
" Evangelift is faid to have made an
" image of the Bleffed Virgin, which is
" kept there to this day; the people of
" thofe parts had it in great honours and
" devotions, while they were Chriftians;
" but no fooner did they embrace the Ma-
" hometan religion, than the angels con-
" veyed it to a caftle called Fiuene in
" Sclavonia; yet not being honoured there

" as

" as it ought, the angels carried it over
" the fea, and fixed it in a wood belong-
" ing to a noble woman, called Laurata
" of Recanati, whence it takes the name
" of our Lady of Loretto : but many rob-
" beries and murders being committed,
" by reafon of the great concourfe of na-
" tions to fee it, the angels again removed
" it to a neighbouring hill belonging to
" two brothers, who falling out about the
" prefents made to it, caufed the angels
" once more to remove it to the high
" road, where it now ftands without foun-
" dations, attended by many figns, won-
" ders, and favours.

" The people of Recanati came to ex-
" amine it, and finding it fo, were afraid
" of its falling, and therefore caufed it to
" be fupported by a more fubftantial wall
" and well founded, as is feen to this day.
" During all this, no one could be met
" with, to give any account of its origin,
" or how it came there, until the Bleffed
" Virgin

" Virgin herself appeared to an aged per-
" fon devoted to her fervice, and revealed
" to him the whole, in the year of our
" Lord 1296. He divulged it immediately
" to feveral prudent men, who, bent upon
" knowing the truth, felected fixteen no-
" table fworn men, to vifit the holy fe-
" pulchre and the city of Nazareth: thefe
" taking the meafure of the faid chapel,
" found its foundations left at Nazareth,
" to correfpond to a hair, with an infcrip-
" tion upon a neighbouring wall, fetting
" forth, that there had been fuch a houfe
" there, but that it was vanifhed they did
" not know where; the aforefaid fixteen
" men attefted all this to be true, upon
" oath. From that time forward, all chrif-
" tian people had and have a great vene-
" ration for it, fince the Bleffed Virgin
" Mary has and does favour it with innu-
" merable miracles daily, as experience
" fhews.

" Here

" Here was a hermit called brother
" Paul de Sylve, who lived in a hut in the
" wood, not far from the chapel, and went
" to it every morning to recite the divine
" office. He was a man of a very abfte-
" mious and fanctified life, and faid, now
" about ten years ago, that upon the feaft
" of the nativity of the Bleffed Virgin,
" viz. the eighth of September, two hours
" before day, and the wind blowing clear,
" he faw a bright light defcend from hea-
" ven upon the faid chapel, about twelve
" feet in height, and fix in breadth; it
" difappeared as foon as it came to the
" chapel; this, he faid, was the Bleffed
" Virgin that came there on her feaft.

" To render all this the more credible,
" two worthy men of this town, the one
" called Paul Ranalduece, and the other
" Francis, alias Prior, have often attefted
" the fame to me, the provoft of Tere-
" mani, and governor of this church.
" The firft affirmed, that his grandfather's
" grand-

" grandfather faw the angels carry 'it
" acrofs the fea and place it in that wood;
" and that he, with feveral others, had of-
" ten vifited it in the fame wood: the
" fecond, who was then one hundred and
" twenty years of age, often told me, that
" he himfelf had vifited it in that wood;
" he alfo faid to many other creditable
" people, that his grandfather had a houfe
" in that wood, in which he lived, and was
" tenant to the faid chapel; but that it
" was carried away, and placed upon the
" hills of the two brothers as aforefaid,
" during his own time. So ends the ftory.
" I believe I could cite a hundred that
" have written in defence of the above,
" and only five or fix againft it: but the
" oddnefs of its circumftances, as evident to
" fenfe, have greater influence with me,
" than all authority. It could not be built
" in one night, fo as to look a thoufand
" years old next morning. It is built
" without a foundation (a thing never done
" before

" before or fince to any other houfe) and
" yet has ftood even here near five hun-
" dred years, with walls near half a foot
" out of the perpendicular, and wood in
" the walls as hard as ever, yea a beam
" under everybody's feet has outlafted
" marble floors. The walls are of ftone,
" cut out of the living rock, of a fort not
" to be found in Italy, but only in a quarry
" yet exifting near Nazareth; it is not
" fupported by any thing, and never was
" yet repaired : facts are ftubborn proofs,
" and can never ply to prejudice. Excufe
" the liberty of declaring my fentiments,
" and reft affured of my being in every
" thing elfe, dear Sir,

 " your moft obedient humble fervant,

   " R. Gillibrand."

 " P. S. I fhould be glad to know where
" you are and how you are, from any part
" of the globe."

LETTER XLVIII.

Ueı   Ancona, May the 2oth, 1771.

LAST night I fent a letter for you to
the poft; as every ftep we now take
brings us nearer to you, my letters will
reach you in more frequent fucceffion.—
We have been this morning to fee the famous triumphal arch, erected in honour
of the Emperor Trajan, his wife, and fif-
ter. Its fituation is upon an eminence
above the mole, and muft make a fine appearance when viewed from the fea, being
built of marble of Paros, of a beautiful
kind, and full of fhining particles, which
glitter in the fun: it is in good preferva-
tion though in fo expofed a fituation;
and before it was fpoiled of its bronze
ftatues, trophies, &c. muft have been a
moft noble monument of Roman magnificence. From this arch there is a fine view
of the Adriatic and the coaft. The mole
when completed, will be a ftupendous
work;

work; it is carried on folely by the galley-
flaves; the cement ufed in the building is
Pouzolane, brought in boats from Puoz-
zoli and the coafts of Baïa: we do not
think it worth while to lie by here,
although Laland mentions fome pictures
in the church; fo fhall depart as foon as
the poft-horfes are ready, and prefs forward to reach Bologna as foon as poffible.
This fea-port is not an ugly town; the
fituation is eligible, and the people appear
more induftrious, richer, cleaner, and hap-
pier than in moft other Italian towns; I
except the great capitals : the caufes of this
difference are felf-evident, viz. toleration of
all religions, and a permiffion to people of
every nation to fettle here : it is moft remarkable, that this place fhould belong to
the Holy See and yet enjoy fuch privi-
leges. On one of the gates of the town is
this infcription,

Alma fides, proceres, veftram quæ condidit urbem.
Gaudet in hoc, focià vivere pace, loco.

On

On this coaft they take a moft extraordinary fpecies of fifh, which are generally
fent to Rome and much efteemed there;
they are found enclofed in ftones; have a
difgufting, naked, and raw appearance;
and refemble more a kind of clear tranfparent flefh than fifh : I believe the high eftimation they are held in, arifes more from
the difficulty of procuring them, than
from any other reafon, as we thought them
but very indifferent eating. The horfes
are ready, fo adieu for the prefent.

Rimini, 12 o'clock at night.

This has been a hard day's journey, and
though tired, I refume my pen for you :
we have come to-day eight pofts and a
half, which is about fixty-feven miles, and
did not leave Ancona as early as we fhould
have done; the viewing the arch and mole
took us up fome time, and accounts for
our late arrival at this town : half our
road lay clofe to the fea-fide, and fometimes a little in the fea till we reached Pe-

faro.

faro. The prospect is very agreeable the whole way; on one side the Adriatic, and on the other a fertile country well cultivated and well peopled. Sinegalia, Fano, and Pefaro are places noted in history, but do not contain any very remarkable antiquities, pictures, &c. Our road lay over great part of the Flaminian way, which terminates with this town. It is famous in antiquity for being the firſt place that Cæſar poſſeſſed himſelf of after he had paſſed the Rubicon. On entering it, we paſſed under a famous triumphal arch of Auguſtus; this place is now an inconfiderable fea-port. Good night, to-morrow we hope to reach Bologna.

Bologna.

May 22, Bologna. Here we fafely arrived laſt night, after a long day's journey; at leaſt I thought it fo, the hot weather greatly augmenting the fatigue of travelling. We quitted Rimini yeſterday morning, and paſſed the river Mareccia, over

Antique Bridge.

the beautiful marble antique bridge, compoſed

poſed of five arches of equal dimenſions.
From Rimini our road lay through Santa
Giuſtina, and we croſſed a river called the
Luſo. Savignano is a ſmall village a few
miles from thence: leaving this place, we
croſſed another river, called the Fiumeſino:
but the moſt remarkable of the many rivers
that cut this road, is the Piſatello or Rubicon, the ancient and famous *Rubicon*,
which at this day is but a very inconſider-
able ſtream. Ceſano our next poſt is a
pretty little town, ſituated at the foot of a
mountain: this place, as alſo Forli and
Faenza, are all mentioned in hiſtory. Before we reached Forli, we paſſed through
Ravenna alſo, where we experienced the
truth of what is ſaid concerning the bad-
neſs of the water, as well as of its ſcarcity;
they boil it, in order to make it wholeſome,
and it is ſo thick from the numbers of *ani-
malculæ* contained in it, that it is neceſſary
to ſtrain it alſo; after all this cookery it
ſtinks abominably: the wine is excellent,

richer

richer than Cyprus : the people of this place look fhockingly ill; they are of a kind of lead colour. When we changed horfes, we obferved the poft-boys had brought water with them, to exchange for an equal quantity of wine, from the former poft-houfe, which was done in our pre-fence. Imola is famous for having pro-duced feveral celebrated perfons and excel-lent poets, one of whom is now alive and refides there, the ingenious Count Camillo Zampieri. We paffed rivers fo frequently in our road from Rimini hither, that it grew at laft extremely tirefome, otherwife the road is good.

The moment our arrival was known though paft eight o'clock at night, feveral of our Bologna friends called upon us, and others fent us the moft obliging meffages; we can never forget, nor fail to acknow-ledge, the very friendly and kind manner in which we were at all times treated by the Bolognefe families in general, and in particular,

particular, by our much efteemed friend the Vice-Legate. We find it indifpenfably neceffary to ftay here a few days; it would be highly ungrateful not to comply with the prefling inftances of thofe to whom we owe fo large a debt of acknowledgment. * * * * * * * *. * We are extremely well lodged at the *Pelegrino*, where the people of the inn gave us as kind a reception in their way, as if we had conferred an obligation upon them: indeed we always confider it as a duty to recommend to our countrymen, fuch inns and houfes as have lodged and ufed us well; and I think every traveller ought to be careful to make this diftinction, otherwife the infolent and the impofing may fare equally well with the civil and reafonable. Here are letters juft arrived from you and from England. * * * * * * * * I fhall write once more from hence, and am, as ever, *&c.*

LETTER XLIX.

WE have never been out of company
and amufements fince our arrival
here, and the weather has contributed to
make thefe few days pafs away delightfully.
There are feveral pretty villas and gardens
in the environs of this city. We have
paffed our afternoons moft agreeably. One
day, after a fuperb dinner at the Cardinal
Legate's, he was fo obliging as to conduct
us himfelf, with two other ladies and two
gentlemen, to the elegant villa of the ingenious and learned Count Algarotti : you
muft know it is a very great honour in this
country to be invited to accompany a
Cardinal Legate in his own coach; it is
rarely the portion of his moft intimate acquaintance and friends, and this, as it may
have probably been the firft time it has
happened to ftrangers, I acquaint you with,

left

left you fhould *not* be furprifed at it. His *cortege* confifted of two fine gilt coaches, drawn by beautiful horfes decked with trappings and ribbons: his pages and gentlemen on horfeback; his troop of of light-horfe attended as guards: paffing through the town the people all turned out of their houfes, and the ftreets were ex- tremely crowded in order to receive his benediction, which he beftowed upon them by ftretching out his hand. However, as even *Legates* themfelves are fubject to ac- cidents, his eminence's coachman, by way of making a fhort cut, miffed his way, and the coaches very narrowly efcaped being overturned in croffing a fhallow river. This, as you may fuppofe, occafioned fome lofs of time, and not a little vexation to the company. Though we went at a great rate, it was late in the evening when we arrived at the villa, where an elegant fupper was preparing, and the houfe in the niceft order, in cafe we fhould chufe to remain

there

there till the next day; but after viewing the
villa and its very pretty gardens, upon our
expreffing a defire to return to Bologna, it
was immediately complied with, and we
were all fet down at the Opera-houfe,
where the audience had waited a confiderable time, doubtful if the Cardinal Legate
meant to *affift* there or not that evening :
we had the honour of fitting in his box,
and the inftant he appeared the curtain was
drawn up.   This opera is truly fine; it is
complete in mufic, both vocal and inftrumental ; the fcenery and decorations beautiful ; the *ballets* well performed by two
hundred dancers, and admirably adapted
to the fubject of the opera, which is Or-
pheus and Eurydice. The morning of that
day, above three thoufand Jefuits arrived
from different places, whence they have
been exiled, as Spain, Portugal, France,
Parma, the Spanifh Weft-Indies, *&c.*
they are only paffing through the town;
fome going to Rome, others to places where
they

they may with fafety conceal themfelves,
and moft of them appear to be in a very
wretched and ftarving condition: we faw
them pafs through the ftreets in the morning from our windows, but I was more
furprifed to find the pit of the opera crowded with them in the evening. We paffed
another afternoon at the villa belonging to
the once famous finger *Farinello.* General
Angeleli, a very fine old gentleman, re-
commended ftrongly to us to go and fee
Farinello and his villa, affuring us they
were both curious and worthy our notice;
adding, that this once famous finger is
upon fo good a footing here, as to be vifited by the firft families in Bologna. When
we came thither, we were furprifed to find an
elegant houfe built in the tafte of an Englifh
villa, on what is there generally called an
Italian plan: the grounds about the houfe
are laid out in the Englifh ftile, *(ferme
ornée)* his cattle come up to the door; his
hay harveft is juft over, and the hayftacks

are

are made up in the corner of one of his fields as with us; his trees are planted in hedge-rows and clumps, and .the neatnefs and fimplicity is fuch, that I could fcarce perfuade myfelf that we were not in England. He received us moft politely at the gate, and fhewed us into an excellent faloon for mufic, where we found the Vice-Legate and feveral of our acquaintance converfing, and from them we learnt, that they frequented this villa, often paffed their evenings here, and treated it as belonging to themfelves. Signor Carlo (as Farañello* is called at Bologna) is in perfon extremely tall and thin, and though confiderably advanced in years has a youthful air. The moment we had entered his houfe, he began to exprefs his obligations to the Englifh nation, for the kind protection and approbation they had beftowed

* The King of Spain has conferred upon him the dignity of Grandee of Spain.

on him when in London; naming feveral of diftinguifhed rank who flourifhed in his day, and who had treated him in the moft generous manner, by aiding him with their bounty, and honouring him with their protection: he concluded, after having made the moft grateful acknowledgments, with faying, he owed to the *Englifh* that villa and land which he poffeffed, and the means of enjoying the remainder of his life in plenty, tranquillity, and eafe.

Very genteel refrefhments of every kind were brought in, and this man appears in his own houfe as if he was made to ferve all thofe who honour him with their company, and without the leaft confcioufnefs of his being the owner: he bears an excellent character, and is much efteemed by all the Bolognefe; his villa is neatly furnifhed, but very fimple. I obferved a picture of an Englifh lady, at full length, in a magnificent frame; fhe is about the middle fize, of a very genteel make, dreffed in a pink

night-

night-gown, muflin apron, and a chip
hat; I could not prevail on him to tell me
who it was drawn for. He is alfo poffeffed
of one of the fineft harpfichords, I fuppofe,
in the world; the portrait and this harpfi-
chord are what he moft values of all he is
mafter of.

I could expatiate on the environs of this
town till I had filled a long letter, but am
obliged to quit the fubject abruptly, having juft received a moft obliging meffage
from the Cardinal Legate to fay, that he
has commanded the opera to be performed
again this evening, in confequence of our
intention to quit Bologna to-morrow; and
as we approved of it much, he thought it
might be agreeable to us to fee it again before our departure. This is certainly extremely attentive, and a very great compliment in his eminence, as it was not to
have been performed till to-morrow evening. So adieu, for this invitation muft be
complied with, though I had rather employ

ployed the evening in your fervice. We are determined to go to-morrow; for were we to leave it in the leaft doubtful, our kind friends would invent fome *fête* to detain us ftill longer. Adieu, I fhall write again at the firft place we fleep at, on our road to Venice.

I am, &c.

LETTER

LETTER L.

Ferrara, May the 29th.

WE left Bologna this morning at ten
o'clock, and sleep here to-night.
We have come only thirty miles to-day,
Cento. having stopped at Cento for above two
hours (it being but six miles out of our
way), in order to see some remarkable
paintings, by Guercino, who was born
there; his real name was Giovanni Francefco Barbieri, but he was nick-named
Guercino, from his having but one eye.

Church.   In the Church belonging to the Jesuit's
Guercino. college is a St. Jerome, and the Virgin
fuckling the infant Jefus: it is a remarkable circumstance in regard to this picture,
that Guercino, by his will, ordered his heirs
not to permit any person, upon what pre-
text foever, to take a copy of it. It is certainly good, the *chiaro ofcuro* is well preferved,

ferved, and the Ciceroni who fhews it, points out fome peculiarities worthy attention : when you walk backward and forward before it, the infant always appears to follow you with his eyes ; alfo the other figures, as well in front as on either fide, ftill appear in a proper point of view, though not in the fame. This effect muft proceed from his great judgment in the doctrine of vifion, and the effects of light and fhadow. Alfo by the fame mafter, an Elifha raifing from the dead the fon of the Shunamite; great expreffion in this piece.

In the church of the Rofary is a St. Jerome, a St. John, and a St. Thomas; the laft by Gennaro, Guercino's mafter. In another church called *Nome di Dio*, is a prodigious fine picture of Jefus Chrift's appearance to the bleffed Virgin, after his refurrection.

In *il Duomo* is another painting, by Guercino ; the fubject, Jefus Chrift giving the keys of Paradife to St. Peter. At the

Church of the Rofary. Gennaro. Il Duomo Guercino.

2   church

church of the Capuchin Monks without the town, is an agreeable picture by the fame mafter, reprefenting the difciples at Emaus; and a Madonna, which is a portrait of Guercino's miftrefs.

The road from Cento is too rough to be commodious; it lies over the fea-beach, or rather in a fhallow fea. The rivers are difagreeable to pafs, and the journey by no means pleafant.

Ferrara. Ferrara, where they fhewed us fome good pictures, is fituated on a branch of the Po. In the refectory of the Carthufian church, is a reprefentation of the marriage Bononi. feaft in Cana of Galilee, by Bononi; they affured us, that they have been offered for it as many pieces of gold as would cover it.

Church of St. Benedetto. In the church of St. Benedetto is a curious picture, by Bononi; it reprefents Herod and Herodias, but they are the portraits of Alphonfo duke of Ferrara and his miftrefs; here is alfo the tomb of Ariofto.

To-

To-morrow morning we fet forward for
Venice, from whence I fhall immediately
write, left you fhould be idle enough to
think a frefh-water journey more dangerous than a land one, and fo fancy us at
the bottom of the *Po,* which you muft
know is one of the fineft rivers in the
world. Good night, *&c.*

LETTER

LETTER LI.

From the Po, May 30, 1771.

WE quitted Ferrara this morning, proceeding to a fmall village called Francolino, which is only five miles diftant from thence : we embarked at two o'clock on board one of the boats that are kept there, for the purpofe of conveyance to Venice, and fhall reach that city to-morrow about three o'clock afternoon, at the rate of about eight miles an hour; and as the weather is extremely fine, we mean to pafs the night on the *Po*; though there are no luxurious conveniences for fleeping on board : however, it is fo improbable that we fhould find tolerable accommodation at a wretched inn in any wretched village fhould we land, that the fleeping on a table in the middle of the boat, with a broad bench on one fide, feems preferable

to

to us. We are well protected from the sun, and the river is as smooth as a looking-glass; it appears to be about half a mile broad; the banks are not deep, and the verdure meets the water's edge in a gentle slope : at some distance and on each side are cottages and farm-houses, with fine grazing meadows about them; the country appears well planted and cultivated. Our baggage is all on board with us, and our carriage makes a droll appearance in the boat I assure you : we never travelled so agreeably in our lives; our rowers work hard, keeping time in their strokes. I have had the prudence to lay in the following articles for our voyage; in the first place two or three books for our amusement, my mandoline and some music books which I have unpacked, a tinder-box and bougies for the night, a cold ham, cold fowls, Parmesan cheese, wine, good water, and a dozen of lemons : the eatables are from Ferrara, which being the residence of a

Cardinal,

Cardinal, is well fupplied with provifions for the table. It is now night, and the rifing moon feems enamoured of her refulgent charms, reflected in the calm bofom of the Po. We have gone about fix and thirty miles, and are juft entering a canal; here our rowers become ufelefs, as we muft be towed by horfes through feveral canals, and we are preparing to go to reft. Out boat-men fleep on their benches by their oars, within a blanket provided for that purpofe, our courier along with them. By way of kindnefs, a thick black woollen curtain has been put up for us, fo faftened over and about our wooden ceiling, that I thought juft now we fhould have been fmothered with heat; the mufquitos, which are like gnats, begin to infeft us. Good night, I hope thefe tormenting creatures will chufe to fleep themfelves alfo.

May the 31ft. I have paffed but a bad night, through the ftings of the mufquitos and my own timidity. Notwithftanding

my

my .endeavours to fecure my face from thefe tormentors, by covering it all over, fave as much of the end of my nofe as was neceffary for breathing, yet thefe cunning animals, difcovered that vulnerable morfel, and bit me moft barbaroufly; the reft of my face efcaped; but they have taken ample revenge of my hands and arms, which are in a miferable condition with moft violent itchings, and my fkin is much inflamed: they never molefted M—. Notwithftanding their efforts I fhould have flept on, had it not been that I was fuddenly waked by the found of the oddeft groans, accompanied with a kind of fighing and ftifled lamentations, as I apprehended. Though extremely afraid, I ventured to look through a craek in the curtain, when to my great terror, I thought I faw a tall man hanging up, much embarraffed in a quantity of clothes : I fuppofed the wailings I had heard to have proceeded from this perfon. I wakened M— in a hurry,

and told him my fears; he immediately got
up and walked to the end of the boat with
a piſtol in each hand, where this appari-
tion ſhewed itſelf; but judge of my ſurpriſe, when it appeared that the groans
and lamentations proceeded from the ropes
by which we were towed ; and the hanging man was nothing but a parcel of weeds
'which had collected and ſtuck about them.
Drawing nearer to Venice when the ſun
was riſen, we perceived the ſides of the
canals to be prettily embelliſhed with ſmall
pleaſure-houſes, gardens, and coffee-houſes:
about eight o'clock the people of one of
theſe latter ſtepping into our boat brought
us coffee, upon which we breakfaſted, continuing our voyage at the ſame time.

Two o'clock. We are now within two
miles of Venice; but the wind is riſen, and
being rather againſt us, are obliged to take
the aſſiſtance of another boat, come out to us
for that purpoſe, being no longer towed by
horſes. I think my letter would make an
admirable

admirable fupplement to the *Voiageur de St. Cloud, tant par mere que par terre.* Venice has appeared before us for three miles paft: but now, on our nearer approach, I believe the world cannot produce a more furprif-ing, or more beautiful view; a city rifing out of the bofom of the waves, crowned with glittering fpires. This fea we are now upon is called the *Lagunes*, becaufe of its calm property, being in a manner like a lake of fea-water; it is fhallow, and not fubjeā to agitation by ftorms. Adieu for the prefent, having juft gained the great canal of Venice.

Venice. We are lodged in a large pa-lace, now converted into an *hotel* for ftran-gers; it is called the *Palazzo Contarini*. We have the fame apartment our acquaint-ance lord L— lately occupied; it is much too large, but there is not a fmaller that is commodious; judge of the fize, when our anti-chamber, or outer faloon, is an hundred and twenty feet long, and wide in propor-

tion;

tion; our fitting-room within is a cube of
forty; our bed-chamber and dreffing-rooms
exceedingly good and convenient; the faloon
is ftuccoed, but the reft of the apartments
richly furnifhed, and hung with crimfon
damafk. The faloon opens into a large
balcony, from which is a beautiful view of
the *Rialto* and the grand canal, to appearance about a quarter of a mile broad,
bordered with feveral fine palaces and well
built houfes; fome of which are painted
in frefco on the outfide. The canal is covered with gondolas, thefe though black
have not fo difmal an effect as you would
imagine. This hotel is kept by a French-
man, who is married to a Venetian woman; they appear to be good fort of people, and I think very reafonable in their
demands: we are to give them twenty
paols a day for our lodging, dinner, and
fupper, not including breakfaft or wine.
Our gondola is to coft us eight paols *per*
day. I fhall fend this letter directly to the
poft,

poſt, as I am ſure you cannot be too ſoon informed of our having made a happy voyage. I am as ever, on land or on water, &c.

LETTER LII.

Venice, June the 6th, 1771.

I Have juſt received three letters from you * * * * * * * * *; I thank you for the news, and I aſſure you the Engliſh papers, which are ſent here, have furniſhed us with a great deal of amuſement: theſe contain ſome extraordinary anecdotes reſpecting ſome well-known perſons, which I ſhall mention, as perhaps you may not yet have heard them. * * * * * * * * Although it is carnival almoſt the year round at Venice, it is not ſo juſt now, which I cannot in the leaſt regret; for though I think a maſqued ball a very elegant amuſement in France and

R 3 Italy,

Italy, yet to be obliged to go about every where in mafquerade, muſt be extremely difagreeable, and fubjeā to many inconveniences, which is the cafe here in carnival time.

The Engliſh envoy Sir J— W— is not here at prefent, nor the French either; the conful of the latter nation, Monfieur le Blonde de la Motte, fupplies his place. Mr. Udney the Britiſh conful is here, and his very genteel manners make him extremely agreeable to Engliſh travellers : he lives well with the Venetians, has an admirable taſte in piāures, and poffeffes himfelf no inconfiderable colleāion. There is no conveyance in this town but by water; out of the door of your lodging, you ſtep into your gondola inſtead of your coach ; the motion of them is extremely agreeable : two gondoliers manage it fo dexteroufly, that they will whip round a ſharp corner of thefe watery ſtreets with more agility, than the beſt coachman in London can take a ſhort

turn

turn there. He that governs the helm,
ſtands in the moſt graceful attitude imaginable. The firſt orders we gave to our
gondoliers, were to conduct us to the *Place* Place St.
St. Mark, which is the only ſpot one can Mark.
call *terra firma* in this city. We were ſoon
there, and found it anſwer all its deſcrip-
tions. This is the center of Venetian amuſement; here you ſee every body; hear all
the news of the day, and every point
diſcuſſed: here are the ſenators, nobles,
merchants, fine ladies, and the meaneſt of
the people: Jews, Turks, puppets, Greeks,
mountebanks, all ſorts of jugglers and
ſights. Although ſuch a heterogeneous
mixture of people throng this place during the day, and often paſs great part of
the night here, yet there is no riot or diſ-
turbance: the Venetians are ſo accuſtomed
to ſee ſtrangers, as not to be the leaſt ſurpriſed at their being dreſſed in a faſhion
different from themſelves; nor inclined to
eſteem them objects of ridicule, on account

R 4   of

of their not fpeaking the Venetian lan-
guage: in fhort, from the moment you
enter the Place St. Mark, the advantage a
free government has over a defpotic is ob-
vious in the eafy and liberal manners of
the people; the fame air extends to their
faces, and it is rare to meet any body at
Venice with a dark fufpicious countenance.
Here are arcades or *piazzas*, extremely
convenient for fhelter from the fun, wind,
or rain; under fome of them are coffee-
houfes and fhops: in the former, the women enter as freely as the men, make their
parties, are ferved with all kinds of refrefhments, and converfe with as much
eafe as if they were in their own houfes.
The two columns of granite, which terminate this Place St. Mark on the fide of the
fea, were brought hither from Greece, and
give the entrance a noble air.

The portico or piazza which is under
the palace of St. Mark, is called the *Bro-*
The Bro- *glio*, and is deftined to the noble Venetians,
glio.
who

who repair to this walk in the morning to
converfe at their eafe about the bufinefs
of the ftate; the people and others are
careful not to mix with them on thefe occafions, nor even by walking too near the
Broglio hazard the interrupting them.
There is an univerfal politenefs here in
every rank; the people expect a civil deportment from their nobles towards them,
and they return it with much refpect and
veneration; but fhould *a noble* affume an
infolent arrogant manner towards his inferior, it would not be born with. I was
at firft furprifed at the quick tranfition,
from the frothy compliments which fall
from the fervile mouths of thofe who
champ the bit of a defpotic government, and the ftyle of compliment here;
the higheft expreffion in this way at Venice being *Gentil Donna,* which fignifies
honeft woman, or woman of honour, which
I think has much the fame fenfe; and

upon

Manners
of the peo-
ple.

upon entering a fhop, the tradefman addreffing me to know what I would have, called me *cara Ella*: when at Rome or Naples, fuch a man would have ftyled me *Eccellenza*, *Illuftriffima*. I own I feel myfelf infinitely more obliged to a Venetian, who ftyles me and believes me to be a *gentil donna*, than to a flave lavifhing all the titles

Place St. Mark.

he can invent to flatter me. But to return to a defcription of the *Place St. Mark*.

Ducal Church.

The Ducal Church dedicated to St. Mark, is in the old abfurd Gothic ftyle of architecture; before you enter, the four bronze

Antique horfes.

horfes (antique) are worthy obfervation; they have been covered with plates of gold; are the fuppofed workmanfhip of the celebrated Lyfippus; are recorded to have ftood over that of Auguftus, and from thence to have been removed and placed over the triumphal arches of other Emperors, till at laft Conftantine had them conveyed with him to Conftantinople, from whence they were taken by the Venetians

in

in the year 1206, after the conqueſt of that capital.

The lion, the ſymbol of the ſaint, and the arms of the Republic is ſo much in repute here, that you find him multiplied, from his firſt appearance on the top of one of the Greek antique columns, to the extremity of the ſquare, wherever room could be found for him. The body is like a lion, but the head and face human, with a ſtern and forbidding countenance; ſo that it is become a common ſaying here, when ſpeaking of a very ugly perſon, *Brutto figure come il lione di San Marco.* The interiour of the church is highly ornamented with fine antique marble, moſaics, &c. brought from Greece. The decorations over the altar are of ſolid gold, ſculpted in *baſſo relievo;* the figures in ſort of ſhrines, enriched with rubies, emeralds, and pearls. Behind this altar is another where the *hoſtie* is kept; it is ſurrounded with beautiful pillars, four of which

which are of oriental alabafter of an extraordinary beauty, and the two others of ferpentine ftone. The bronze door of the fanctuary, is by Sanfovino. The ducal chapel is richly adorned with the moft precious marbles. This church contains a *miraculous* picture of the Bleffed Virgin, by St. Luke: this is the moft famous of all the pictures done by that holy evangelift: they affured us, that the emperors of Conftantinople carried it with them in all their military expeditions, verily believing it the work of that faint; and that it was in the year 1204, when the Venetians and French took Conftantinople, that the Doge Henry Dandolo caufed it to be tranfported to Venice.

The treafury contains many articles of great value, but I do not believe equal to what it was eftimated at in former days; there are a numerous collection of relic, which are in this age much fallen in their value. Amongft the curiofities, they affert themfelves poffeffed

poffeffed of a manufcript of the gofpel of St. Mark, written with his own hand : and amongft the rich and precious articles, here are feveral candlefticks and vafes of pure gold. Twelve rock rubies, which weigh feven ounces each; prefented by an Emperor to the Republic, in the year 1343. A very large pearl. A fapphire which weighs nine ounces. A difh of an entire and perfect turquoife fix inches diameter; four rabbits are engraved upon it, and fome Arabick characters : here are feveral other valuable and curious gems. In the pavement of the portico of St. Mark is a fmall morfel of porphyry, frequently kiff-ed by the people, who hold it in the higheft veneration : on this piece of marble the Emperor Barbaroffa proftrated himfelf at the Pope's feet (Alexander the Third), in 1177, when his holinefs gave him abfolu-tion. This ftory is reprefented in the grand faloon of the Ducal Palace, where the Pope is feen treading on the neck of this Em-

peror;

peror; there is a tedious and foolish piece of hiftory belonging to it, which I fhall **Ducal Palace.** fpare myfelf and you. The Ducal Palace where the Doge lives, is a vaft Gothic pile; one front in the *Place St. Mark*; another looks upon the land; the principal door of entrance (for there are eight) is on the fide of the fquare, or Place St. Mark; by this you enter a large court, where are placed feveral antique ftatues, the moft remarkable, a *Cicero* and *Marcus Aurelius.* After having afcended the ftaircafe, called that of the giants, you come to a corridore, where are the famous mouths (*Denunzie Segrette*) for receiving letters relative to the ftate. This corridore conducts to an anti-chamber, the ceiling of which **Tintoretto,** is painted by *Tintoretto*; the fubject Juftice prefenting a fword to the *Doge Priuli.* On the walls are paintings in compartments, fome by *Paolo Veronefe*; the beft are the following fubjects, Our Saviour on **Paolo Veronefe.** the mount of olives, by P. Veronefe. St.

John

John the Evangelist, by *Francifco Baffano*; the Angel waking the Shepherds, alfo of Baffano. In the Sela *delle quatre porte*, all the paintings are fo much injured as to be fcarcely worth noticing. In the room called *Anti Collegio*, the ceiling is painted by *P. Veronefe*, where is an allegorical reprefentation of Venice, *&c.* The Rape of Europa, one of the pictures which adorn this *fala*, is efteemed the *chef d'œuvre* of *Paolo:* this piece reprefents three different parts of the fable; the colouring is rich and glowing; the ftuffs, of which the drapery is formed, of that peculiarity and beauty that *Paolo* is fo remarkable for. The bull is of the fineft and moft noble fpecies of that animal, his countenance expreffes great tendernefs; the moft ftriking beauty in Europa is her naked foot, which is of the moft elegant fhape and delicacy of flefh. A picture by *Giacoppo Baffano*, reprefenting a paftoral fcene; it is finely done. The *Real fala del collegio* is adorned with

Francifco Baffano.

Giacoppo Baffano.

.5   paintings,

paintings, fome of which relate to the
Venetian hiſtory, others are ſcripture ſub-
jeꝗts : but I will not attempt to enter into
the detail of any pictures, but ſuch as appear to me particularly remarkable, either
for their great merit, or ſingularity ; as I
think you have already been ſufficiently
obeyed on the article of pictures from
other places in Italy, and I fear tiring you
with catalogues. All the apartments, which
conſiſt of council chambers, courts of juſ-
tice, &c. very large and convenient, are
adorned with hiſtorical paintings, chiefly
in freſco, by no means in good preſerva-
tion ; they have been much ſpoiled by the
clouds of powder that fly out of the law-
yer's perukes when pleading, at which
time they uſe a vaſt deal of action and
agitation. However they are curious, and
worthy the examination of a traveller; as
a knowledge of the moſt intereſting part
of the Venetian ſtory may be more
agreeably collected from them, than by
reading

reading the hiftory of Venice. I fhall not attempt to defcribe the prifons in this palace; we have not feen them, but by what I hear am convinced the writers of travels have made a true report of them when they affert, that between the rafters, and immediately under the covering of the palace, is a hollow place fufficiently large to confine unhappy wretches, but too low to admit of their ftanding upright ; that their fuffering muft be dreadful from the burning heat of the fun, till death puts an end to their mifery; as the covering confifts chiefly of copper, and in fome places of lead : and this difmal fentence had effect not long fince, upon a young man of the *Mocenigo* family, who (I think) was charged with no other offence than that of an intended mifalliance ; his family concurred in the infliction of this punifhment. The Place St. Mark is particularly agreeable to walk in by night ; the lights in the coffeehoufes illuminating the piazza render it ex-

tremely cheerful : a concourfe of people re-
forting here to breathe the cool evening air,
is fo confiderable as to fill the whole fquare.
The little ftreets leading from this *Place*,
are well furnifhed with elegant fhops,
which make the moft brilliant appearance,
from the curious arangement of their articles ; and ftrike me, as far exceeding the
coup d'œil of the *foire St. Germain* at Paris.
The ftreet of the filverfmiths makes a
fplendid fhow, there being no other fort of
fhops in it. That of the milliners and
mercers is like a *parterre* of flowers, the
goods, of the moft glowing colours, being
ingenioufly mixed in fuch a manner in the
windows, as to produce a ftriking effect.
Other ftreets confift folely of poulterers,
and fome of green-grocers fhops for all
kinds of garden ftuff: thefe laft are dreffed
in fuch a manner, as difcovers a furprifing
tafte in the common people; a perfect
neatnefs reigns throughout, and I obferved
that ideas drawn from architecture were
the

the favourite fancies of the gardeners, who
pile up cabbages, lettuces, &c. as columns,
and form their capitals, friezes, &c. of
turnips, carrots, and cellery; the flowers
and herbs are linked together, and difpofed
in feftoons after the *antique*. The confec-
tioners and paftrycooks fhops are alfo curioufly contrived. I fhould not trouble you
with this detail, but that the appearances
are fo ftrikingly odd and fingular, that I
thought it worth mentioning. The provifions here are tolerable, but the Venetians are wretched cooks : they told me,
that almoft all the meat comes from Dal-
matia; it is coarfe and lean; their poultry
is good, as is the fifh; the fcuttle-fifh difgufts at firft fight, for when dreffed it fills
the difh with a black juice like ink, but
taftes agreeably when you have conquer-
ed your prejudice to its colour. They
have an odious cuftom here, of ufing
the blood of animals in their foups and
ragouts; not liking the foup they ferved

up

up yefterday, I defired our hoft to have it
made better to-day; when it came upon
the table I thought it of an odd colour,
and the tafte was extremely difagreeable;
upon inquiry I was told, it was made after
the Venetian manner, and particularly
delicate and elegant, even *eccellentifimo*,
there being a greater quantity than ordi-
nary of fowls and pigeons blood in it:
guefs if I had any further appetite for Venetian foup.—We do not propofe making
any long ftay here. As foon as our curiofity is gratified we fhall depart, but our
day is not yet fixed. Adieu.

I am, as ever, yours, *&c.*

LETTER LII.

THE very day after I wrote laſt I was attacked by an indiſpoſition, occaſioned by the water we drink having a brackiſh taſte, which I did not perceive for ſome time, having always mixed it with wine. The common Engliſh remedies had not the deſired effect, I believe I ſhould have been extremely ill, (and would not hear of a Venetian phyſician) had not M— mentioned my diſorder to Mr. U— who was not at all ſurpriſed at it, the water of Venice having frequently a like effect upon ſtrangers: he adviſed my drinking a mineral water of *Nocera*; I took his preſcription, the firſt glaſs relieved me much, and half the bottle completed the cure. This water is extremely clear and light, and has no taſte. My indiſpoſition occaſioned me ſome

S 3

dif-

difappointments. I could not comply with
the obliging invitations we received to two
wedding balls and fuppers: one was the
marriage of the Doge's fon *Alvife Mocenigo,* e la *nobil Donna Poliffena Contarini*;
the other was of *Aleffandro Barziza,* e
Andriana Berlenda Berlendis: though I
could not partake of the amufements in
the evenings, I thought I might poffibly
venture to fee the ceremony in the church;
we were accordingly prefent at the firft of
thefe, that of *Mocenigo.* I was extremely
well pleafed that I had not permitted fo fine
a fhow to efcape me, though afflicted with a
tormenting pain in my ftomach the whole
time. The proceffion of the gondolas
to the church was very fine; the gondoliers, droffed in gold and filver ftuffs,
made a moft brilliant contraft with the
blacknefs of their boats. We got into the
church before the bride and bridegroom
with their *fuite* arrived, where the pillars
and walls were covered with crimfon damafk,
fringed

fringed with gold; the altar richly adorned with lace and flowers, and the fteps up
to it fpread over with Perfian carpets; the
whole church was illuminated with large
wax tapers, though at noon-day.

As foon as the company were difem-
barked from their gondolas, they formed
themfelves into a regular proceffion; the
ladies walked two and two: they were all
dreffed in thin black filk gowns (excepting
the bride), with large hoops; the gowns
are ftrait-bodied, with very long trains,
like the *robes de cour* at Verfailles; their
trains tucked up on one fide of the hoop,
with a prodigious large taffel of diamonds.
Their fleeves were covered up to the
fhoulders with falls of the fineft Bruffels
lace, a drawn tucker of the fame round
the bofom, adorned with rows of the
fineft pearl, each as large as a moderate
goofeberry, till the rows defcended below
the top of the ftomacher; then two ropes
of pearl, which came from the back of the

neck,

neck, were caught up at the left fide of the ftomacher, and finifhed in two fine taffels. Their heads were dreffed prodigioufly high in a vaft number of buckles; and two long drop curls on the neck. A great number of diamond pins and ftrings of pearl adorned their heads, with large *fultanes* or feathers on one fide, and magnificent diamond ear-rings.

The bride was dreffed in cloth of filver, made in the fame fafhion and decorated in the fame manner with the other ladies; but her bofom was quite bare, and fhe had a fine diamond necklace and an enormous *bouquet* of natural flowers. Her hair was dreffed as high as the others, with this difference, that it was in curls behind as well as before, and had three curls which fell down her back from her poll, the two fide ones reaching half way down her back, and the middle curl not quite fo far : thefe three curls had a fingular appearance, but not near fo good an effect as the heads

of

of the other ladies, whose hair was plaited
in large folds, and appeared much more
graceful: her diamonds were very fine, and
in great profusion. She is but seventeen
years old; is of a comely sort of beauty,
and very full grown of her age. All the
ladies that walked, about sixty in number,
were relations or intimate friends to the
young couple; many of them extremely
handsome. The men appeared to me to be
all alike; they were dressed in black gowns
like lawyers, with immense periwigs. The
bridegroom is a slender fair little man, seemed to be much charmed with his new wife;
he very politely sent us the *epithalamiums*
and other poems made on the occasion,
elegantly covered and adorned with en-
gravings. I was extremely sorry at not
being well enough to go to the ball and
supper; however I persuaded M— to comply with their very polite invitation: he
danced English country-dances, but did
not stay to supper. I was not well enough

to go to the other wedding; but he went, and it paſſed much in the ſame manner with the firſt. Is it not ſingular, that the Doge's dignity ſhould forbid his being preſent at his own ſon's wedding? I have employed my mornings, ſince my recovery, in ſeeing a few of the moſt remarkable churches and palaces, which are here ſo numerous, that I thought it adviſable to make a ſelection of thoſe moſt worthy of notice; ſo, during my confinement, I made out a liſt of ſuch as contained the beſt pictures, &c. To begin with the churches: St. Zaccaria is a church belonging to a convent of noble ladies of the Benedictine order; it is fronted with marble. The beſt picture this church poſſeſſes is by P. Veroneſe; it repreſents the Virgin, the Infant Jeſus, St. John, St. Joſeph, St. Catherine, St. Jerome, and St. Francis; St. John is upon a pedeſtal, and St. Francis is ſhewing him his *Stigmates:* the colouring is beautiful, the figures all expreſſive of the characters,

ChurchSt. Zaccaria.

P. Veroneſe.

the

the Virgin extremely handfome, and St. Catherine, whofe profile only appears, is of a moft amiable countenance; her hair is finely done, is braided with pearls, and in the picture Veronefe had a good opportunity of difplaying his powers of reprefenting rich and ornamental drapery. The grand altar is finely decorated with porphyry, and other precious marbles.

St. Fantino is worth feeing for its fine ornaments in marble and opake gems; here are alfo two good pictures, by Palma.

St. Fantino.

Palma.

Scuolo di St. Fantino is the *confraternata* of St. Jerome. Thefe brethren vifit the condemned criminals, and exhort them to repentance, &c. in their dying moments. The church belonging to this convent is highly ornamented (but is not the fame with that above mentioned); the ceiling is painted by Palma, and is amongft his beft performances; the fubject an Affumption, with the Apoftles and St. Jerome. Here are introduced the portraits of Tiziano and

Scuolo di St. Fantino.

Palma.

I   Vittorio

Vittorio (a ftatuary), Palma, his wife, and feveral celebrated muficians, friends of his. The whole hiftory of St. Jerome is painted on the walls.

St. Lucca. St. Lucca ; this church is fituated in the center of Venice ; over the grand altar is P. Vero- a fine picture by P. Veronefe; it reprefents nefe. St. Luke, who, having drawn the portrait of the Virgin which is placed in the cor- ner of the picture, is admiring it, leaning on his ox ; behind him ftands a prieft: this is a very fine picture. Over another altar is a picture by Benefatto, a nephew of Veronefe; the fubject, a Laft Supper: in this piece appears a man with a large beard, which is the portrait of Aretino, who lies buried under the pulpit.

Church St. Salva-
doro. St. Salvadoro is famous for its architec- ture, from the defigns of Julio Lombardi, and for two or three good paintings by Tiziano.

Church I Mira- coli. I Miracoli, a church belonging to the fe- male convent of Clarifts, is encrufted within and without with fine marbles, ferpentine

7 ftone

ftone and porphyry. Over the organ are two ftatues of children in marble; they are antique, of the laft beauty, and attributed to Praxiteles, the celebrated Athenian fculptor. Near the church is the houfe Tiziano lived in; he is efteemed with juftice the firft painter of the Venetian fchool: he drew the picture of Charles the Fifth three times, and was fo highly favoured by this monarch, as to be created a *Count Palatino:* this celebrated artift is interred in the church of I Frari (where are fome good paintings of P. Veronefe); he died of the plague in 1576, aged ninety-nine years.

St. Giorgio Maggiore is a church belonging to the Benedictins; Palladio was its architect; the front is entirely of marble: in my opinion, this is the fineft church in Venice; I fay in my opinion, as its architecture has been criticifed by good judges. The refectory belonging to it contains the famous picture by P. Veronefe, which re-

Antique Statues.

P. Veronefe.

Church St. Giorgio Maggiore. Architect Palladio.

P. Veronefe.

prefents

prefents the Marriage Supper at Cana in
Galilee. I was not permitted by the
monks to enter their refectory, *as no women are fuffered to penetrate fo far:* I therefore waited for M— in the church; he
made a note of it : he thinks it a very fine
picture, and believes there are more portraits amongst the perfonages, than the
monks apprehend : amongst the muficians
they point out thofe of Tiziano, Tintoretto, and Baffano; he thinks the colouring, ordonnance, grouping, &c. in Veronefe's beft manner. As a proof of the
great difference between the prices now
paid for pictures, and what they fold for
at the time this was done, it appears by
an entry in the convent houfehold book,
which M— faw, that P. Veronefe was
paid for this picture the fum of twenty-
two fequins, fix meafures of wheat, and
two veffels of wine : I wonder how Sir
J— R— would look, if he was offered for
one

one of his beft family pictures ten guineas,
an hundred of cheefe, and a hogfhead of
ftrong beer !—

I have but two more churches to mention. Church
St.Sebaftiano contains feveral pictures by Ve- St. Sebaf-tiano.
ronefe; here is alfo his tomb. The fanctuary Veronefe.
is furnifhed with a very good picture of his,
which reprefents St. Marco and St. Marcellino, who are defcending the ftaircafe of
the Prætor, fuppofed to have juft quitted
him after he had condemned them to die:
their mother appears earneft with them to
renounce their faith, and fave their lives;
but St. Sebaftian exhorts them to be fteady
in their refolutions: it is a very interefting
picture, the colouring frefh, and in high
confervation. Here are a great collection
of excellent paintings: the martyrdom of
St. Sebaftian, and feveral circumftances of
his life, with fome fcripture hiftory, are
all worthy the attention of the curious.

In the church of St. Maria Maggiore Church
are fome remarkable paintings. One by St. Maria Maggi-ore.
Baffano

Baſſano. Baſſano is a moſt entertaining ſcene; the ſubject, Noah's ark: it is incredible what a number of ſtrange animals he has introduced, how highly he has finiſhed the plumage of an amazing variety of birds, and the accuracy with which he has drawn the various beaſts, &c. The Four Seaſons in the *naif* of this church are by the ſame painter, and well done. I ſhall now mention ſome of the palaces, for I think I have introduced you to as many churches as are neceſſary to give you an idea of the reſt, but be aſſured I have not named a fourth of the number this city contains. We had a great deſire to

Pallazzo Piſani. ſee the *Pallazzo Piſani*, on account of one famous picture by Veroneſe, repreſenting the family of Darius proſtrate before Alexander; but were much diſappointed at hearing it had been ſold: this was the boaſt of the palace, the remainder I think but indifferent.

Pallazzo

Pallazzo Barberigo. This palace contains feveral excellent paintings by Tiziano;
amongft the moft remarkable are the following : a woman and a fatyr; a Prometheus; Tobias and the Angel, a fingular
reprefentation; a Venus at her toilette, fhe
is extremely handfome, and appears to be
a portrait; a Cupid brings her a crown,
and another holds the mirror. Venus
diffuading Adonis from the chafe. A Virgin and infant Jefus, to whom the Magdalen prefents a box of perfumes; this is
a very fine picture. A weeping Magdalen,
full of the moft pathetic expreffion. The
miracle of the five loaves by Baffano; a
winter fcene by the fame mafter.

Pallazzo Graffi contains a fine collection
of pictures. Here is a Venus by Tiziano;
fhe ftrongly refembles that at Florence, and
is fuppofed to be the portrait of a miftrefs
of a duke of Ferara. A rape of Europa
by Veronefe, an admirable picture. Acteon
and Diana by the fame. A very fingular

(margin notes: Pallazzo Barberigo. Tiziano. Baffano. Pallazzo Graffi. Tiziano. Veronefe.)

picture ; its fubject the parable of the
beam and the moat, *particularifed* by Feti.

Feti.

Vandyke.

Some portraits by Vandyke. The anoint-
ing our Saviour's feet at the table of the
Pharifee, by Rubens. A Cupid by Guido.

Rubens.
Guido.

David bearing the head of Goliah. The
Ifraelites rejoicing precede him, by Guer-

Guercino.

cino. The triumph of Galathea by Schia-
vone; the women are elegantly caft.

Schia-
vone.

The palaces at Venice are much in the
fame tafte ; having feen one or two,
you have in a manner feen all. The Venetians cover their walls with pictures,
and never think their apartments properly
furnifhed, until they have fuch as fhall
fill all the fpaces from top to bottom, fo
as completely to hide the hanging. This
being their object, there are in all the collections many more bad pictures than good;
and on entering a room, the number of
paintings are fuch, that it is not till after fome recollection you can difcriminate
thofe pictures that merit attention, from
amongft

amongft a chaos of glowing colours that furround them ; and which are frequently fo ill claffed, that a picture which requires to be hung high, is perhaps the loweft in the room, whilft another that cannot be feen too clofe, touches the cornice : this is occafioned by their great object of covering the walls, never confidering what light, &c. may fuit their pictures.

The palaces in general are furnifhed with velvet and damafk, fringed or laced with gold. The floors are of a compofition which imitates various marbles, and has an excellent effect ; but what I admire very much, and is univerfally found in all the houfes as well as palaces, is the elegant manner in which they paint the doors, architraves, fkirting boards, and all their wainfcotting : it is fmooth as viory, of very pale tints for the ground, and prettily ornamented with various devices, feftoons, fruits, &c. They alfo paint in frefco on the walls with a great deal of facility and

T 2   tafte,

tafte, having an exceeding good idea of
perfpective : this is to be met with in the
pooreft houfes, and where they do not go
to the expence of painting the walls, their
white-wafh is of an uncommon neatnefs;
it is gloffy, of a foft colour, and never
comes off. I fhall write again before we
leave this city, and muft break off now,
the time being come for our engagements
to two Caffinos this evening. Adieu, &c.

P. S. I live almoft the whole of the day
when at home in the balcony, which is to
me the moft agreeable part of this great
hotel, I fhould fay *Pallazzo*. The people
are fo mufical here, that all day long the
houfes fend forth the moft melodious
founds, which die off charmingly along
the water; till they again awake the
ftrings, and at the fame time draw off my
attention fo much from what I am about,
that I believe were I to refide here for any
time, I fhould do nothing but liften to
mufic the whole day.

LETTER LIII.

Venice, June the 17th, 1771.

TO-morrow we leave this city, and proceed on our route to Milan. I ſhall write from every place we ſtop at as uſual, and ſend my letter by the firſt opportunity, if any offers before we reach that city.

The *Caſſinos* I mentioned to you in my laſt letter, are ſmall houſes of one or two rooms on a floor; neatly fitted up, but never fine: thoſe I ſaw were papered with India paper, and furniſhed with chintz. It is the faſhion here for every perſon of diſtinction to have one Caſſino at leaſt, and very frequently more: they have little pleaſure in inhabiting their palaces, which are really uncomfortable, and by the plans and dimenſions rendered extremely melancholy. A ſilent and ſolitary magni-

Caſſinos

T 3

ficence

ficence reigns throughout, interrupted only
by the hoarfe wafhing of the fea againft the
walls, which is not exhilarating to the
fpirits, you muft confefs. I fuppofe it was
in fearch of cheerfulnefs, recreation and
fociety, that *Caffinos* were originally refort-
ed to; the greater number of them are
fituated behind St. Mark's Place. Here
fmall *Cotteries* meet, play at cards, generally fup together on fome trifle they procure from the paftrycooks-fhops and coffee-houfes; and often pafs the night in
converfation, mufic, or in walking about
the *Place St. Mark.* I do not pretend to
fay thefe Caffinos are not often made
an ill ufe of:—all I can affert is, that
in thofe to which I was introduced, I neither faw nor heard any thing but what
was extremely well bred and liberal; the
fmallnefs of the rooms, and the card-par-
ties, prevent the formality of a circle.
The fociety was compofed of people who
feemed perfectly well acquainted with each
other,

other, and who fhewed us the kindeft attention as ftrangers. To us indeed thefe
Caffino parties was not very amufing, as
we could not poffibly find in them the
pleafures the Venetians feemed to do; we
had much rather have been at an opera, or
a play; but there is no theatre open
at this feafon of the year. The only
amufements at this time are thefe private
parties, walking in *la Place St. Mark,*
taking the air in our gondola amongft the
little iflands near Venice, or walking in
the *Giardini Giudecca,* as they are called,   Giardini
near Venice; which are extremely ill laid   Giudecca.
out, in dirty walks and vulgar arbours; the
garden itfelf is divided into quarters, and
contains little elfe than common kitchen
garden ftuff. Here the fenators and people
refort; and are ferved with refrefhments
in the arbours: there is no diftinction
fhewn to one more than another, by
thofe who attend upon the company, yet we
never could learn that any accident hap-

T 4   pened

[280]

pened from this mixture of people and ranks. M— has been to fee the Arfenal and the *Bucentaure:* as to the firft, he fays, it agrees with the defcription the writers of travels have given of it, but does not think it contains any thing that might compenfate to me for the trouble of vifiting it this hot weather. He thinks the *Bucentaure** the uglieft, moft tawdry, worft contrived veffel he ever faw; loaded with ornaments and gilding, and totally void of grace.

Arfenal and Bucentau:e.

We have feen fome of the Charitable Inftitutions, or convents here; one is called *la Pieta*, it is an hofpital for foundlings of the female fex: all I fhall fay at prefent concerning this convent is, that I was in, and all over it, and that I faw noting curious: that we were prefent in the church when there was fome very good mufic, both vocal and inftrumental, performed in

Charitable Inftitutions.

* The ftate veffel in which the Doge performs the annual ceremony of marrying the Adriatic.

a tri-

a tribune, by the women of the convent:
that the tribune having a lattice before it,
we could not diftinguifh the performers;
I therefore begged to be permitted to go
into the tribune, that I might fee as well
as hear the concert: my requeft was granted; but when I entered I was feized with
fo violent a fit of laughter, that I am furprifed they had not driven me out again.
You cannot wonder that my rifibility was
excited, when, upon entering the tribune,
my eyes were ftruck with the fight of a
dozen or fourteen beldams ugly and old;
one blowing a French horn, another fweat-
ing at the bafs-viol, another playing firft
fiddle, and beating time with her foot in
the greateft rage; others performing on
baffoons, hautboys, and clarionets; thefe,
with feveral young girls who formed the
choir, and one who played upon the organ,
compofed the concert, a concert I never
can forget; but after I had feen it, I could
no longer bear to hear it, fo much had the
fight

fight of the performers difgufted me. As
to other anecdotes relating to this convent,
I fhall referve them for you when we meet.

Hofpital I
Mendi-
canti.
I Mendicanti is an hofpital deftined for
the relief of indigent girls, and decayed
old age. From what I have feen of thefe
charitable inftitutions, I think they admit
of great improvements and better regulations.

Glafs-
houfes.
The Glafs-houfes are for the moft part
built in the iflands near the city. We went
to fee the beft manufacture of this kind,
but think it falls infinitely fhort of our
Englifh fine cut glafs. The only thing I
faw that appeared fingular or curious, was
certain feftoons of flowers intended to decorate luftres, and large *bouquets* for *faints
in churches*; the effect of thefe flowers
when finifhed is not very pretty, they have
a fragile and tawdry appearance. It is an
univerfal cuftom at Venice, to drefs up
wooden figures, as large as life, of *madonnas*
and faints, *&c.* and to clothe them in various

rious modes; their faces and hands are painted, to imitate nature; but they have the appearance of gigantic dolls, and are quite fufficient to make one ftart when placed in a darkifh corner. At the above-mentioned manufactory, they fhewed us complete furniture for a room in the Grand Signior's feraglio, which had been befpoke at Venice, and made exactly to the orders received from the Porte. The moft re-markable article was the principal fofa; it was not raifed above four inches from the ground, the back and arms carved and gilt, its carving forming curves and fcrolls, and the back rifing to the height of about eight feet. In the moulding were inferted or inlaid, broad pieces of thick blue glafs (not cut), and here and there fmall oval and round looking glaffes, fo placed as to reflect with variety every contiguous object. It was covered with fine Lyons gold filk, and was to have three or four mattraffes of the fame. Though

in

in defcription this fofa may not ftrike you
as pretty, yet the effect was really fo and
very odd; as the fculpted wood, which
formed and guided the plan of the whole,
was elegantly executed, and defigned in a
good tafte. The reft of the furniture confifted of very broad and low ftools, the
frames and feet of which were decorated
with gilding and pieces of blue glafs.
There were luftres and feftoons of flowers,
&c. to ornament the fame room.

I think I have not yet mentioned the
manners of the Venetians, at leaft not entered into any detail on that fubject, nor
will my time now allow me, were I much
better qualified for the tafk than I really
am. However, not wholly to difappoint
you, take this account of fome of their women at leaft, particularly the nobility. The
cuftom of *Cavalieri Serventi* prevails univerfally here : this ufage would appear in
a proper light, and take off a great part of
the odium thrown upon the Italians, if the

Cavalieri

Cavalieri Serventi were called hufbands; for the real hufband, or beloved friend, of a Venetian lady (often for life), is the *Cicifbeo*. The hufband married in church is the choice of her friends, not by any means of the lady. It is from fuch abfurd tyranny of the relations and friends of young girls, not fuffering them to chufe for themfelves, that this chufing of Cicifbeos, or Cavalieri Serventis, has taken its rife, and will never be relinquifhed in Italy, whilft the fame incongruous combinations fubfift : this furely leffens the criminality, at leaft in fome degree. The Venetian ladies have a gay manner of dreffing their heads, which becomes them extremely when young, but appears very abfurd when age has furrowed over their fine fkins, and brought them almoft to the ground. I felt a fhock at firft fight of a tottering old pair I faw enter a coffeehoufe the other evening ; they were both fhaking with the palfy, leant upon each other, and fupported themfelves by a

crutch-

crutch-ftick; they were bent almoft double
by the weight of years and infirmities,
yet the lady's head was dreffed with great
care; a little rofe-coloured hat, nicely
trimmed with blond, was ftuck juft above
her right ear, and over her left was a
fmall matt of artificial flowers; her few
grey hairs behind were tied with ribbon,
but fo thinly fcattered over her forehead,
that large patches of her fhrivelled fkin appeared between the parting curls : the *Cavaliere* was not dreffed in the fame ftile,
all his elegance confifted in an abundance of
wig which flowed upon his fhoulders. I
inquired who this *venerable* couple were,
and learnt, that the gentleman had been the
faithful *Cavaliere* of the fame lady above
forty years; that they had regularly frequented the *Place St. Mark* and the coffee-
houfes, and with the moft fteady conftancy
had loved each other, till age and difeafe
were conducting them hand in hand together
to the grave. However, a forty years conftancy

cy is far from *univerfal* at Venice; *coquettes*
are to be found there, as well as elfewhere:
I have feen fome inftances of coquetry at
fourfcore; a *Donna Nobile*, whom a catarrh
and Satan had bound, " lo, thefe eighteen
" years !" was fuftaining herfelf on the
arm, of a brifk Cicifbeo about twenty-
five, in the *Place St. Mark*; fhe had often changed *Cavalieres*, as you may fuppofe. Several inftances of the moft fatal
effects from jealoufy are to be found in
the annals of modern Venetian gallantry;
but fuch anecdotes, with fome of a lefs
tragical kind, I fhall communicate to you
when we meet, as they would confume too
much time to narrate them with my pen.
A new regulation in the coffee-houfes
had juft taken place before our arrival:
the partitions, which formed kind of
cells in the interior of them, into which
two or three people might retire and
faften the door, are now taken away, and
the rooms quite open and public. At

firft

'firſt the ſenate had determined to exclude the women entirely from entering the coffee-houſes, but they remonſtrated ſo violently and effectually againſt this meaſure, that they were allowed the liberty of appearing publickly, but abſolutely forbid to retire in private into any room, and the little rooms were without exception ordered to be thrown into the large ones. Another law has juſt been promulgated, which is, that if any *fille de joie* is found walking the ſtreets about the *Place St. Mark, &c.* for the firſt offence ſhe is to have her head completely ſhaved, and ſuffer impriſonment for a time ſpecified; and for the ſecond offence, her eye-brows are alſo to be ſhaved, ſhe is to be branded between the eyes, and baniſhed the Republic. The ſingularity of the ſituation of this town, I believe, will account for its tiring ſtrangers ſooner than moſt others ; I fancy myſelf a priſoner, from being ſurrounded with water, at the ſame time nothing can be more

2   con-

convenient and eafy than the gondolas. I
fhall quit Venice with lefs regret, than I
have hitherto done any other refidence in
Italy.

Adieu, you fhall hear from me again
as foon as poffible. I am as ever, &c.

P. S. I forgot to mention to you, that
the celebrated Rialto does not anfwer the
idea I had formed of it. The arch is indeed large, but wants a certain dignity that
fhould accompany architecture of a bold
ftyle; it does not ftrike one with awe, there
is no greatnefs in the appearance. The
Bridge has paltry fhades built on each fide
of it; thefe are fhops, and their merchan-
dife is brilliant and coftly, for they fell nothing but pearls and gold ornaments.

LETTER LIV.

WE arrived here laſt night, and find
Padua an old, ſtraggling, ugly
town, though founded by Antenor, and
celebrated by claſſic authors; it is but
twenty-five miles from Venice. We embarked at Venice in a boat called a *burchio*,
in which is a pretty room glazed, painted,
and extremely convenient. Four rowers
conveyed us from Venice to the canal,
formed by the *Brenta*, when two horſes
towed us along. Before you gain the
Brenta, your route is indicated by piquets
fixed at certain diſtances in the water,
that you may not loſe your way through
the Lagune; and the firſt *terra firma*
you come to is called Fuſina, five miles
from Venice. From that city to Padua
the views are delightful; for the firſt five
miles, Venice alſo gives you a variety of
appear-

Fuſina.

appearances: the iſlands of the Lagunes are fertile, and under a plentiful cultivation. While we were towed along the Brenta, the banks preſented us, on each ſide, with gardens planted down to the water's edge, crowned with palaces and beautiful villas. One of the moſt elegant of the former is that of Foſcari; another that of Piſani, twenty miles from Venice, and five from Padua: the gardens belonging to this laſt are very large, and laid out in the taſte of thoſe of Marli near Paris. We paſſed by ſeveral villages after having entered the Brenta: the name of the firſt is *Mira*, in which are ſeveral good houſes: the next *Doglio*; the third *Stra*; the fourth *Noventa*, but two miles from Padua. Palaces Foſcari and Piſani.

Lalande aſſerts the fortifications of this town to be in good repair; and ſays ſo much of them, that M— had the curioſity to go round and viſit them; but found them all in ruins. *Lalande* moſt Fortifications.

certainly

certainly never faw them, but took his account from fome old defcription of them, as (all he fays in regard to Padua, (the hiftorical part excepted) is entirely falfe. I think, in a well governed ftate, there fhould be a fevere punifhment inflicted upon travellers, who do not make truth their guide: the leaft inconvenience attendant on fo bafe a conduct, is the giving a great deal of unneceffary trouble and difappointment to thofe who credit their reprefentations. In the Cathedral church of this city is a Virgin, painted by the famous Giotto; Petrarque once poffeffed this picture, and bequeathed it to Francefco di Carrara. The Sacrifty holds a collection of curious pictures; that of the Virgin and Infant, announced to be of Tiziano, is fine; but as the Virgin is not in the fame ftyle with moft of thofe painted by that mafter, it has been conjectured Pardenone drew the Virgin, and Titian the Child. Here is an excellent portrait of Petrarque, placed amongft the

the *other* canons of the cathedral. The library is worth feeing, as it contains fome curious manufcripts.

The Church of *St. Antonio* is an old Gothic building. Here are fome *baffo relievos* by *Donatello* in bronze, tolerably good. In one of the chapels is a decollation of St. John, by *Piazzetta*; this is a very fine picture, but the fubject, with the circumftances here depicted, is fhocking to contemplate. A Martyrdom of St. *Bartelemi*, by *Tiepoletto.* Alfo the martyrdom of St. *Agatha*; an executioner cutting off her breafts by the fame painter: horrible objects of notice.

St. *Antonio's* chapel is much adorned with marble ftatues, *baffo relievos*, pillars, &c. In the interior are nine pieces of fculpture in *baffo relievo*, with figures nearly as large as life, reprefenting the moft remarkable events of the faint's life; which, though but indifferently executed, afford amufement from the oddity of the

U 3   adven-

Church St. Antonio.

Donatello.

Piazzetta.

Tiepoletto.

adventures they reprefent. In the firft
compartment appears St. Antonio, who is
fo defirous of the glory of martyrdom,
as to quit his canonical habits, to become
a member of the pooreft order of monks;
this is by one *Minello di Bardi*. In the
fecond compartment appears the faint, who
making the fign of the crofs, faves the life
of a woman that her hufband had *kindly* thrown out of a window. The third
is by *Campagna*, and is one of the beft.
St. *Antonio* in this performs a very ufeful
miracle, for he raifes a young man at Lif-
bon from the dead, in order to clear his
father from the unjuft accufation of having
murdered him. Another extraordinary
miracle of his, is the joining on to his leg
the foot of a child, who had cut it off, as
a punifhment for having kicked his mother. The converfion of an heretic, appears alfo amongft them; the heretic's
name was *Alcardino*; he faid he fhould be
converted and become a difciple of *St. Antonio*,

Minello
di Bardi.

tonio, if a drinking-glafs thrown out of
the window fhould receive no fracture,
through the power or interpofition of the
faint. The experiment was made, and
the glafs, inftead of breaking, broke the
ftone to pieces on which it fell; upon the
fight of this miracle, the heretic was (as
you may fuppofe) immediately converted. About the middle of the chapel is
a fine altar of granite, in which is enclofed the body of St. Antonio; this
altar is richly decorated with columns of
verd antique, bronze ftatues of faints,
fome beautiful filver candlefticks of curious workmanfhip, and of great weight.
One fine gold lamp and twenty-four of
filver burn conftantly in this chapel.
The *Ex-votis* of gold and filver, cover
the walls over. In the church are fome
monuments worthy obfervation; I noticed one in particular to the memory of
Helena Cornaro Pifcopia, a noble Venetian lady, who was honoured at Padua
with

[296]

with the degree of Doctor in Philofophy for her great learning; I believe it would not be eafy at this day, to find a Venetian lady capable of anfwering for a doctor's degree.

Church St. Giuf- tina.

P. Vero- nefe.

The Church of St. *Giuftina* deferves notice; there are fome good pictures in it, particularly one over the great altar, by P. Veronefe, which has much merit, though confiderably damaged by the damps. Several of the churches here are worth feeing, and fome palaces. The hall of audience called *il Salone*, is one of the largeft In all Italy; it is principally vifited upon this account.

Famous Monu- ments.

Here you fee feveral remarkable Monuments, two of them are to the memory of two as virtuous ladies as ancient Rome ever boafted of; one *La Marchefa Lucrezia Dondi Orologia*, wife of *Pio Enea, marchefe de gli Obizzi*, who died in defence of her honour: the other, *Bianca de Rofs*, who was facrificed upon the tomb of her hufband, rather

rather than fubmit to the tyrant *Ezzelino.*
The ftories of thefe ladies would take up
more time than I can now command; befides, they are too fhocking for relation.
Adieu, for the prefent.

Verona, the 20th of June, 1771.

(In continuation.) Laft night we reached Vicenza, which is about eighteen miles
from Padua, and paffed this morning in
viewing the famous amphitheatre, &c.
From Vicenza to Verona is thirty two
miles; the road very tolerable, and the
country well planted with mulberries and
vines.

The face of the country is covered with
water meadows, in which rice is generally
cultivated. Nothing looks prettier than
thefe meadows when the fun fhines on
them; the trenches for the water are cut
in ftraight lines, and I do not know any
thing fo like a field of rice, as a fine pale
green filk ftriped with filver.

Vicenza

Vicenza. *Vicenza* makes a fingular appearance; as at firft fight it prefents you with nothing but commencements of noble palaces, which have been left unfiniſhed. Theſe edifices (by Palladio), if completed, would have made this a beautiful city: two rivers *Bridge Palladio.* run through the town, over which are three bridges, one of them, by Palladio, is of beautiful proportions; it has but one arch, and on the parapet walls a baluſtrade of marble; the whole is fimple, and in a noble ftyle.

Theatre Olympi-co. Palladio has alfo built *il teatro olympico,* 'tis his *chef d'œuvre* taken from the plans of the antique theatres; its form a demi-oval divided the long way; no boxes, but *gradins* or fteps ferve as feats for the fpec-tators. There is but one fcene, and that is fixed at the extremity of the ftage, be-ing a view of feven ftreets which feem to terminate there: thefe ftreets are decorated with temples and other public edifices, all in wood and immovable; they leffen in real

per-

perfpective; I could walk through fome of them, but the furtheft grew too narrow to admit my paffing. *The Profcenium* repre-fents a triumphal arch, dedicated to Her-cules; this theatre is efteemed one of the moft perfect morfels of modern architecture the world can boaft of.

In the *Piazza d'Ifola* is a beautiful front of a palace by *Palladio*. He was an ac-ceffary to the ruin of many of the great fa-milies at *Vicenza*, by drawing them into a tafte for architecture. It is afferted here, that it was done from a motive of revenge, for their having imprifoned his fon, who was an extravagant fpendthrift, during the father's abfence from *Vicenza*, who on his return gave them plans and falfe eftimates, to induce them to begin upon what he knew they never could finifh.

Here are fome churches worth feeing: that of *la Santa Corona* contains a fine pic-ture, by *P. Veronefe*, of the Adoration of

Church la Santa Co-rona.

the

the Magi. The country about *Vicenza* is rather pleafing. A flat field, furrounded with a ditch, and planted with trees, is the place frequented by the inhabitants as a public walk. You enter by a triumphal arch erected by Palladio; it is of fine proportions, very much and very defervedly admired.

There are fome elegant gardens and cafinos in the neighbourhood of this city, **Verona.** but we had not time to vifit them. Your accommodation in the inns, provifions, beds, &c. are better through the Venetian ftates than in moft others of Italy. The river *Adigio* paffes through this city, over which are three bridges: one in particular is re- **Ponte di** markably fine; it is called *il Pente di Caf-* **Caftello** *tello Vecchio.* **Vecchio.**

The *Arena*, or antique amphitheatre, is the firft object of curiofity at Verona; it is fuperb, and built in the fame tafte with the *Coliffeo* at Rome: the fhape

is

is oval. There are forty-five rows of gradins (fteps) carried all round, formed of fine blocks of marble about a foot and an half high each, and above two feet broad. Twenty-two thoufand perfons may be feated here at their eafe, allowing one foot and an half for each perfon. This amphitheatre is quite perfect, and has been lately as well as frequently repaired with the greateft care at the expence of the inhabitants. They frequently give public *fpectacles* in it, fuch as horfe-races, combats of wild beafts, &c. It is fuppofed to have been built in the reign of the emperor Trajan. Near the amphitheatre in the *Piázza Bra* is a mufeum, or collection of rarities and antiques, fome very curious infcriptions, ftatues, &c. but we had time only to take a very curfory view of them. In this building is a kind of public room for converfation and cards, where the people of fafhion of the town meet every evening. There is fcarcely a fmall town

in

in Italy that has not fomething of this kind. It is a much more fociable plan than the receiving their acquaintance in their own houfes, which occafions much trouble and fome expence. I fhould think, that were this practifed in fome of the country towns in England, under proper regulations, it might be productive of more fociety and rational amufement, than the continual dining about with country neighbours, and the teafing importunity of vifitors, not always in themfelves agreeable.

Theatre. The theatre is fpacious, and very convenient; it is almoft circular, has five rows of boxes one over the other; each range confifts of twenty-feven in number. To my great regret, there is no opera here at prefent; but they affure us that the mufic is excellent in the month of November, when they have as fine fingers as any in Europe. They boaft much of a *Cantatrice* of the name of *Aguiari*, commonly called the *Baſtardina* of Ferrara, whofe voice, they

say,

say, is of a wonderful compass and flexibility. Mentioning this finger reminds me, that when at the *Pieta* at Venice, they told us the famous Gabrieli was educated there; and a long story of the manner in which she contrived to escape from thence. I think I have mentioned this singer to you before, whose musical talents and capricious temper have given trouble to every body she has had to do with.

Here are some vestiges of antique arches and gate-ways, but none very fine. Most of the houses and other buildings in this city are marble. Several churches contain pictures and sculpture not unworthy the traveller's notice: but we had not time this morning to visit them, and the other objects already mentioned, at our ease. We have employed the evening in viewing some cabinets of natural history. Amongst many rare and curious articles of the fossile kind, the petrified fish are the most surprising; I have packed

ed

ed up fome to travel with us, as M——
thinks they are a good addition to the
little collection I have fent to England.

Petrified fifh.

Thefe petrified fifh are found at about
eighteen miles diftance from Verona,
in the mountain *Bolea,* where are certain
ftones in layers, of a dufky, greyifh, and
brownifh hue; of about an inch thick in
general, not rough, but of a fuperficies as
fmooth as a flate; they feparate in flivers
when taken from the quarry, by the application of the chiffel; if that part is hit right
which contains the print of the fifh, the
head, bones, fins, tail, &c. are fo extremely well preferved, that it is eafy to diftinguifh the fpecies. They alfo find the
impreffions of leaves, plants, &c. but
never any kind of petrified fhell, or fhell
fifh.

Though we have feen but little of
the Veronefe, yet are we inclined to
think them ingenious, and more knowing in phyficks, and the fpeculative

branches

branches of science, than the Italians in general.

To-morrow morning we mean to continue our route with as much expedition as pof-fible towards Milan, from whence you fhall hear from us on our arrival. I am as ever, &c.

P. S. Though the poft does not go from hence to-night, they affure me my letter will be equally fafe with them.

L E T T E R LV.

OUR arrival here laſt night, was through a violent ſtorm of thunder and lightning, accompanied with guſts of wind and rain. We are well lodged at the beſt inn; the ſign the Woman of Samaria, which I mention on account of its ſingularity. The night before laſt we ſlept at *Breſcia.* From Verona to Milan is about one hundred and four miles, through a very rich ſoil and fertile country, cloſely cultivated with vines, mulberry-trees, and corn, *&c.* ; its face is flat ; at length the horizon is bounded by mountains, covered with ſnow: this ſort of proſpect continued to Bergamo. We had diſagreeable rivers to paſs, which are ſubject, it ſeems, in winter, to overflow their banks, and make

the

the road extremely troublefome, if not dangerous. Some good pictures are to be feen at
Brefcia, as well in the churches as in private   Brefcia.
collections; but we did not make any delay
in this town, arriving in the evening, and
leaving it the next morning. The weather
was fo extremely hot and ftormy, 'that
there was no poffibility of going to fee any
thing, unlefs we had determined to ftay here
a day or two, which did not appear to us to
be worth while. This town is remarkable
in hiftory, and mentioned as the fcene of
many extraordinary events, both in ancient
and modern times. I fhould have been
glad to have feen the houfe the *Chevalier*
Bayard occupied, when *Gafton de Foie* took
the town. I dare fay you recal the circumftances of this remarkable event, as mentioned in the reign of Lewis the Twelfth
by the French hiftorians.

Bergamo is the native country of Har-
lequin: here that abfurd character origi-   Bergamo.

nated,

nated, and although we did but change
horfes at that town, we had an opportunity of difcerning the characteriftics of the
Italian harlequin. The poft-mafter, the
poftilions, &c. have a fpecies of humour-
ous repartee, an arch manner of being
alert, and an agility which participates both
of mifchief and folly in all their actions:
they are quite different looking people
from any other Italians we have yet
feen. The road from Bergamo hither
lies through the rich and delightful plains
of Lombardy. For about twelve miles be-
Milan. fore we reached Milan, it was perfectly
good; and the meadows, enclofed with
hedge-rows and watered by trenches calcu-
lated for that purpofe, prefent the richeft
pafturage that can be feen. This city
feems very large and confiderable ; we are
already provided with Milanefe fervants, a
coach, &c. The prices are, for a very handfome town carriage, *fifteen pauls* per day,
the *laquais de louage, four pauls* a day each;

our

our own dinner, *ten pauls* a piece; fupper,
the fame; *four pauls* for the valet de chambre; *ten pauls* more our bed-chamber; and
no charge for our dining-room. We are
admirably well ferved, fed, and lodged.
The trout of the Barromean lake are as
large as the largeft Englifh falmon, and
much better than any fifh I ever tafted.
The turkeys and all their fowl of every
kind, being fed upon rice and milk, are not
only the fatteft, but I believe the beft in the
world. All other forts of provifions, as
well as game, in the greateft plenty and
perfection. I fhall write once more from
hence; we fhall not ftay longer here than
to fee this city, &c. and then direct our
courfe to Turin. Adieu, &c.

LET-

LETTER LVI.

Milan, June the 28th.

WE set out on our journey to-morrow, and might reach Turin the same night, though it is ninety miles from hence, did we not prefer travelling in the cool of the day, and lying by during the heat; so we must sleep one night on the road. Milan, in my opinion, though very large and considerable, is not beautiful: some of the environs are pretty, and very convenient for taking the air in coaches. The Duke of Modena resides here (he is Vice-governor of the Milanese), with the princess his grand-daughter. Count Fermian represents her Imperial Majesty, he shares the government with the Duke: Count Fermian's very amiable character is so well known, that it is needless for me to repeat those praises which natives and foreigners

foreigners fo liberally beftow upon him; we wifhed to have feen fo remarkable a man, but at this time he is abfent from Milan.

Determining to make no acquaintance here, but to remain as little known as pof-fible, we have funk all our letters of re-commendation; forefeeing that, inftead of paffing a few days at Milan, we might be induced, by the civilities of thofe to whom our letters are addreffed, to a refidence of at leaft a month or fix weeks, which would have deftroyed our prefent plan of opera-tions, and fruftrated our intention of re-turning to you within the time propofed. The *Milanefe* character is univerfally that of hofpitality and kindnefs to ftrangers, and with our letters of recommendation, no doubt we fhould have found as much difficulty in leaving Milan, as in quitting Bologna. By this prudent meafure we have feen all that is curious in this city,

X 4   and

and fhall depart to-morrow without regret. Should you be defirous of a defcription of the Duke, I will give it you another time, *if poffible*; for to do him juftice, I think he " *beggars all defcription;*" afk me not in what fenfe.—His grand-daughter has an amiable character; fhe is to be married immediately to a brother of the Emperor. I fhall now mention what we have feen : *Il Duomo*, the Cathedral Church, is fituated in the center of the city: it is the moft confiderable edifice at Milan, and efteemed by many, the fineft church in Italy after St. Peter's at Rome. The columns that adorn and fupport it are fuperb; particularly four pillars under the dome or cupola, which are each about twenty-eight feet in circum-ference : it is profufely decorated with marbles, ftatues, ornaments, &c. fo that one fine thing hides another : whoever loves an extenfive view, may find one that will content him from the top of the dome. The famous Chapel of St. Charles

Barromeo

Church Il Duomo.

Barromeo is under part of the church;
his body is entire, and lies in a cryſtal
caſe, finely dreſſed in rich pontifical habits; his face is quite perfect, excepting
juſt the tip of the noſe, but his ſkin is of
the colour and conſiſtency of parchment:
it has a ſhining appearance, like a burn
or ſcald newly healed; he has ſilk gloves
on: his portrait is preſerved in a little
chapel juſt by; it is done in embroidery
by the famous Peregina, and exhibits a
ſtrong likeneſs to what he is at preſent.
He cauſed his catacomb (which is very
near his chapel) to be dug out before
his death, where his body had remained
an hundred and eighty-ſeven years, at
the time of its removal into this cryſtal
caſe. The octagonal panes of rock cryſtal,
of which the caſe is formed, are each ten
inches long and eight broad; they are ſet
in ſilver gilt: his croſier, which lies by
him, is richly ornamented with diamonds.
The walls of this chapel are lined with

ſilver

silver pannels, wrought in *baſſo relievo*; whoſe ſubjects are, the birth, life, and death of this Saint: this chapel is always illuminated, and is a rich treaſure in itſelf. In the church, over the grand altar, is placed *il ſacro chiodo* (the ſacred nail), a relic for which the Milaneſe have a great veneration; encloſed in cryſtal, and ſurrounded with a gilt glory: it is what Conſtantine uſed for a bit for his horſe, when he went to battle: Theodoſius preſented it to this church, and 'tis carried in proceſſion every third of May. The ſculpture, in marble and in wood, of the choir, is highly finiſhed, and demands an accurate obſervation. The famous ſtatue of St. Bartholomew is finely done, but there is ſomething ſo ſhocking in the contemplation of a man flayed alive, that I could not look at it long; on the pedeſtal is this inſcription,

Non me Praxiteles, ſed Marcus finxit Agrati.
The treaſury contains a great number of

articles

[315]

articles in gold, filver, and precious ftones, to a large amount. Next to this church the Ambrofian Library is highly efteemed here, which by no means anfwered the defcriptions I had read of it, either in refpect to the number of books, or the collection of paintings, fculpture, medals, &c. that are afferted to be contained in it. This library is really appropriated to the ufe of the Public *gratis*, being open every day, and a great many people frequent it, and read commodioufly whatever books they think fit; their time is not limited, nor is there any kind of reftraint put upon them. The *Gabinetto*, or Mufeum, belongs to the library; this collection was made by one Manfredo Settala, a *Milanois*, remarkable for his learning and application to the ftudy of natural hiftory, antiquities, &c. One of the moft curious articles, in this collection, is a lump, or ball of cryftal; in the center of which you plainly diftinguifh a drop of clear water. Amongft the pictures the

following

Ambrofian Library.

Mufeum.

Pictures.

following are the moſt remarkable; a
Carraccio. Virgin, by Carraccio. A portrait of a
Corregio. doctor, by Corregio. A Madonna, by
, Rubens, encircled in a garland of flowers.
The *Cartone* of the School of Athens, of
the ſame ſize with the picture in the Vati-
Raffaello. can, by Raffaello. A Virgin, a Dutcheſs
of Milan, a Doctor and a Phyſician who
Leonardo graſps a dagger, by Leonardo da Vinci.
da Vinci.
Peter Nef. A beautiful Peter Nef, repreſenting the
cathedral at Anvers. The four elements
J.Brughel. in miniature, in oils, by J. Brughel. This
Flemiſh painter has diſcovered ſome lit-
tle degree of fancy in the repreſentations
of the elements: the figures are ſo diminu-
tive, that they cannot be clearly diſtin-
guiſhed without a microſcope. There are
many other morſels of his to be ſeen here;
in general, his temptations of St. Antonio
are the beſt and moſt humorous of his
paintings. They ſhew in this cabinet certain manuſcripts of Leonardo da Vinci,
on which they ſet an immenſe value, conſiſting

fifting chiefly of notes and figures, and
here and there a very rough fketch indeed;
however, it appears by a bufto of one Ga-
leas Arconati, a citizen of Milan, placed
in this mufeum as a reward for his generous conduct, that James the Sixth of Scot-
land offered three thoufand piftoles for one
of thefe volumes; but this citizen, whofe
property they were at that time, preferred
the giving them to the Ambrofian Library,
to the piftoles the King had proffered him.
While we were examining the contents of
the mufeum, the *Ciceroni* who fhews them
beckoned to us to follow him, and conducted me to a cafe, in which was placed
a fkeleton; he bid me (with the utmoft
gravity) confider it attentively. I did fo,
and then afked him what there was extraordinary or remarkable in that fkeleton ? He replied, that it was the fkeleton of the greateft beauty Milan had ever
produced. By this lady's will, her heirs

were

were enjoined to have her body diſſected, fixed in a caſe, and placed in the Ambroſian Library, that every one of her ſex, who ſhould come to ſee that collection, ſhould be ſhewn her ſkeleton; and be informed at the ſame time, that that ſkeleton once poſſeſſed ſuch charms as made all the artiſts of Milan pronounce her perfect in every perſonal beauty; that ſhe was eſteemed and beloved by all who knew her, prizing her ſuperior talents, uncommon underſtanding, and wit, for which ſhe was as remarkable as for her beauty.—After a long harangue in words to this purpoſe, he at length informed me, that I muſt come at laſt to ſuch a ſtate. Whether he thought I ſhould have wept at ſuch an extraordinary piece of information, or what he expected, I know not, but I made him no other anſwer than burſting into a laugh, and aſking him, whether he took me for a *ſtolta* (a fool), he ſeemed greatly ſurpriſed prifed and difappointed, and I fuppofe thought me a very wicked wretch, quite hardened in herefy.

The church of San Vittore is a very ele- Church San Vit-gant edifice, highly decorated with gilding tore. and other ornaments. Here is a picture of the bleffed *Bernardo Tolomeo,* by Battoni Battoni. of Rome ; the fubject is the above *bleffed Bernardo* affifting people who are dying of the plague. This is the beft painting the church contains. *Le Grazie,* the church of Church le the Dominicans : this church was founded Grazie. by *Luigi Sforce,* Duke of Milan; Beatrice his wife is interred here : the beautiful pro-portions of the cupola are much admired. Here is a picture by Tiziano, that the Mi- Tiziano. lanefe efteem one of his very beft paintings; the fubject is, Chrift crowned with thorns. In one of the chapels is a St. Paul, by Godenzio Ferrari da Novara : this is a Godenzio Ferrari da good picture, and the firft I ever faw by Novara. this mafter, to the beft of my remem-brance. In the refectory of this convent,

is

is the moſt famous of all the pictures done
by Leonardo da Vinci; it repreſents the
Laſt Supper, and is painted in freſco on the
wall; it is a very large piece, occupying the
whole end of the refectory. On the table,
at one end, Leonardo has repreſented a diſh
of fried trout, of the famous lake near Milan; at the other end, a paſchal lamb
larded: the diſh placed before our Saviour
is empty; before each diſciple ſtands a
goblet of wine, and the table is garniſhed
with rolls of bread and apples. The figure
intended to repreſent our Saviour, is pretty
well done, particularly the face, which ex-
preſſes the utmoſt benevolence, clemency,
and grace. You readily remark, that the
painter has given ſix fingers to St. John:
the diſciples are poorly done, excepting
Judas, which Leonardo exerted his utmoſt
abilities to finiſh. This picture, upon the
whole, is finely coloured, although much
ſpoiled; the perſpective is good; there is
much vigour in the deſign, and a very fine
air

air in all the heads : it is in a great ftyle
and manner, without being much ftudied,
or highly finifhed. I fhall give you a curious anecdote concerning this picture: Some
time paft, the fuperior of thefe holy
brethren was fo ftrikingly like the Judas
both in perfon and mind, that every one
perceiving the refemblance, the monk, in
a fit of vexation, ordered it to be white-
wafhed all over : thus it remained forgot
and loft to the world for feveral years; till
an Englifh traveller, who had read of fuch
a painting, by diligently examining the wall
difcovered its concealment; the monks had
its white fkin taken off, by which ope-
ration the picture was injured in feveral
places. In the frefco paintings of the life
of St. Dominique, purgatory is reprefented
at the bottom of a well, and the Virgin
is employed in drawing up fouls by means
of her chaplet, in the fame manner as a
bucket is drawn up by a rope.

Unfortunately for me, who am so fond of music, there is no opera here at this feason; the *comedia* is the only theatrical amusement.

The Theatre is a very large building, consisting of five ranges of boxes, thirty-five in each range: its plan is almost square. The boxes are large enough to receive and return visits, to play at cards, and to sup in, which custom is practised here as much as at Genoa. As to *la Comedia*, I could not enter much into the humour of it, never having read, or seen it before; but it seemed to me to be a kind of satirical piece, somewhat in the style of the French comedy of *le Bourgeois Gentilhomme*: what diverted me, almost as much as it did the Milanese, was the part of Harlequin in the farce; his blunders, action, attitudes, were worthy a true son of *Bergamo*. When he serves his master at supper, he is ordered to make the sallad,

fallad, and to obferve particularly to put
falt enough, and then to ftir it well
about. To obey the firft order he brings
a meafure of falt as much as a large difh
can hold, and flings it all in; then having
forgot the oil, fetches a great lamp, fuppofed to be burning in the hall, empties it entirely of the foetid train-oil, and upon deep
reflection puts the cotton wick in alfo; he
then brings a veffel, *not* intended for vine-
gar, and flops in the contents; he laftly
fetches the ftable dung-fork, and ftirs the
fallad till he is almoft extenuated. His
mafter, at length lofing all patience, frightens poor Harlequin out of his wits, who
implores pardon on his knees for his giddi-
nefs and want of thought. The mafter
takes him again into favour, on promife of
amendment, and orders him to cut him a
flice of *pane col, molto delicatezza:* here
Harlequin errs again; he goes out to fetch
a knife, but meeting with a marble faw in
his way, thinks that may do the bufinefs

much

much more effectually; he brings it with
difficulty, and commences fawing the loaf.
I really am afhamed at taking up your
leifure with fuch a nonfenfical narration,
but the truth is, the foibles here alluded to,
are not much exaggerated; and as I have
feen fome Italian fervants of the tribe of
Harlequin, I was more diverted than I
fhould have otherwife been.

The weather is fo extremely uncertain,
that I am afraid to venture to the Barromean iflands: the palaces, or pleafure-
houfes, which were once fo delightful, they
tell us, are in a moft ruinous condition, and
not worth feeing; M— would fain go,
but I have diffuaded him from it. As there
has been an holy day fince we have been
here, we had the pleafure of feeing how
extremely opulent the citizens and their
families appear, even down to the loweft
mechanic; though I cannot fay I liked to
fee blackfmiths and fhoemakers with gold
and filver ftuffs in waiftcoats, long fwords,
and

and embroidered knots; tailors in brocade, and fine laced ruffles, &c. This is carrying opulence into luxury; at the same time, waving these ridiculous excesses, I was rejoiced to see every body appear rich, and happy. The women are in general very handsome. The nobleffe and great ladies dress in a more noble style than at Paris, and have a very genteel air and manner; their clothes are of the richest materials, and better made than any I have yet seen in Italy.

Adieu for the present; it is now late, and I must be up early to-morrow.

Y 3 LETTER

LETTER LVII.

Turin, June the 30th.

WE reached this, our firſt acquaintance of the Italian towns, yeſterday. Having lain at Novara, a very
indifferent inn, where we had no reſt from
the vulgar and brutal noiſes made by the
poſtilions and helpers, &c, who, playing
and quarrelling at cards all night, long
ſo frighted me, that I expected to hear
in the morning they had aſſaſſinated each
other, but happily no miſchievous conſe-
quence enſued. Our journey here was
made very diſagreeable by the frequent
croſſing of rivers; ſome by means of a raft,
others we were obliged to ford. The cur-
rent of the *Teſſin* in particular was ſo
ſtrong, that we had like to have met with
an ugly accident; it was as much as could
be done to avoid being carried forcibly

2   down

down the river. We alfo croffed the *Doro*, whofe fands are mixed with grains of pure and fine gold. The road was not very fafe neither, as there was a banditti who lay concealed in a foreft not far removed. Armed peafants were ordered by the magiftrates to patrol, four or five in a company, in their turns, between one village and another, in order to affift travellers, in cafe of neceffity; and as the road lies through both the king of Sardinia's territories and the Milanefe, it is a convenient circumftance that thefe villains fometimes avail themfelves of, to efcape into the one or the other ftate, when they ply on the borders of both.

We fhall leave this city as foon as we have feen our acquaintance, then proceed to Lyons, and after a few days ftay there, prefs on to the fouth. Our intention is, that this excurfion fhall not take up more time than three weeks, being anxious to fee thofe monuments

of

of Roman magnificence, which still remain at Nifmes, Orange, Arles, &c. of which you shall have a full and true account.

When in France, which we shall be in a few days, you muft fancy us very near you. We, it is true, fhall be in the fouth; and you in the north; but you know, in this inftance, that north and fouth are not very far afunder. I can give you one circumftance which will afford you pleafure, that we are affured the roads through the Savoy have been fo well mended, previous to the young princefs's journey to *the Comte de Provence*, that travelling over them is no longer inconvenient or dangerous. We like this town as much as before we had feen all the others of Italy: I fhall go again to vifit the King's Palace, from an affurance of finding it as much to my tafte as formerly.

The weather is delightfully fine, and the environs in high beauty. His Majefty

has

has not neglected his works at the Valentin in our abfence, there is a great deal of earth moved and much done; it may probably be completed before winter. We are lodged at an hotel called *les Armes d'Angleterre*; the apartments are good, and we are well ferved. As we propofe being here but a few days, we thought it more convenient to lodge in an hotel, than to have the trouble of a houfe and houfekeeping. Adieu, *&c.*

APPEN-

A P P E N D I X.

Defcrizzione orittograffica del ponte Naturale di Veja ne' Monti Veronefi, e d' un tratto di paefe all' intorno.

Al chiariffimo Sig.ʳ Giovanni Arduino, publico Sopraintendente all' agricoltura, &c. ALBERTO FORTIS.

NON Signore, io non ho fatto un autunno oziofo, come voi forfe lo credete l'amenita di Verona tutti gl' incanteffimi dit focietà, de quali e' poffeditore, ed artefice il Capitan Lorgna, quando fi fpoglia della fua ifpida fopravefte di xxii, e difcende a noi, i lampi, ci fulmini originali del divino Riviera, che fa' ful noftro Globo cio, che il Giove d'omero minaccia di far in cielo agli Dei minori ; l'apparizione in afpettata dell' amabiliffimo noftro Abate Talier, che contro l'ufo ricevuto fotto tanta modeftia e foavità di maniere copre fi eftefa erudizione, e profonda dottrina la domeftica compagnia del voftro eftimatore. P. Vivorzio, prefiatiffimo amico mio, che agran paffi cammina per ottenere in eta frefchiffima un diftinto pofto fra Matematici d' Italia ; e mille altre cofe atte radicare un uomo, non che a trattenerto per pochi giorni in una città, non mi v' hanno poputo fermare.

- Lo Sapeva beniffimo, che un amatore della chimica non dee altron anarfi due dita da Vincenzo Bozza, il quale ne poffiedè le ultime fineffe : ne aveva di bifogno mi foffe detto che un ricercatore di Foffili trouva pofeolo per parchi giorni nella ricea

e futta

e foto colezzione del noftro Giulio Moreni, e che un cultore divoto delle mufe non puo in cofcienza allontanarfi volontariamente dalla patria di Cattullo, del Cotta, del Bonfadio, del Fracaftoro, lo fpirito dequali prefiede ancora alla letteratura Veronefe. Mi fi Moltiplicavano poi ad ogni paffo per la via degli occhi gl' inviti a reftare, perquanto per quanto dalle circoftanze m' era permeffo, fra quelle fortunate.

Ma ora, che vantano per loro Cittadino l' immortale Paolo Calliari, ed oltre tanti altri rinomati Pittori di quella età, un Zotari, un Cagnaroli, eccellenti pennelli del noftro fecolo.

Ad onta però di tutto quefto, io feci le mie fcappate montane, d'una delle quali, che mi conduffe a fcorrere un tratto di paefe del tutto nuovo per me, vi rendero conto tanto piu volentieri, quanto che il ritorno follecito del noftro impareggiabile Sig. S. diligente, e infaticabile indagatore di quanto l'arte, o la natura ha prodotto di fingolare, m' ha fatto ribbattere il camino medefimo pochi giorni doppo la prima gità, e riconfermare le mie offervazioni. Voi avete un diretto incontraftabile di fapere prima d'ogni altro il rifultato de miei Viaggiacci d'offervazione, voi, che fe non me da ifpirafte-da prima, fortificafte certamente un inclinazione nata con me.

M' era da molto tempo giunta agl' orecchi la fama del celebre ponte naturale di Veja, lavorato da quelli operarii, che fervono alla gran Madre, fra le rupi de Monti Veronefi, non piu che dodeci Miglia lontano dalla Citta a Settentrione, frai Vilaggi di Prun, e di Fane.

Una defrizione di effo ponte publicata dal celebre Sig. Zaccaria Betti del 1767. Mi venne alle mani in queft' autunno per la prima volta; le grazie dello ftile, e l' afpetto del ponte medefimo, ch' egli fe incidere in rame, mi rifvegliarono il defiderio antico di vederlo cogli occhi proprj; il corfo ftravagante de gli ftratti efpreffi nella figura m' avea mal prevenuto dell' ezatezza dell' artefice; io avei giurato ch' egli s' era prefo qualche arbitrio, non fofpetando d'opporfi diametralmente infacendolo alle coftanti leggi della natura in fatte di montagne.

Ne

Ne parlai cogli amici; e L' Ab. Willi mi fi efibì cortefe-
mente per focio, còme pratico del paefe. Più opportuno re-
galo d'un compagno pratico non poteva efferni fatto; ne piu
atto ad iftruirmi, e togliermi la noja del camino lo aurei fapùto
defiderare. Il valorofo Sigʳ Bona comune amico ci benedì
una mattina per tempo con una pozione coroborante di per-
fetto ciocolate; e quindi noi divotamente montati fu due pru-
denti cavalcature prefimo fuor di porta S. Zenone la via de
Monti.

La Nebia denfiffima, che ingombrava la pianura, e la piu
baffa parte dé colli, mi tolfe il piacevole fpettacolo, che i varj
ponti di profpetiva doveano farmi godere; v' avea però un
vantaggio in quefto danno: tutti gli oggetti mi riafcivano af-
fatto nuovi, a mifura che mi s' avicinavano al nafo, oltre la
portata del quale non fi vedea motto.

Noi non avevamo prefa dirittamente la via del ponte di
Veja, la guida, gentilmente maliziofa, e foverchiatrice, abu-
zava del ignoranza mia per furmi nafcere improvifo un pia-
cere, cui io avea moftrato defiderare, fe foffe ftato combinabile
col camino naturale del noftro viaggio. Lo mi trovai, doppo
d'effer poffato da Gargagnago, ore dicefi abbia villeggiato
Dante, che v' aveva de poderi, e doppo forfe 12. Miglia di
cavalcare fra il bujo cenerognolo delle nebie, poco difcofto da
Mazurega, e dalla deliziofamente fituata abitazione dé quattro
Frattelli Sigʳⁱ Lorenzi ciafcun de quali cofi felicemente riufcì
nello ftudio, cui volle applicarfi, che nella ftella famiglia un
egregio oratore, un eccellente poeta, ed improvifatore, un pit-
tor valorofo, che par bazzica in Parnaffo ed un bulino finiffimo
fi ritrova. Copriva un mare di nebia la Val Policella di cui
una gran parte fi fcopre dall'altezza di Mazurega; e fu bello
fpettacolo per me, che finalmente era giunto all'aria ferena,
il vedermelo fotto i piedi agitato come da una procella alzare
di gran fiatti e cavalloi, che ora barcollando ofcillavano, ora
infeguivanfi rapidamente l'un l'altro cacciati dal vento la baffa
parte de colli, ch' io aveva battuta, non mi fomminiftro curio-
fità foffili; la pietra vi e' ordinariamente roffigna, e di pafta
analoga

analoga al marmo di Verona comune; non atta pero al lavoro
fe dalla fuperficie del fuolo fi prenda, perche tutta fcrepoli, e
fenditure, é quafi trinciata in quadrelle. V' ha benfi una inte-
reffante cofa per voi alquanto piu fu, é vicino immediatamente
alla cafa fudetta degli amici, ed ofpiti miei. V' ha della terra
calcaria, ch' é marna véra e reale, bianca, leggiera, quafi pol-
verofa. Il Sig.r Francefco Lorenzi, non contento di adope-
rare con applaufo il penello, e la cetra, coltiva molto attenta-
mente la Georgica, e in un fuo praticello magro, e fterile,
anzi che non, ha' con ottimo efito fparfa di quella terra, doppo
d'averla purgata da faffi, che forfe in troppo numero vi fi tro-
vano mefcolati. Il praticello adeffo e oltre modo erbofo; ed
il celebre Sig.r Al. Lorenzi, che fta lavorando colla ufata feli-
cita ed eleganza fua un utile e dilettevoliffimo Poema fopra la
coltivagione de monti, vi parlera di quefta trasformazione, e
arrifchiera di perdere la grazia di quel dabbene, e pacifico cita-
dino, che non correbbe, fi cercaffe la marna o fi ftudiaffe ch'
egli non ha creduto ben fatto di ftudiare.

A Mazurey non abftano folamente le mufe, e belle arti v é
anche un'abitazione di Gnomi, e delle offervabili eh'io m'abbia
vedute, quantunque non delle piu vafte. E quefta una cava
di marmi, in cui fi lavora da foli quarant anni. La pafta
d'effi marmi difpofti a ftrati parrallele orizzontali dolcemente
inclinati, fi rafomiglia fempre, parrebe che le matterie groffe
componenti gli ftrati de monti beronefi e d'una parte de vicentini foffero per tutto quel vafto tratto quafi cottantemente le
medefime; e che folo dalle torbide carlche di terra ora in
un modo ora in un altro, fiano rifultate e varieta del marmo
roffo del bianco, e loro gradazioni. V'e eziandio notabile,
differenza tra le groffeffe didetti ftrati e di quefta non meno
che dalla fituazione che hanno eglino tratti i differenti nomi,
co' quali dagli fcavatori fono difegnati. Vedeffi fovente fra
l'uno ftrato e l'altro un filo piu omeno fottile d'ocra femipe-
trofa; et alvolta non v'é cofa, che li divida vifibilmente al
di fuori; quantunque reale divifione e feparazione orizzontale

tale v'abbia nell'interno fra quelle gran laftre probabilmente prodotto dalla varietà détempi, e de 'modi dell'induramento loro, la caverna ha r una bocca affai regolarmente tagliata di dodeci piedi quadrati all'incirca ; il vano s'internà profondo cento piedi feguendo l'indole degli ftrati, che afcendo no foavemente, ne avrà di larghezza intorno a 70. i pilàftri lafciati nel vivo per foftenere la, volta, fono cosí bene fcarpellati, che adorna l'irregolarita loro, prefentano un ruftico maeftofo, che piace. A, vedere la fattica la pafienza, l'induftria, il tempo che cofta a poveri fcarpelini l'eftuazione di quei laftroni fi direbbe che ogni quadro di marmo dee valere un teforo. Lo ftrato che ferve di volta ha ogimai fentito il muneamento de 'fondamenti, egli fi e feffo, edifquilibrato poco lungi dell'entrata, della caverna le acque concorrono alla fenditura dal di fopra, e ne fcolano ; benche la quantitá loro fia poca eleno faranno delle rovine col tempo. Gli offervatori non avari d'anni, fanno, che non folo una gocciola oftinatameñta cadendo fcava la pietra ma che poche ftile hanno a poco a poco rovefciato i piu pezañti maffi aprono nelle piu campatte pietre gran fenditure deftinate a divenire valli, egran divifioni di monti, collo fcorrere dé fecoli. Mi pare che i contemplatori degli angoli falienti, ed entranti non abbiano efaminato bene il l'avoro de' torrenti. Eglino fi farebbono ria parmiata peraventura la fatica di domar l'acque del mare prefcrivendo legge a loro irregolári movimenti. E verita conofciuta nella ftoria degli uomini, che picciole caufe hanno mai fempre prodotti i piu ftrepitofi ed importanti avvenimenti ; chi fa leggere ben adentro negli annali del noftro Globo ritrova migliaja d'efempfi di quefto anche nelle di lui rivoluzioni fifiche, ed e vero i motivi che i piu minuti, edagli occhi del volgo fpregevoli offervazioni in fatto d'orittologia, conducono a intendere fenomeni molte rimoti, e aftabilire le Teorie, che fembrano ftrane oltremodo ed ardite a timidi Filofofanti. A molti maftri eruditi par ampollofo e ftrano il raggionare cui non intendono, ma voi farete d'opinione, che di coloro i quali odiano l'offervare, gli offervatori e il linguaggio loro liberamente efpreſſivo, qualunque ſiano, non ſe ne debba far conto. Un Galantuomo, che trova qualchecoſa di nuovo, perche non potra efprimerla con nuovi modi? puo vietarſelo ſenza taccia di ſtravaganze.

Paſſammo quella giornata tutta, e la ſera in compagnia di qué coltiſſimi fratelli. La Mattina ſequento ci poſſimo di nuovo in camino verſo il ponte. So che non avea veduti per anche ſegni di Vulcani nel mio viaggio, ſe alcuni ciottoli ſe ne eccettuino, che coſteggiando i monti alla lontana, ſi erano incontrati per lapianura i'dorſi di S. Fiorino, á quattro miglia, forſe da Mazurega, verſo Veia, me ne offerirono i primi, ſegni, io diedi all'improviſo in un area ſerigna dura peſante, e neriſſima. La paſta degli ſtrati vicini é analoga alle pietre calcarie di Nanto, di Coſtoza, di S. Gottardo, &c. nel vicentino. Su'quelle cime, e ne contorni v'hanno tutte le apparenze, che ſi debbano trovare dé petrefatti, anche fuor del matone, che coſi e chiamata quella ſpezie di pietro poco dura di Veroneſi.

Andand'oltre, incontrammo il paeſe di Marano. Gli ſtrati petroſi veggonſi colá ſollevati da un vulcano e ſtanno come una gran tavola ſu la cima di quel monte, peſando ſopra materie cretoſe, granite, di varj colori, e ſopra ribollimenti Vulcanici ravultolati a guiſa di gran cipolle, ſomiglianti a quei che ſi veggono preſſo di Vicenza, alle ſalde, e ſu le cime del Berico piu Baſſo ſi ſcopre, tutto all'interno di quella vetta rotonda, la continuazione dello ſtrato ſuperiore, che forma una voragine, ſe quella ſommita ſi ſprofondaſſe un giorno quanto s'alzo con violenza. Queſto rialzamento ſi trova a finiſtra della ſtrada comune; a deſtra ſi vede gia nella valle una collina ſterile, e nuda, tutta di materie, vulchaniche verdaſtre, e oltre eſſa il fianco del monte della medeſima paſta ſembra che il vano della valle foſſe tutto pieno di quelle eruzioni, che, ſcarſa porzione di materia vitreſcente contenendo, rimaſero poco compitte, e per conſequenza aprirono un agevole paſſaggio alle acque de piu alti luoghi che apoco apoco
ſcavarono

ſcavarono quella gran veſcica, l'arſiccio collinetto nel mezzo
laſciandovi, diſpoſto a ſcemare ſgretolandoſi ad occhi veggenti
forſe du qualche antica bicocca, di cui non reſta veſtigio
chiamaſi quel promontorio Caſtel Beleno ; uno degli abitanti
ci diſſe, che nel vicino monte detto Noroni ſi trovavano produzioni di mare lapidefatte ; e che un D. Stefano Ruzenente
ne portava a Verona : rilevammo anche dai diſcorſi del Vil-
lano, che il buon collettore D. Stefano era diluvianiſta.

Il paeſe, cui attraverſammo, non e orrido, non ameno,
ma ſquallido, e diſguſtoſo. Tutto v'e magrezza, ſterilità,
ſparatezza e nemmeno il Biancheggiante colore de ſaſſi ſparſi
per le falde coltivate appaga l'occhio coll'aſpetto d'una in fe-
condita non diſaggradevole, poiche anche i ſaſſi vi ſono foſchi.
Ci fermammo, con intenzione di pranzare a Prun, paeſe
ſituato alla parte oppoſta di Marano, e che diede anticamente
il nome alla valle Policella, chiamata da noſtri arcibifavoli
Praina : Ma l'intenzione ando a voto per metá : proviggioni
non v'aveano, ne coſa ragionevole da mangiare nè naſce, o
muore in quelle coſte ſcaglioſe: non viti, non caſtagni ne v'allig-
nano, non erbe da cuocere; io credo la poca gente, che v'e, viva
di numeri : ma non ſaprebbe far bene i ſuoi conti chi dovendo
andarvi, non ſi portaſſe qualche ſorta di cibo, Uſciti di la trovammo la ſtrada molta comoda, e delizioza per un buon tratto,
coſteggiando la valle detta di S. Anna. Finalmente giugnimo
a Creſtena, caſolare meſchino, dove, importa da chi voleſſe
far il mio viaggio ſi ſappia, che v'é un corteſe ſacerdote, non
ſomigliante all'inoſpitale Aruprete di Bolea ; e di la ſummo
guidati alponte cento paſſi prima di giungervi s'attraverſa un
prato, che ha ilfondo quaſi tutto di focaja ; la ſtrada che v'e
aperta n'é piena, Ve ne hanno de pezzi di Vago colore e
che ſarebbono atti a Lavori. Voi Sapete che grandiſſima
quantitata di calcedonio, edi ſelci variamente colorate s'incontra
per li monti Veroneſi, d'onde ci vengono per la maggior parte
le pietre focaje da u'o.

Lo áveva bene ſtadiuto il libretto del Cel. Sigr Betti e
tratto tratto me lo andáva traendo di ſaccoccia per rinfreſcar-

mene la memoria, quindi fono andato facendo qualche an-
notagioncella margionale, ch' io ho attualmente fotto gli
occhi e vi trafcrivo, egli e per aventura un tratto d'audacia
quefto mio volervi defcrivere una magnificenza della natura
da cofi elegante penna illuftrata : ma fe porrete mente alla di-
meftichezza ch'io ho colle rupi, e cogli orrori grandiofi, che
fra greppi s'ammirano bene fpeffo, e vi ricorderete che non
folo in piana profa, ma in verfi talvolta ardifco defcrivere l'af-
prezza rigogliofa, e le interiori tenebre eterne, troverete ;
che mi fi puo perdonare.

Arrivai camminando, quafi fenza vedermene, all'orto d'una
gran bocca circondata da ciglioni tagliati a piombo tutto all'
intorno, fe non che l'acque vi fi hanno aperto, qualche angufto paffaggio logorandoli alcuna feffura. Vi fi difcende
dalla parte di mezzo giorno per uno s'drucciolevole fentierino;
a finiftra fcendendo fi vede un foro verticale nel maffo, che e
tutto foderato interiormente di accutiffime criftallizazioni
fpatoffe; la preffo v'ha una cava incominciata di terra gialla
da Pittori d'affai buona qualita, pezzata di verde fine. Uno
ftrato peró molto piu ricco, e da cui fi trae gran quantita
della terra medefima, trovafi piu alto dall'altro lato adeftra
del ponte, fuori della Vallicella. Quefta affetta la figura
circolare irregolarmente, ed e ingombra da un capo all'altro
fin fotto il ponte di maffi fmifurati. L'impofto di que gran
pezzi di fcoglio moftra, ch'eglino appartennero ad uno degli
ftrati piu alti, e fuperiori alla fuperficie prefente del vivo
dell'arco ch'e planiffimo faffo di roffo di Verona; e vale
adire, che probabilmente piombarono da intorno a fettanta
piedi d'altezza perpendicolare.

A levante l'area della vafca afcende un cotal poco verfo il
ciglione che fa fronte ; di la deefcendere qualche copia d'acqua ne tempi piovofi, che fi fcarica formando un rigagno poco
affervabile pel volume, ma molto per gli effeti, per di fotto il
ponte, dal di cui arco e chiufo l'avallamento a ponente. Meritano rifleffione gli ftrati di breccia componenti il ciglione
che

che sorge di facciata all'arco, eglino sono piu alti, ne hanno
dietro se monti superiori dalle materie de quali possano dirsi
fabricati l'arco, e formato dalla continuazione degli strati,
che corsono tutto all'intorno di quella profondità, la di cui
estensione d'oriente in occidente sara di circa 150 piedi da
Mezzogiorno a Tramontana di 100 le divisioni di questi gran
fogli (passatemi l'ardita espressione) del libraccio, che contiene
una parte dell'antica storia del nostro pianeta, sono assai
visibili; e vi si ponno contare parechi strati di varie grossezze,
e colori. Nel vivo dell'arco del ponte ch'e grosso 20 piedi,
si noverano stando abosso da chi ha buoni occhi oltre trenta
divisioni piu o meno espresse, lequali non sono conveniente-
mente segnate nella figura fatta esseguire dal Sig.r Betti, che
avra infalibilmente comandato bene ma che su per certo servito
male. Io ho vivamente dipinto nella fantasia quel grand
arco che dalla parte interna ha piu di 114 piedi Veronesi di
corda, secondo le misure prese dal suo illustratore alle quali mi
sono stimato in dovere di quasi sempre riportarmi. Confron-
tandone sopra il luogo la figura espressa nella T. 11. del Sig.r
Betti ho veduto che l'architetto disegnatore non e stato esatto,
strapazzando, e ravolgendo nell'ombra un magnifico frontale,
che sporge in fuori forse dieci piedi ad angolo retto, e mal-
trattando i canali divisorj, e parrà stelli de' lastroni; ha però
soplito lo scrittore ingegnoso con quella elegantissima sua pena;
La facciata interna del ponte, che guarda l'oriente, e molto
piu dilettevole ad osservarsi che l'opposta, per la forma regolare dell'arco assai gelosamente osservatavi, non meno che per
la prodiga magnificenza colla quale visono i materiali disposti.
Vi grandeggia quella spezie di concorenza superiore che rende
originali le opere de piu eccelenti imaestri; e vi si scorge una
certa armonia colle aggiacenze, che apaga e sodisfa del pari
gli occhi e la mente. Immaginatevi qualche cosa di strana-
mente grandioso. Un Ponte tutto d'un Pezzo largo cinquanta piedi dove l'arte non ha messo le mani, che forma un
arco regolare piu di venti piedi grosso ne ha sessantadue di sesta,

e riposa

e ripofa fu d'un paio di paliftroni di fcoglio alti ottantafei, dec
fare una grande impreffione. E pure la faciata, che guardia
l'occidente appagandomi meno, miha fbalordito di piu. Non
vi circate regolarita; non ve n'e veftigio. Ella e uno fboz-
zaccio gigantefeo e fcoretto; da finiftra fa un brutto verfo a
cagione d'uno fconcio moffo che forge a gombito importuna-
mente vicino alla caduta della picciol acqua fpergendo in-
dentro, e adeftra fbardelatamente ftendefi in lungo, e in largo,
facendo quafi un atrio, o un portico di mezza volta fenza fof-
tegni alla caverna vicina. L'ardita irregolarita di quefta
facciata la rende un oggetto totalmente differente dall' altra,
e che quindi fa tutto diverfa impreffione. E pare che molte
mara viglife cofe vi fi veggano in un colpo d'occhio, non una
folo aggiungete a quel grand arco gettato lá come in fogno
fopra 154 piedi di corda, l'orrore magnifico delle rupi ignude,
e tayliate a piombo, che lo fiancheggiano, eftendonfi a deftra,
e a finiftra per lungo tratto, la profonditá della valle, in cui
da di fotto il vafto Ponte precipita fuftenendo il burrone é
il fondo di quella bocca che fi vede fuor per gran varco
della curvatura, ingombra, é circondata da maffe torreggiante,
adornate quefto alpeftre ignudo, rovinofe difabitato orrore
di pochi arbofcelli nati a ciocche qua e colá fra le fenditure
degli fcogli come a difpetto ftorpj, e rabbaffati; interompete
tratto tratto la regolarita eo corrifpondente fi degli ftrati con
ifpacature, osfaldature perpendicolari, e colla negrezza degli
antri e fpeloache Inacceffibile che s'internano fia que gran
letti di marmo, e avrete come da una camera ottica lo fpettacolo che mi forprefe, allorche paffato fotto il ponte mi fermai
ad offervarne le fchiene i fianchi e le appendici.

Il Ponte di Rialto me la perdoni; ma io non lo poffo pia
guardare—con quella maraviglia di prima. Eglié un miracolo
dell'arte; dell'una e dell'altra parte e fiancheggiato da Pa-
lazzi fuperbi, va tutto bene; ma chi ha veduto il ponte di
Veia con quelle fue magnifiche vicinanze abitate da lupi, e
dall'aquile, puo vedere Rialto fenza fcomporfi, il maffimo

difetto

difetto della figura delineata dall'architetto Coroni fi é di non
dar anche lo fpaccato del ponte, che avrebbe potuto portare per
confequenza il difegno della portentoza orridezza aggiacentevi
a deftra, e a finiftra, e dirimpetto. Tutti qué dirupi, che
da difotto il ponte fi vedono, meritano d'ufcire da bofchi per
opera del Bulino. Una diligente ftoria naturale, che ne pre-
fentaffe i foffili, le piante, e gl'infetti, ed uccelli che v'abbi-
tano, farebbe imprefa del noftro fecolo, e del genio Veronefe.
Non fi vorrebbe rifparmiare fpefa, o diligenza in fiffatte cofe.
Ella e gran vergogna per noi, che i foreftieri vengano ad illuf-
trare come va la curiofita naturali de paefi noftri, e ne portino
in lontane terre le produzioni che ci mancano né mufei, e che
appena noi conofciamo. Un de piu raguardevoli perfonaggi
dell'Inghilterra, gran miniftro prottettore dichiarato delle belle
arti tutte, e promotore generofo della fcienza naturale; cui
poffiede fondatamente, ha fatto difegnare le Valli di Ronca e
Brendola nella ftate paffata cofa che invano s'avrebbe fperato
d'ottenere da noftri. Il celebre M. Seguier e venuto a farci
la Fiera Veronefe; ma quefti fi e troppo ben pafato portando
cón fe in Francia la ricca collezione del fu'Arciprete fpada,
noto per catalogo de Foffili Veronefe da lui publicato.
Dobbiamo arroffire in penfando al miferabile prezzo, per cui
e ftata venduta a quel dotto ftraniere una ferie di produzioni
naturali, che avea coftato tonto denaro, fatica ed attenzione.
Ma lafciamo quefte malinconie, delle quali abbiamo a vergogna noftra affai di fovente nuovi e fempi, e torniamcene al
ponte.

Tanto a deftra, che a finiftra fotto l'arco v'ha una caverna.
La meno vafta e lunga intorno a cinquanta piedi, larga quindeci, e molto alta; vi fiorifce quantitá di falnitro. L'altra
che s'interaa di molto, é a deftra di chi offerva il grand arco
al di fuori; la fua bocca é coperta da quel magnifico capellone
a mezza volta ch'io v'ho defcritto; uno ftratto non continuo
d'ocra da pittori femi-petrofa, meglio colorita di quella, che
ho accenata le fta dinanzi; un letto di breccia compofta d'an-

Z 3   tichiffimi

tiebiffimi rottani vi fi fcopre quafi parallelo, ed ha molto di
che penfare a chi fa come fi formino le breccie. Il capitan
Iorgna ha ben acconciamente offervato, come accenero piu
fotto, che v'era della differenza fra quaefto ftrato, e i fuperiori.
Queglino che immediatamente vi fopraftanno, fono di pietra
morta, o matone fecondo il dialetto Veronefe. Là caverna e
fcavata per entro aquefta materia, e merita offervazione la
grotefca fcabrofitá della volta, prodotta forfe da fluori ftalat-
titici ; ella é affai fpaziofa per alquanti paffi, ma poi s'abaffa
all'improvifo, e coftringe chi vuol ire innanzi a curvarfi quanto
piu é poffibile. Per otto o dieci paffi fa d'uopo camminare
incofi incomoda pofitura. Ad onta della noja, che quefta
facenda recavami, io profittai della vicinanza della volta al
fuolo, per offervare, che la fcabrofitá dell'una corrifpondono
cofi perfettamente a quelle dell'altro, che fe da unaforfe pro-
porzionata foffe abbaffato il di fopra, o follevato il difotto,
eglino fi combacierebbono colla pia fcrupoloza efattezza.
Voi vedete, che quefta offervazione non poteva reftare del
tutto fterile, ella conduce a quelche cofa un uomo, che non
per nulla fiafi internato fra quelle tenebre. L'acqua che
raddoppia l'incomodo del cammino inquel fito, e s'apre fot-
terra di nafcoflo una via per calare nel burone non offervata,
dovea venire da qualche parte. Di fatto, pofti in libertà
d'alzare la tefta, ci trovammo in un luogo alto, ma angufto, e
voltici adjetro vedemmo, che lungo il maffo fcendeva l'acqua
tacitamente, incroftando il fuo camino quafi perpendicolare di
tartaro impuro. Avanzammo a doppo breve viaggio per
quella fpezie d'andito, le di cui pareti logore moftrano a
fcoperto una gran quantita d'entrocheti, e d'altre minute produzioni di mare, giunfimo ad una galleria fpaziofa, quafi
rotonda feminata di maffi capovolti. Il vano fuperiore, che
afcendendo s'interna nelle vifcere del monte non é però pro-
porzionato a que'materiali, che pur d'alto cuddero certamente
ci arrampicammo con qualche difficoltá fu per que'gran rot-
tami a deftra ; il limo, ond'errano lordi ci facea fdrucciolare ;
io rifletei, che non ifpregevole volume d'acqua lutolente dovea

vea paſſare di là, ſe giungeva a ſommergere qué gran ſaſſi; queſt'acqua ſi perde ſotterraneamente. Sermontati i maſſi ci ſi affacciò un camino anguſto di molto, cioé non piu largo di trepiedi all'incirca; mi venne in capo di badare ſe le due pareti di quella catacomba ſi corriſpondeſſero nel modo medeſimo in cui gia addietro ſi corriſpondono la volta e il ſuolo. Mi ſembrò che né grandi angoli, e nelli piu oſſervabili curvature v'aveſſe una corriſpondenza perpendicolare, analoſa a quella orrizzontale ch'io avea tocata con mano. Temendo ci mancaſſe il tempo per arrivare la ſera a Paeſe abitato vitro cedemmo; io reſtai col diſpiacere di non aver potuta veder il fine di quel ſotterraneo, ma colla ſoddisfazione d'aver veduto quanto baſtava. Forſe andando bene innanzi s'avrebbe trovato qualche atra ſpezie d'abitatori di quella notte eterna oltre a pipiſtrelli. Voi ſapete che nell' acque de cavolli d coſtoza v'hanno de viventi, che mai vedono ſole ne Luna. Feci con iſcarſezza eguale di tempo il ſecondo viaggio al ponte di Veja col noſtro amabiliſſimo ſignor S. e molte coſe potei oſſervare oltre a quelle ch'io avea notate nel primo; ma non iſpinzi piu oltre il camino ſotteraneo. Nel uſcire da quella Bocca portai l'occhio ſu d'un diſtico fatto ſcrivere nel maſſo vicino alla di lei bocca; le lettere ne ſaranno in breve ſmarrite. Eccolo.

Si tantum dum ludit opus natura peregit
   Quid faciet proprio docta majeſterio.

E da ringraziarſi la providenza, che non ſia ſtato ſcolpito, come ha creduto il Sig.r Betti, che atorto ha lodato queſti due verſi puerili; e coſi poco latini, io non la poſſo perdonare a coloro, che della natura fanno un pulcinella, e mi ſembrano ancora piu condannevoli del Robinet, che ama di mandarla alla ſcuola, e la fa imparare dell'eternita fino attempo noſtro a far l'vomo. La natura non fa coſ'alcuna o tentomi, o per iſcherzare, e io non vorrei ſi proferiſce inqueſto ſecolo una ſi fatta beſtemmia in cattivi verſi ne inproſa. Egli e vero, che v'hanno alcune teſte, alcuni caratteri, alcuni cuori coſi ſtra-

manente

nascente Lavorati, che sembrano fatti al bujo o per ischerzo: ma i buoni, e ragionevoli filosofanti oggimai sanno benissimo, che le stravolte idea d'un vomo sono necessariamente legate alle conseguenti, e adeguate d'un altro, che il Polipo invisibile ha la sua necessità esistezza relativa all'esistere della Balena, e la pulce leggiera ha la sua parentela di questo genere coll' elefante. Non v'ha cosa nel mondo per quanto disparata sembri dall'altre, che lo sia infatti; e le leggi regolatrici di quel che ci pare stravaganza quantunque ricorrenti men di sovente sono egualmente costanti che le diretrici degli avvenimenti piu ordinarij, o forse sono conbinazioni, e risultati delle medesime. Parrebbe che agli uomini convenisse lo studiarsi l'intendere la cagione delle cose che destano la loro sorpresa e che doppo d'aver fatto ogni sforzo senza profitto (come purtroppo sovente accade) dovessero confessarsi ingenuamente non atti a penetrare ne misterj della natura. Nel caso però del ponte non v'ha d'uopo, che ci umiliano la natura, che non ischerza giammai, e nasconde spesso all'umana penetrazione le leggi che s'e prescritti nell'operare, non lo ha fatto a Veia.

L'eruditissimo Sig.r Betti riferisce due opinioni altrui intorno alla formazione di quell' arco, e stabilisce poscia la sua, che partecipa d'entrambe il celebre amico nostro Sig.r Capitan Lorgna lo ha creduto un lavoro delle pioggie, che fra gli strati meno compatti aprendosi apoco apoco il passaggio, e profitando della sconnessione di alcuno di essi, scomposero la base degl'immediatamente sopra stanti, i quali per conseguenza fendutisi lasciarono libero ad altre acque il cammino; e coll' andar degli anni di se qui liberati del tutto si lasciarono rovesciar finalmente. Chiunque ha un po di pratica della strattora attuale dé monti troverá molto ragionevole questo parere, anzi il sole che sia incontrastabilmente ragionevole, e piano V'hanno per aventura poche divisioni fra le montagne epoche valli, per quanto sian elleno vaste, che non si debbano al tardo Lavoro dell'acque. La corrispondenza degli strati, che si vede girare regolarmente d'intorno alle pianure chiuse da monti, é

una

una prova incontraſtabile d'antica continuità. Di queſta ſorta di corriſpondenze da un braccio all'altro di monti veggonſene bene ſpeſſo coſteggiando gl'Appennini fra Bologna e Firenze. E fra quella fortunata città dove paſſai giorni ſi lieti, e Siena, dove ho'tanti detti amici, Colli di Val d'Elſa hanno dall'una all'altra parte perfetta corriſpondenza di ſtrati formati da ciottoli fluctati. Poc'acqua baſta ad aprire un paſſaggio fra ſtrato, e ſtrato, dove ſovente ritrovaſi materia atta a diſſoluzione come la creta, o a ſcompoſizione come la breccia e i ciottoli non ben comentati dalla ſtalattite.

I tremuoli ponno aver contribuito ad accelerare gli avvallamenti, ſcuottendo vaſti letti petroſi prioi di ſottegno, e tenuti, fermi ſoltanto dalla forte coeſione delle lor parti atta per qualche tempo a render vana la tendenza d'un peſo enorme. E quando dico per qualche tempo io non intendo di meſi, o di anni, ma di quanto e combinabile colla ſtrattura interiore, col carico ſuperiore, colla reſiſtenza delle aggiacenze più omeno ſuſcettibili d'alterazioni. Ne perche l'acque s'aprono per le viſcere di tutti i monti paſſaggi, e raro s'incontrano di coſi magnifiche arcate, ſi dee eſitare ad attribuirne a logoramenti loro l'origine. Aſpettiamo prima di ben conoſcere la Natura de varj ſuoli, che formano l'interiore delle montagne né differenti paeſi; e quando ſaremo ſicuri d'aver trovate un luogo del tutto ſimile a un altro, potremo ſgridare la natura s'ella v'avrá operato in maniera diverſa.

Io mi ricordo d'aver veduto in Iſtria, e particolarmente nel Territorio di Pola una quantita ſorprendente d'avvallamenti di figura ſomigliantiſima a quella d'una Arena; gli ſtrati all'intorno vi ſervono come di gradini, e, con ſimmetria non del tutto rozza, o indegna di rifleſſo, quelle grandi bocche circolari ſi vanno riſtringendo verſo il fondo aguiſa d'un cono tronco roveſciato. In quelle picole archi, dove concorrono le foglie, e lapoca terra del circondario ſogliono gl'abitanti ſeminare con profitto. Le acque dell Iſtria ſi perdono quaſi iſtantantamente doppo le pioggie per vie ſotterranie e non vi ſono comuni i torrenti, come per monti noſari, né quali é
meno

meno frequente l'alternagione degli strati cretosi. Quello smarrimento quasi subitaneo dell' acque piovane é tutto ad un tratto la casione della siccita, dacui e pur troppo sovente afflitta quella Penisola, e delle inumerabili voragini, e avvallamenti che vi s'incontrano. Doppo d'aver bene esaminata l'interna struttura del paese, io trovai molto conseguente l'operare della gran mastra. Mi risovviene d'aver pensato, trovandomi inquel paese, che gli abitanti aveano forse potuto far uso di sì fatti Anfiteatri naturali prima di averne d'altra forte; o che forse doppo d'aver fatto reflesso all' uso che sene potea fare, ne aveano eseguiti inpiu picciola forma i modelli nelle città. Io sono dunque costantemente d'opinione, che l'acqua (se in poca o in molta quantita non lo saprei dire, ma certamente in non pochi secoli) abbia travolto, e spezzato tutto quel gran pietrame, che riempieva la Vasca, o Vallicella che sta dietro al ponte di Veja, perdi sotto alquale in qualonque modo si voglia deve essere uscito. Credo dimostrato, che l'acqua medesima abbia portato sico, e stritolato tutto cio che formava la continuazione degli strati al di fuori a destra, e a sinistra dell' arco, e si congiungeva con quéí massi chi gli sono dirimpetto. E finalmente tengo per fermo, che fosse tutto d'un pezzo quel tratto di paese ora intersecato da burroni, e torrentelli, le sommitá del quale mostrano una corrispondenza parallela, e orizzontale pochissimo inclinata; poiche stimo un osservatore debba essere meno avaro di secoli, i quali ajutino il tardo Lavoro d'una causa semplice, che di congetture composte, ed intralciate.

L'opinione di coloro che credono quel ponte fatto di prima creazione dalla natura, non merita confutazione; ella si dec mettere co sogni di quelli, a quali sembrano scherzi o moltiplicazioni primitive di forme ipesci, i testacei, e le piante fossili. Se questa razza di gente, che regnunó tempo nelle seccole, dove spiegava comodamente la majior parte delle cose altrate colla natura scherzante, o colla volenta primitiva di Dio Creatore, non fosse un poco scemata di numero per dar luogo a genj meno

3   poltroni,

poltroni, le fcienze, e l'arti, e ogni forta d'umane cognizioni farrebbefi poco inottrate.

Per quello poi riguarda il parere del Celeb. Sig.^r Betti, che ftimar poffa effere ftato quel grand arco una porzione di ampia caverna, ad efempio delle due laterali lafciata vuota dalla natura, che in quello ftudiofiffimo fito pare fi fia dilettata di fcarpellare a gran vani, direi, che fe d'ogni fenomeno s' adduceffero origini fimili, faremo fempre da capo. Suppofta la gran caverna (d'onde potrebbe anche aver avuta una profima origine il ponte) refta a chiedere da chi ella fia ftata Scavata, edove fieno andati i materiali, che fervirono a continuare gli-ftratti fuperiori, e inferiori della Vallicella, ed el ponte. Fara d'uopo ricorrere al noftro compiacentiffimo ed amabile Capitan Lorgna, perche ci prefti quell operatore filo d'acqua, e le giffre da calcolare gli anni neceffarj a un lavoro fi grande. Non e fupponibile che dalle mani della natura, primitivamente fia ufcito quel vano; poiche primitiva opera della natura non fono que faffi, ne quali fi offervano preffefpoglie di mare, come nautili, Cornammoni, Entrochiti, Afterie colonari, &c. ne fi puo dire, che nella decantazione di quelle materie vi fiano reftati de vani, fenz' addurre di bon raggioni, o efferne ftati teftimoni oculari. I vulcani, i tremuoti, le acque le combinazioni, egli anni, cioe gli operaj della natura fono quelli che fcavano le caverne, e le riempiono alternativamente: io rifpetto troppo la Madre comune per affomigliarla ad una donnicciuola, che fa ilpane, e fi diverte a far de buchi, o de rilievi nella pafta molli, e fo poi di certo, che il noftro pianeta nonpuo effere ftato cofi alla lettera al tempo della formazione delle caverne una pafta molle. Quindi fono ben lontano da cio, che pende a credere l'elegante illuftratore del ponte di Veja. Egli " offervando la frequenza delle" grote, di cui non v' ha per cofi dire paefe che non vanti lafua, e non ne " efageri la belezza, credette di doverne quafi neceffariamente dedurre, ch' eleno " fono una confequenfa del modo con cui fi formarono imonti fin da principio," Io confeffo la mia inperizia ; monti,

chefi

cheſi poſſano francamente chiamare formati fin da principio, non ho peranche veduti, equanti m'accadde di vederne portano i ſegni plutonici, o del tridente, o' dell' una o'dell altra forza ad un tempo. E avvertano gli aſſertori di opinioni analoghe, che ſe nel giorno in cui ſi diviſero l'acque dalla terra, giuſta il Geneſi, per opera del fuoco ſotterraneo qualche cavita nelle argille non per anche indurate potea formarſi (coſa di cui e facile aſevire in aſtratto, ma pero malagevole a provarſi la poſſibilita in caſi determinati) le caverne di veja non ponno eſſere del numero. Il Celeb. Sigʳ Betti non ha forſe avuto campo da riflettere, che quelle acque doveano eſſere per anche diſabitate: poiche furono creati doppo il giorno della diviſiſione, giuſta il citato libro ſacro, quelli animali, le ſpoglie da quali formano principalmente l'oſſatura de monti Veroneſe d'origine Mavina, e di Veja in particolare

Or voi che ne dite,
Maeſtro di color che ſanno?

Io vi ſcrivo tutta queſta cicalata, perche rettifichiate quanto v' ha di mal penſato; ſono diſpoſitiſſimo a laſciarmi correggere da chi ne ſa del meſtiere quanto voi: del reſto de giudici non competenti v' immaginerete ch' io non cerco i ſuffraggi.

L'acqua che paſſa ſotto il ponte mezzo coperto cade nel buvone da forſe cento piedi d'altezza; il ſabro, ond ella precipita, ſerve come di grondaja a una vaſta cavita, che merita particolare menſione. Poco ſotto a quello ſtrato che ſta coſi in aria, vedeſi un arco aſſai minore del gia deſcritto, ma ſenza pareſare piu architettonico. Egli aria da 50 a 55 piedi di corda, ed e ſoſtenuto da due pilaſtroni alti circa 90. Queſt' arco, e queſti gran pilaſtri, formano l'ingreſſo della caverna, che aſcende ma non s' interna di molto, ella ha la volta maeſtrevolmente rotondata a foggia di cupola, cui ſerve di tetto il piano ſotto poſto al ponte. Dinanſi a queſt' apertura ſa come un velo l'acqua cadente, e vi move un accretta, che ſarà gentil coſa in tempo di ſtate. In queſto luogo ho veduto con ſorpreſa varj ciottoli di l'acca nera, e pezante, ſenza che d'intorno

torno

torno abbia potuto fcoprire lo ftrato, o la fenditura, d'onde vennero. E pero importante offervagione quella, che ne avrete effervi ftat un Vulcano anticamente in poca diftanza, e forfe immediatamente fotto il ponte di Veja.

Scendendo per abbandonare il ponte, appena abbimo fatti pochi paffi, che a deftra vidimo un burroncello, in capo al quale v' hanno pur archi, e caverne e caduta d'acqua, ed elementi d'un ponte futuro fullo fteffo piano dell' altro. A deftra e afiniftra dell alveo veggonfi molti antri, e fcilla vetta ftrana fraftagliature di ciglioni, e rovine fcogliofe.

Lafciatoci'l ponte di Veja, e il di lui fucceffore prefuntivo alle fpalle, ci avviammo a lugo, ora caminando per torrente, ora cofteggiaudolo. Non molto lungi dal ponte, fi trova il camino coperto per tratto di molti paffi da uno ftrato, che fporge in fuori forfe tre braccia. L'ofcuritá, che fi colfe per qué deferti, non mi avea permeffo nel primo viaggeo d'offervare le variazioni de corfi petrofi a mifura, che ci accoftavamo al piano, ma nel fecondo l'ora mi fu piu favorevole. Vidi fcoperto nel letto del torrente, in cui fi fcarica il burroncello di Veja, uno ftrato affai profondo di lumachella, cioe un ammaffo di bivalvi d'una fola fpezie, appartenente, fecond ogni apparenza, al genere delle oftraciti, di cui é fconofciuto totalmente l'originale Marino. Quefte Lumachelle congiurano colle Nummularie, coi cornammoni, colle Grifiti, e con parechie altre fpezie di foffili a far che gli Orrittologi faltino apie pare una quantita di argini fattizij, ed efcano a cavalchioni del Globo fuori de confini, ne quali egli e coftretto a girare prefentemente.

Si ponno offervare nello fcendere per quella Valle poche varieti foftanziali negli ftrati; eglino fono alternativamente Roffo, o Bianco di Verona, Breccie, e Lumachelle. A un miglio in circa dal ponte, nel luogo detto la bufa, fopra il molino, la ftrada paffa fra due Maffi incinati l'uno verfo l'altro, e diftanti intorno a 70 piedi. Le due faccie di effi, che fi guardano, fono incroftate dall alto al baffo di ftrie ftalagmi-

5   tiche,

tiche, che moftrano effere eglino anticamente ftati porzione
d'un grand arco, o di una gran caverna; chi cavaffe fotto la
ftrada troverebbe il refto. Uno de due maffi l'ifolato; en-
trambi fono impaftati di breccia. La natura fi compiacque in
qué contorni di far ifcavare delle acque fpelonche, ed archi.
Nello fcogliere che s' alfano perpendicolarmente rimpetto a
lago, v' hanno molte caverne ridotte ad ufo di cafe provifionali
dagli abitanti. Eleno hanno la bocca ben murata, e porta, e
fineftre. Per quale ftrada vi vadano que Montagnaj, io non
ve lo diro; perche.

      " Vaffi in fan Leo, e difcendeffi in Nole

      " Montafi fu Bifmantova in cacume

      " Con effo i pie : ma qui convien che vuom voli.

    Forfe l'interiore della Corfica, e di Monte Negro e ben
proveduto di fiffatti alberghi, e quindi e cofi difficile il pene-
trarvi. Prima di giungere alla chiefa di lafo offervai ne faffi
vicini alle cafe de Bellori grande abbondanza di Terebratole,
e di quel curiofo oftracite che lo Spada ha figurato T. IX.

    A Lugo ripofai nel primo mio viaggio la note, e nel fecondo
ci volea coftringere a far il medefimo la cortefia ofpitaliffima
di quel Reverendif mo Arciprete; di fronte alla di lui cafa v' ha
un ciglione magnifico; io penfai, che prima di montare a cavallo mi correffe un doverere d'andarlo a vifitare. Vándiedi
in fatti ; e per non perdere di troppo tempo mi vi aggrappai
a quattro gambe per la piu ripida, e impraticabile, preferendola
come la piu corta. Vi raccolfi tanta quantitá, e varietá di
Corna, d'Ammone, che gia vicino alla meta cioé alla fom
mitá, dove m'era prefiffo di giungere, io non avea piu fiato ;
ful coftretto a deporne qualche pajo de Maggiori, e un gran
faffo che da ogni parte ne ha belliffime impreffioni. Quando
mi refolvero di fare una Collegione per me, li andero a difep-
pellire con parachij altri tefori fimili; chio ho fparfi pe Monti
Vicentini, e fu gli Euganei. In quefti ultimi ho un depofito
dello fteffo genere fatto dieci o undeci anni fono; lo che
prova la lunga etá, e l'incurabilitá del mio male. Al di

forto

fotto di qué ciglioni v'é una fpelonca molto opportunamente fcavata in luogo, dove la pioggia farebbe una ftrana burla, fe vi forprendeffe un galantuomo. Ella ha quattro aperture ragionevolmente grandi, il fuo diametro e di trenta piedi all' incirca; la volta rufticamente ineguale, ma intorno a quindeci piedi alta. S' entra da una fola parte a finiftra; a Greco Levante v' ha l'ingreffo maggiore fatto come un portone di cafa; di fopra ha una fpecie di fineftra ovale; da quel portone non s'entra, perche il ciglione, in cui fu aperto, e tagliato apiombo. Dalla parte oppofta a quefte apperture ve ne un altra, quafi nel tetto, orizzontale, d'onde efce probabilmente l'acqua per ifgonbrare quel ricovero da orfi. Sotto quefto buco v' ha una fenditura perpendicolare nel maffo larga due piedi, longa otto in dieci. A deftra di effa, contiguo all' ingreffo praticabile, v' ha un gabinetto molto acconciamente fcavato. In quefta fpelonca reftarono i noftri nomi fcritti nel fito pia afciuto; io non farei lontano dall abitarvi per qualche mefe in perfona. Quegli farebbe un luogo a propofito per lavorare nel mia tenebrofo ed alpeftre Poema. Da lugo a Verona non trovaj cofa che fermaffe la mia attenzione.

Eccovi pafuto una fpecie di tributo, ch' io credo dovervi, come archimandrita degli orittologi noftri. Ricevetelo con quella amicizia con cui trattate me fteffo. Io non mi lufingo di poter fare altretanto di tempo in tempo, come avrei pur voluto, effendo perfuafo, che conveniffe ad un amatore della ftoria Naturale il conofcer bene quella del proprio paefe prima di penfar ad efaminare gli altrai.

Credetemi coftantemente animato da qué Sentimenti, che meritate e per confeguenfa,

Voftro Servitore ed Amico, &c.

GENERAL INDEX

(*N. B.* The Roman Numerals refer to the Volume, and the Figures to the Page.)

A

ACADEMY of painting and sculpture at Parma, i. 412.

Academy of sciences at Bologna, ii. 50.

Addison, Mr. miftakes in his account of the gallery at Florence correcfted, ii. 155.

Adrian's villa near Tivoli, iii. 119.

Agnese, St. church of, at Bologna, ii. 44.

Agoftino, St. church of, at Piacenza, i. 372.

Aiguebelle in Savoy, i. 41, 45.

Aix in Savoy, i. 30. The medicinal fprings there, 31.

Albani, villa, near Rome, iii. 130.

Albano, mountain of, near Rome, fome account of, iii. 115. The town, 116.

Albergo di Poveri at Genoa, i. 299.

Alberoni, cardinal, the principal events of his life, i. 381.

Aldrobrandini, villa, near Rome, iii. 134. At Frafcati, 157. The gardens, 158. Mufical ftatues, *ibid.*

Aldrovandi, his manufcript colleftions in natural hiftory at Bologna, ii. 51.

Aldrovandi palace at Bologna defcribed, ii. 9.

Aleffandria on the river Tanaro, i. 230.

Vol. III.　　　　A a　　　　　　*Al-*

INDEX.

Altieri palace at Rome, iii. 94.
Amazon, a Sardinian one defcribed, i. 46.
Ambrofe, St. in Piedmont, i. 86.
Ambrofian library at Milan, iii. 315.
Amphitheatre at Verona, iii. 300. Is ftill ufed by the inhabitants for public fpectacles, 301.
Ancona, the town, port, and mole of, iii. 219. Road from thence to Rimini, 221.
Angelo, Michael, character of his famous picture of the Laft Judgment, in the chapel of the Vatican palace, iii. 58.
Annonciato church at Genoa, i. 287.
Antonio, St. church of, at Padua, iii. 293. Baffo relievos of the events of his life, *ibid*.
Apothecary, anecdote of one at Genoa, i. 238.
Appenine, the road over to Genoa, i. 233.
Aqua di Pifciarelli, a famous medicinal water near Puzzuoli, ii. 343.
Aqua Zolfa, near Tivoli, iii. 116.
Armoury for women at Genoa, i. 326.
Arfenal at Turin defcribed, i. 143.
———at Genoa, i. 297.
———at Venice, iii. 280.
Arfinelli, the leaning tower of, at Bologna, ii. 63.
Affietta, detail of the battle of, and defeat of the French by the Piedmontefe, i. 220.
Affignations, common in the Italian churches, i. 248.
Avernus, lake, ii. 345. The Sybil's cave, 346. Temple of Apollo, 347.
Auguftus, the maufoleum of, at Rome, iii. 44. Coloffal head of, at the villa Mattei, 143.

B

Baia, near Puzzoli, ii. 316. The baths and prifons

prifons of Nero, *ibid.* Agrippina's tomb, 322. Temples, 326. Ponte di Caligula, 328. Hiftorical anecdotes of Baia, 329. The village of Bauli, 331.

Balbi palaces at Genoa, paintings in, i. 251.

Balbus, father and fon, equeftrian ftatues of, in the palace of Portici near Naples, ii. 253.

Barberiga palazzo, at Venice, iii. 273.

Barberini palace at Rome, iii. 79. Characters of the paintings in, 80. Of the buftos, 82. Library, 83. Villa Barberini, 138.

Barromeo, St. Charles, the church of at Turin, i. 141. Chapel of, in the cathedral at Milan, iii. 313.

Beacons, defcription of thofe in Switzerland, i. 12.

Belrefpiro, villa, near Rome, iii. 134. The garden, 136. Water organ, 137.

Belvidere palace at Rome, fome account of, iii. 65.

Bergamo, the birth place of Harlequin, iii. 307. Traits of his character obfervable in the inhabitants, 308. The road from thence to Milan, *ibid.*

Bernis, cardinal, fome account of, and his mode of living, ii. 192.

Bois de Bramant, i. 58.

Boleyn, queen Anne, character of a picture of her in the palace of Marcellino Durazzo at Genoa, i. 278.

Bologna, entertainment at the Pellegrino there, i. 457. Vifit from the cardinal legate, 462. And other diftinguifhed perfonages, 463. The opera, 465. The boxes at the opera, and the entertainment in them defcribed, 466. The palazzo publico, ii. 2. Capua palace,

7. Palazzo Aldrovandi, 9. Palazzo Bovi, 10. Palazzo Sampieri, 13. Palazzo Monti, 19. Palazzo Zambecari, 24. Palazzo Tanaro, 28. Palazzo di Buono Figlivoli, 31. Palazzo Pepoli, 35. Palazzo Ranuzzi, 36. Church of Madona di Galiera, 37. Church of Giefu and Maria, 39. Church of Mendicants di Dentro, 40. Corpus Domini church, 43. Church of St. Agnefe, 44. Church of St. Dominico, 45. Chapel of the Rofary, 47. Inftituto palace, 49. Academy of fciences, 50. The great theatre, 55. The little theatre, 56. Affemblies, 58. Manners, 61. Drefs of the inhabitants, 62. Leaning towers, 63. Fountain in the Piazza Maggiore, 64. Buildings in general, 65. Manufactures and provifions, 66. Natural curiofities, 69. Arrival of fugitive Jefuits from Spain and Paraguay, 73. The road from thence to Florence, 76. A vifit to count Algarotti's villa, in company with the cardinal legate, iii. 226. Arrival of exiled Jefuits, 228. Vifit to the celebrated Farinello, 229.

Bolfena, defcription of the lake of, ii. 188.

Borghefe palace at Rome, iii. 74. The villa near Rome, 145. The garden, 152. The park, 155.

Bofcovick, father, employed to take the level of the lands between Rome and Rimini, but obftructed by the peafants on the fuppofition of his being a magician, iii. 177.

Iovi palace at Bologna, ii. 10.

Bracciano palace at Rome, iii. 93. Villa at Frafcati, 163.

Brefcia,

INDEX.

Brescia, a town remarkable in history, iii. 307.
Bron, the boundary between the dominions of Sardinia, and those of Parma, i. 357.
Bucentaure at Venice, character of, iii. 280.
Buono Fighvoli, palazzo di, at Bologna, ii. 31.

C

Caduta della Marmora, description of the cascade so called at Terni, iii. 180.
Cambeaces of Genoa, five families distinguished by their munificent charity, i. 305.
Campo-marone, in the Genoese territory, i. 234.
Capitol, at Rome, ii. 392.
Capo di Monte, palace of, described, ii. 356.
Caprea palace at Bologna, ii. 7.
Caracallo's baths at Rome, iii. 38. His circus, 41.
Carameli, a monk, his peculiar talent of painting miniatures with woodcock's feathers, i. 113.
Carignan, the bridge of, at Genoa, i. 299.
Casserta, a palace for the king of Naples, building there, iii. 231. Royal ball, 234. Description of the theatre, 237.
Cassinos at Venice, a description of, iii. 277.
Cassius, his villa near Tivoli, iii. 123.
Castel Gondolfo, near Rome, iii. 111.
Castello lake near Rome, iii. 111. Ancient canal to drain off the superfluous water, 113.
Catacombs at Rome, some account of, iii. 51.
Cavalieri serventi, or cicesbeios at Venice, iii. 284.
Cennis Mont, i. 57. Manner of passing, 65. Plants and flowers, 71. The chamois goat, 72. Some account of Pere Nicolas, 74. 76. 88.

88. The lake, *ibid.* The defcent from *La Grand Croix*, 80.

Cento, paintings in the church belonging to the Jefuits' college there, iii. 234. In the church of the Rofary, 235. In the church Il Duomo, *ibid.* In the church of the Capuchin monks, 236.

Cefi, near Narni, precarious fituation of that town, iii. 176.

Chamberry in Savoy, i. 35. The church, 36. The caftle, *ibid.* Convents, 37. Anecdote of a cobler's family there, 39.

Chambre, La, in Savoy, i. 52.

Chamois goat on mount Cennis, defcribed, i. 72.

Chiaia, fuburb of, at Naples, ii. 385.

Chiefa nova, an unfinifhed church at Modena, i. 450.

Chigi palace at Rome, iii. 96.

Chriftine, St. the church of at Turin defcribed, i. 141.

Cicefbeios, the fafhion of at Parma, to what owing, i. 420. At Venice, iii. 284.

Civetta Caftellano, its peculiar fituation, iii. 171.

Clitumnus, temple of, iii. 189. River of, *ibid.*

Cocagna, a popular entertainment at Naples, defcribed, ii. 247.

Coffeehoufes at Venice, new regulation introduced into, iii. 287.

Collicipoli, derivation of the name of that town, iii. 177.

Collifeo, at Rome, ruin of, iii. 29.

Colonna palace at Rome, iii. 91.

Comteffa, the convent la, at Foligno, iii. 191.

Concert, defcription of a curious one at La Pieta in Venice, iii. 281.

Conofa, the fortress of, between Parma and Modena, i. 430.

Confervatori palace in the capitol at Rome, ii. 393. The adjoining gallery of pictures collected by pope Benedict XIV. 397. The Museum, 402.

Contarini palace at Venice, converted into a public hotel, some description of, iii. 243.

Conti, villa, at Frafcati, iii. 160.

Cornigliano bridge near Genoa, i. 235.

Corona, la Santa, church of, at Vicenza, iii. 299.

Corpus Domini church at Bologna, ii. 43.

Corregio, critical examination of his famous picture at Parma, i. 402. Character of the fine copy of his picture *Il Notte*, at Modena, 440.

Corfini palace at Rome, iii. 76.

Corfo at Naples, some account of, ii. 375.

Cuma, description of the ruins of, ii. 350. Temple of the giants, 351. The Sibyl's cave, 352. The burial places there called Colimperia, 354.

Cyprefs almonds, how used at Florence, ii. 176.

D.

Danae, description of a beautiful picture of, by Tiziano, at Florence, ii. 174.

Dance, Mr. George, his academical drawings at Parma, i. 413.

Daphne, her metamorphofis into a laurel tree, a modern group by Bernini, at the villa Borghefe near Rome, described, iii. 147.

Deo Ridiculo, temple at Rome, on what occasion erected, iii. 43.

Doge's palace at Genoa, i. 293.

Dominico, St. church of, at Bologna, ii. 45.

INDEX.

Domitian's palace near Rome, account of the ruins of, iii. 112.

Dorias, inscriptions on the statues of, in the Doge's palace at Genoa, i. 294.

Dragone, villa, at Frascati, iii. 162.

Ducal church at Venice, iii. 250. The treasury of, 252. The palace, 254. The prisons in the palace, 257.

Duomo church at Naples, ii. 369. At Gento, iii. 235. At Milan, 312.

Durazzo, Philip, his palace at Genoa, paintings in, i. 271. Paintings in that of Marcellino Durazzo, 274.

E

Earthquake at Florence, ii. 93.

Emerald vase at Genoa, an imposition, i. 326.

Estense villa, near Tivoli, iii. 128.

F

Farrinello, some account of, and of his house near Bologna, iii. 229.

Farnese, equestrian statues of some of this family, at Piacenza, i. 363.

Farnese palace at Rome, iii. 85

Farnesini villa, near Rome, iii. 140.

Ferrara, paintings in the Carthusian church, and church of St. Benedetto there, iii. 226.

Fierengola, village of, between Bologna and Florence, ii. 90.

Filippo di Neri, St. his church at Naples, ii. 371. At Spoletto, iii. 187.

Fiorenzuola in the duchy of Parma, i. 389.

Fish, petrified, found in the neighbourhood of Verona, iii. 303.

Flaminian way, its construction described, iii. 170.

Florence,

Florence, good accommodation at Vanini's inn there, ii. 74. Entrance of the city, 90. General remarks, 91. Earthquake there, 93. The famous gallery deſcribed, 95. The palazzo Pitti, 158. The environs, 175. The peaſants, 177. Proviſions, 178. Theatres, 178. Private aſſemblies introduced there by Sir Horace Mann, 180. The road from thence to Sienna, 180.

Foligno, the town of, near Spoletto, iii. 191. The convent La Compteſſa, *ibid.*

Fondi, between Rome and Naples, curious deſcription of the inn there, ii. 209. Dreſs of the inhabitants, 217.

Fountain of the nymph Egeria at Rome, iii. 46.

Fraſcati, or ancient Tuſculum, near Rome, iii. 155.

Friangean in Savoy, i. 26. The road between that village and Geneva, 27.

Functions celebrated at Rome, during the Santa Settimana, iii. 2. On Palm Sunday, *ibid.* The Tenebræ of the Holy Wedneſday, 5. Maunday Thurſday, 7. Of Eaſter Sunday, 20.

G

Gabrieli the ſinger, her character, iii. 303.

Gallery at Florence deſcribed, ii. 95. The building, 96. Equeſtrian ſtatue of Coſmo, i. 97. The Veſtibule, *ibid.* Statues, 98. Contents of the gallery, 101. Of the Tribune, 110. The famous Venus de Medicis, *ibid.* The gabinetto of antiques, 128. Cabinet of arts, 135. Cabinet of medals, 143. The ſaloon of arms, 147.

Galley ſlaves at Turin, i. 148. At Genoa, 242, 307.

Gardens,

INDEX.

Gardens, Englifh, the tafte of, celebrated, iii. 125.

Garifendi, the leaning tower of, at Bologna, ii. 63.

Gavi, in the Genoefe territory, i. 233.

Generofity and Modefty, by *Guido*, in palazzo Monti at Bologna, defcribed, ii. 21.

Geneva, the lake of, i. 9, 18. View of the country about, 20. The city, 26.

Gennaro, St. the liquefaction of his blood no longer credited at Naples, ii. 370.

Genoa, common drefs of the women in the city of, i. 236. Humorous anecdote of an apothecary there, 238. Expences and entertainment at the inn there, 241. The galley flaves, 242. The ftreets and palaces, 244. Church of St. Siro, 246. Affignations common in the churches, 248. Situation of the town, and the houfes, 249. Paintings in the Balbi palaces, 251. Paintings in the palace of Philip Durazzo, 271. Of Marcellino Durazzo, 274. In the palace of Pallavicini, 280. The Jefuits' church, 286. Annonciato church, 287. Curious account of a penitent, 289. Church of St. Luca, 292. The Doge's palace, 293. The arfenal, 297. The bridge of Carignan, 299. Alborgo di Poveri, *ibid.* Munificent charity of five families of the Cambeaces, 305. The galleys and flaves, 307. The Inquifition, 315. The theatre, 320. The villa palaces, 321. The armoury, 326. The emerald vafe, *ibid.* Appearance of the Doge, 327. The manufactures carried on there, 328. The ramparts and lighthoufe, 329. Public charities, 330.

330. Economy of the nobles, 331. Roman inscription unnoticed by Addison, 333. Foreign possessions, 337. The mole, 338. The sbirri, 339. Frequency of assassinations, 342. The gabelle, 348. The nobles, 349. College of Jesuits, 350. Species of native marble, 351. Other natural productions, 352.

Giardini Giudecca at Venice, described, iii. 279.

Giesu and Maria church at Bologna, ii. 39.

Gillibrand, father, his account of the travels of the Holy house of Loretto, iii. 212.

Giorgio Maggiore, St. church of, at Venice, iii. 269.

Giovanni di Latterano, St. church of, at Rome, iii. 47.

Giustiniano palace at Rome, iii. 97.

Giustino, St. church of at Padua, iii. 296.

Glaciere on mount Cennis, i. 69.

Glass-houses at Venice, iii. 282.

Graffi, palazzo, at Venice, iii. 273.

Grazie, Le, the church of the Dominicans at Milan, iii. 319.

Grotta del Cane, near Puzzuoli, ii. 337.

Grotta dragonara, near Puzzuoli, ii. 343.

Grotta di Pausilippe at Naples described, ii. 333. Virgil's tomb, 336.

Grottes of the nymphs on the borders of the Lago Castello, iii. 112.

H

Harlequin, where that absurd character first originated, iii. 307. The style of that character at Milan, 322.

Herculaneum,

INDEX.

Herculaneum, remains of, in the palace of Portici near Naples, ii. 255. When and how deftroyed, 284. Its remains when and how difcovered, 285. Defcent into defcribed, 291. See *Pompeia.*

Horatii and Curatii, monument of, near Rome, iii. 115.

Horfes, four of bronze, at Venice, hiftory of, iii. 250.

Hydropique by Gerard Douw, at Turin, this celebrated picture defcribed, i. 115.

I

Idiots, children artificially converted into, for the amufement of the ancients, ii. 267.

Jean, St. church of at Piacenza, i. 375.

Jean de Maurienne St. in Savoy, i. 51.

Jefuits' church at Genoa, i. 286.

——Convent of, at Chamberry in Savoy, i. 37. College of at Genoa, 350.

——College of at Rome, iii. 101. Remarks on the inftitution, 108.

——Arrival of exiles of that order, at Bologna, ii. 73. iii. 228. Paintings in the church belonging to their college at Cento, 234.

Infant, at Parma, his character, i. 417.

Infanta, at Parma, her character, i. 415.

Inquifition, regal reftraints on the office of, in Sardinia, i. 216. State of, at Genoa, 315. The office at Parma, fhut up, 415.

Inftituto palace at Bologna, ii. 49.

John, St. the church of, at Parma, i. 397.

Iflands, floating, in the Solfatara near Tivoli, iii. 117.

Jougne, the caftle of, i. 6.

Julius Cæfar, his monument at Cuma, ii. 354.

Labor-

INDEX.

L

Labor-mia river, croffed upon rafts, i. 230.

Lago d'Anagno, near Puzzuoli, ii. 337.

Lagunes at Venice, fome account of, iii. 243. 290.

Lanebourg in Savoy, i. 59. No phyfician permitted to live there, 63. The happy fimplicity of manners there, 64.

Laocoon, character of this celebrated group, iii. 67.

Lava of Vefuvius, the nature of, defcribed, ii. 284.

Laura of Petrarch, a copy of verfes found in her coffin at Avignon, i. 119. Her picture in the king of Sardinia's cabinet defcribed, 120.

Lawyers, Venetian, ill confequence of their violent action in pleading, iii. 256.

Lazzaroni at Naples, character of, ii. 383.

Leonardo da Vinci, his famous picture of the Laft-fupper, in the church of the Dominicans at Milan, iii. 320. Anecdote of, 321.

Letters of recommendation, proper caution as to the ufe of, i. 464.

Loretto, the approach to, defcribed, iii. 198. Situation of the town, 199. Trade of, 200. The church, and Santiffima Cafa, 201. The Virgin and Infant, 202. Prefent to, from James II. of England's queen, 204. Relicks, 205. Treafures, 206. Has been greatly neglected of late years, 209. Father Gillibrand's account of the travels of the Holy houfe, 212.

Luca,

Luca, St. church of, at Genoa, i. 292. at Venice, iii. 268.

M

Madona de la Campagna, church of, at Pia-
cenza, i. 374.
Madona di Galiera, church of, at Bologna,
ii. 37.
Mæcenas, ruins of his houfe near Tivoli, iii. 127.
Mann, Sir Horace, the introducer of private
affemblies among the Florentines, ii. 180.
Manufcripts, ancient, difcovered at Hercula-
neum, fome account of, ii. 272.
Marcellus's theatre, ruins of, at Rome, iii. 40.
Marforio, the celebrated ftatue of, at Rome, ii.
402.
Maria Maggiore, St. the church of, at Rome,
iii. 48. At Venice, 271.
Mark, St. the ducal church at Venice, iii. 250.
Treafury of, 252.
Marfigli, count, his collection of curiofities in
the inftituto palace at Bologna, ii. 49.
Marfin, marefchal, infcription on his tomb,
i. 161.
Mafchieri, village of, between Bologna and Flo-
rence, ii. 89.
Mattei villa near Rome, iii. 143.
Maurice, St. the order of, in Sardinia, i. 217.
Mendicants di Dentro, church of, at Bologna,
ii. 40.
Milan, the road from Verona to, defcribed,
iii. 306. General remarks on the town,
308. Provifions, 309. Indabitants, 311.
Il Duomo, the cathedral, 312. The Ambrofian library, 315. The gabinetto, or
mufeum, *ibid*. Remarkable fkeleton, 315.
Church

INDEX.

Church of San Vittore, 319. Le Grazie, the Dominican church, *ibid.* The theatre, 322. The humours of Harlequin there, *ibid.* The common people, 324. Banditti on the borders of the Milanese, 327.

Modane, the village of, in Savoy, i. 58.

Modena, general account of, i. 433. Ducal palace, 434. Paintings, 435. Cameos, 445. Library, 446. The cathedral, 448. The church La Chiesa nova, 450. Theatres, *ibid.* Troops, *ibid.* Illuftrious families, 451. Bourgeoife, *ibid.* Fountains, *ibid.* Strata of the foil, as found in digging wells, 452. The adjacent country, 454. Illuftrious men born at Modena, *ibid.* The road from thence to Bologna, 456.

Mont Callier, a palace belonging to the king of Sardinia, i. 169.

Mont Cennis, fee *Cennis.*

Monte Nuovo, near Naples, hiftory of, ii. 344.

Monts Ferrats, near Turin, natural curiofities of, i. 218.

Monti palace at Bologna, ii. 19.

Montmelian in Savoy, i. 43.

Morges in Switzerland, i. 9. The port there. 18

N

Naples, general remarks on the town, ii. 219. Mrs. Hamilton's affembly, 224. Profpect of mount Vefuvius, 227. *Fete* at the princefs Potera's, 229. The palace at Cafferta, 231. Defcription of the queen's perfon, 234. Royal ball, 235. The Neapolitans curious manufacturers in tortoife-fhell, 243. The little

little notice taken of murders there, 246. The popular amufement called the Cocagna, 247. Cabinet of Portici, 252. Palace of Portici, 253. Remains of Herculaneum and Pompeia preferved there, 255. Defcription of Herculaneum, 284. Puzzoli and its antiquities, 310. The baths and prifons of Nero at Baia, 316. The road to Puzzoli, 333. The grotta di Paufilippe, 334. Grotta del Cane, 337. Solfaterra, 341. Lake Avernus, 345. Cuma, 350. Julius Cæfar's monument, 354. Palace of Capo di Monte, 356. The royal palace, 363. The theatres, 364. The church Il Duomo, 368. Church of Santa Reftituto, 369. The liquefaction of St. Gennaro's blood difcredited, 370. Church of St. Philippo di Neri, 371. Mount Vefuvius, 373. The Corfo, 375. Popular amufements, 383. The Lazzaroni, *ibid.* Government, 388.

Narni, in the ecclefiaftical ftate, fome defcriptive account of, iii. 173. Ruins of Auguftus's bridge, 175. Town of Cefi, 176. Road from to Terni, 178.

Nero, his baths and prifons at Baia, ii. 316. Ruins of his golden palace, iii. 29.

Nicholas, Pere, on mount Cennis, fome account of that good father, i. 74. 76. 88.

Nera, river, its picturefque appearance at Terni, iii. 178.

Notre Dame de Compagna near Turin, i. 160.

Novi, a town in the Genoefe territory, i. 231. The road from thence to Genoa defcribed, 232.

INDEX.

P

Padua, voyage from Venice to, iii. 290. The fortifications, 291. The cathedral, 292. Church of St. Antonio, 293. Of St. Giuſtino, 296.

Painters and poets deferving of punifhment for the choice of fubjects exciting horror and rage, ii. 12.

Paintings difcovered at Herculaneum, with the method of detaching them from the original walls, ii. 274.

Pallavicini palace at Genoa, paintings in, i. 280.

Paix de Gex, the country and inhabitants deſcribed, i. 13.

Palazzo publico at Bologna, ii. 2.

Palladio, his bridge and theatre at Vicenza, iii. 298. His ſuppoſed artful ſcheme of revenge againſt the inhabitants, 299.

Pamfili, villa, near Rome, iii. 134. The garden, 136. Water organ, 137.

Panaro river, that divides the duchy of Modena from the eccleſiaſtical ſtate, i. 456.

Pantheon at Rome, iii. 31.

Paolo, St. church of, at Parma, i. 411.

Paolo di Roma, St. church of, iii. 49.

Parma, general deſcription of the town, i. 392. Its antiquity, 393. The cathedral, 396. Church of St. John, 397. Church of St. Sepulchre, 398. Church of Madonna della Stecatta, *ibid.* Critical examination of Corregio's famous picture, 402. The theatre, 405. Public amuſements, 410. Church of St. Paolo, 411. The palace, 412. Academy of painting and sculpture, *ibid.* The office of the Inquisition there shut up, 415. Characters of the royal family, *ibid.* Hearth tax lately imposed there, 417. Principal families, 418. Remarkable picture in the church of St. Micheli, 419. Cicesbeios, 420. Disturbances occasioned there by the late pope, 423. Police, 425. New road making to Genoa, 428.

Pausilippé, grotta di, ii. 333. Virgil's tomb, 336.

Penitent at Genoa, curious particulars of one, i. 289.

Pepoli palace at Bologna, ii. 35.

Peter, St. weeping, by Guido, in the Sampieri palace at Bologna, described, ii. 15.

Peter's, St. at Rome, description of, ii. 200.

Petrarch, copy of his verses, found in the coffin of his Laura at Avignon, i. 119.

Petroleum produced in a spring at Bagnonera near Modena, i. 453.

Philip de Neri, St. the church of at Turin, described, i. 139.

Phosphorus of Bologna, ii. 69.

Piaggi, padre Antonio, the inventor of a method of opening and reading the ancient manuscripts discovered at Herculaneum, ii. 272.

Piacenza, its disagreeable appearance, i. 361. Equestrian statues of some of the Farnese family, 363. The cathedral, 368. Church of St. Agostino, 372. The church la Madona de la Campagna, 374. Church of St. Jean, 375. The ducal palace, 377. The theatre and corso, 378. Number of inhabitants, convents,

I

INDEX.

vents, and fortifications, 379. Face of the country between this town and Parma, 388.

Pickler, father and son, engravers on gems, at Rome, their characters as artists, iii. 166.

Pietra Mala, between Bologna and Florence, ii. 77, 90.

Pigeons, wild, Italian method of catching, iii. 178.

Pinciana, villa, near Rome, iii. 145.

Piranese, engraver and sculptor at Rome, his character as an artist, iii. 166.

Pisani Palazzo, at Venice, iii. 272.

Piscina Mirabile, near the Mare Morto in the neighbourhood of Naples, ii. 349.

Pitti palace at Florence, described, ii. 158.

Place, St. Mark at Venice, described, iii. 247. The Broglio, 248. 257.

Po, the passage on that river from Francolino to Venice, iii. 238. View of Venice from the river, 242.

Polceverra, in the Genoese territory, i. 234.

Pompeia, its situation, ii. 251. How destroyed, and since discovered, 292. The discovered parts described, 293. Skeletons found, 294, 295. A house and garden, 297. A gate and a street, 300. A temple of Isis, 302.

Pontarlier, the road between that town and Ornon, described, i. 3.

Pope, his reasons for declining having ladies presented to him, ii. 415. Functions performed by him during the Santa Settimana, iii. 2. His mode of life, 18. Anecdote of, 36.

Portici, its situation, ii. 251. Cabinet of, 252. The palace, 253. Remains of Herculaneum and Pompeia, preserved there, 255.

B b 2

Potera,

I N D E X.

Potera, princefs, defcription of a *fete* given by her at Naples, ii. 229.

Prejudices, national, corrected by travelling, i. 421.

Pretender, fome account of, ii. 196, 199.

Puzzuoli near Naples, defcribed, ii. 310. The cathedral, 311. Curious antique pedeftal, 312. The fuppofed Academia of Cicero, 313, Labyrinth of Dædalus, 314. The columbarias or tombs, 315. The gulph or bay, 316.

Pyramid of Caius Ceftius at Rome, iii. 44.

R

Radicofani, defcription of the accommodations for travellers there, ii. 183.

Raffaello, curious picture of the Virgin by, in the convent La Comteffa at Foligno, iii. 191.

Randan, a village in Savoy, how deftroyed, i. 47.

Ranuzzi palace at Bologna, ii. 36.

Ravenna, remarkable badnefs of the water there, iii. 223.

Reggio, between Parma and Modena, i. 429, 431. Paintings in the churches there, 432.

Relics, general reflection on thofe preferved at Rome, iii. 48.

Reno, river, in the ecclefiaftical ftate, i. 456.

Rialto at Venice, fome account of that celebrated bridge, iii. 289.

Rivers in Italy, fubject to change their beds, i. 389.

Rivoli in Piedmont, i. 86. The road from thence to Turin, 87.

Roads, why excellent under defpotic governments, i. 209.

Rome,

I N D E X.

Rome, the accommodation at Pio's hotel there, ii. 189. General remarks on the city, 190. Account of some diftinguifhed families there, 191. Entertainment at cardinal Bernis's, 192. and at the duchefs of Bracciano's, 194. Account of the Pretender, 196. 199. St. Peter's church, 200. Road from thence toward Naples, 208. Defcription of a fuite of private apartments hired there, 379. The capitol, 392. Confervatori palace, 393. Adjoining gallery of pictures, collected by pope Benedict XIV. 397. The mufeum, 402. The ftatue called Marforio, *ibid.* The pope, 415. Functions celebrated during the Santa Settimana, iii. 2. Impediments to the viewing public buildings, 25. Ruins of temples, &c. 26. The collifeo, 29. The Pantheon, 31. Evening amufements, 34. Caracalla's baths, 38. Marcellus's theatre, 40. Tarpeian rock, 41. Temple Deo Ridiculo, 43. The maufoleum of Auguftus, 44. Pyramid of Caius Ceftius, *ibid.* Fountains, 46. The church St. Giovanni di Latterano, 47. Relics, 48. Church of St. Maria Magiore, *ibid.* St. Paolo di Roma church, 49. Church of St. Urbano alla Caffarello, 50. Church of St. Sebaftiano alle catecombe, 51. The catacombs, *ibid.* Vatican palace, 56. Belvidere palace, 65. The Laocoon, 67. Borghefe palace, 74. The Palazzo Corfini, 76. The Palazzo Barberini, 79. Palazzo Farnefe, 85. Palazzo Spada, 90. Palazzo Colonna, 91. Palazzo Bracciano, 93. Palazzo Altieri, 94. Palazzo Chigi, 96. Palazzo Giuftiniano, 97.

B b 3   Palazzo

INDEX.

Palazzo Rofpigliofi, '99. The Jefuits' college, 101. Tivoli, 123. Villa Albani, 130. Villa Aldrobrandini, 134.' Villa Pamfili or Belrefpiro, *ibid.*—Villa Barberini, 138. Villa Borghefe, 145. Principlo artifts now there, 165. Englifh ftudents there, often diftreffed by the parfimony of their friends at home, 167. Road from hence to Narni, 170.'

Rofary, chapel of, at Bologna, ii. 46. Church of, at Cento, iii. 235.

Rofpigliofi palace at Rome, iii. 99.

Rotunda, or Santa Maria ad Martyres church at Rome, iii. 31.

Rumelie in Savoy, i. 29.

S

Sacrifices, ancient heathen, curious method of producing white victims for, iii. 190.

Saint. For all thofe towns and churches having *Saint* prefixed, fee their refpective proper names.

Salvadoro, St. church of, at Terni, iii. 179. Ditto at Venice, 268.

Sampieri palace at Bologna, ii. 13.

San Vittore, church of, at Milan, iii. 319.

Santa Corona, church of, at Vicenza, iii. 299.

Santa Reftituto, church at Naples, ii. 369.

Santa Settimana, functions performed during, iii. 2.

Sara, the town of, i. 8.

Sardinia, peculiar character of the kings of, i. 118. Manner of feizing the late king, 169. Œconomy of the prefent king, 201. Troops, 203. The king's table, 205. Public employments, *ibid.* Politics, 206. Jews, 207. Silk-

INDEX.

Silkworms, 208. Roads, 209. The king's farms, 211. Salt fprings, 212. Peafants, 213. The Bourgeoife, *ibid.* Nobles, 214. Poft-letters all examined by the minifters, 215. The Inquifition, 216. Order of St. Maurice, 217. See *Turin*.

Savoy, mountains of, i. 9. Dangerous roads in, i. 53.

Sbirri at Genoa, fome account of, i. 339.

Scaricalafino, convent of, between Bologna and Florence, ii. 98.

School of Athens, a capital painting of Raffaello in the Vatican palace, fome account of, iii. 62.

Scuolo di St. Fantino at Venice, iii. 267.

Sebaftiano, St. church of, at Venice, iii. 271.

Sebaftiano alle catecombe, church of, at Rome, iii. 51.

Seneca in the bath, comparifon between the painting of, in the palace of Marcellino Durazzo at Genoa, and that in the poffeffion of the duke of Marlborough, i. 274.

Sepulchre, St. the church of, at Parma, i. 398.

Seraville, in the Apennines, dreadful thunder-ftorm there, iii. 193. Account of the village, 196.

Sybil's cave at the lake of Avernus, ii. 346. Another at Cuma, 352. Temple of, at Tivoli, iii. 124.

Sienna, the appearance and accommodations of, ii. 182.

Siro, St. the church of, at Genoa, i. 246.

Skeleton, remarkable one in the Ambrofian library at Milan, iii. 317.

Solfatara,

Solfatara, lake of, near Tivoli, iii. 117. Floating iflands, *ibid.*

Solfaterra, near Puzzuoli, ii. 341.

Somma, a ftupendous Apennine mountain in the road between Terni and Spoletto, iii. 181. Terrible ftorm on the road over, 185.

Spada palace at Rome, iii. 90.

Spoletto, the town of, defcribed, iii. 186. The cathedral, *ibid.* Famous aqueduct in the neighbourhood of, 188.

Strange, Mr. the engraver, his high repute at Rome, iii. 168.

Stupenige, the king of Sardinia's hunting palace, i. 161. The paintings, 163. The gardens, 168. Defcription of a royal chafe there, 187.

Suaire, St. the chapel of, defcribed, i. 137.

Sudley, lady, her memory much revered by the Neapolitans, ii. 356.

Superga, la, the church of, near Turin, i. 174. Infcription over the entrance within, 177. Bas reliefs, *ibid.* Miraculous image of the Virgin, 179. Adjoining convent of the Channonines, 180.

Supplice des razoirs, a Sardinian inftrument of death, defcribed, i. 56.

Sufa, a village in Piedmont, i. 84. The road from thence to Turin, 85.

Switzerland, the flourifhing ftate of agriculture there, i. 12. The beacons there for fpreading an alarm, *ibid.*

T

Table Ifiaque at Turin, defcribed, i. 135.

Tanaro

INDEX.

Tanaro palace at Bologna, ii. 28.

Taro, the river of, in the duchy of Parma, i. 389.

Taverna villa at Frafcati, iii. 161.

Terni, picturefque appearance of the river Nera there, iii. 178. Defcription of the town and its antiquities, 179. Church of St. Salvadoro, *ibid.* Cafcade, 180. Road to Spoletto, 181.

Terre Majore, obfervatory erected on that eminence to take the level of the lands between Rome and Rimini, iii. 177.

Thefeus, defcription of the ancient picture of, found at Herculaneum, ii. 275.

Tillot, M. the duke of Parma's minifter, i. 414. 416.

Tivoli, in the neighbourhood of Rome, iii. 116. 123. Temple of the Sybil, 124. Cafcade of, 126. The Cafcatella, *ibid.* The villa Eftenfe, 128.

Tobacco, great plantations of, about Turin, i. 203.

Tombs of the illuftrious dead, reflections on the ancient manner of erecting, compared with that of the moderns, iii. 45.

Trajan's arch at Ancona, iii. 219.

Travelling, of ufe to correct national prejudices, i. 421.

Trebia, battle of, between Hannibal and the Romans, where fought, i. 380.

Truffles, method of preparing and dreffing on the Apennines, iii. 184.

Turin, a defcription of that city, i. 87. The royal gardens, 94. The palace, 97. Paintings in the palace, 101. The theatre, 130.

3   Palace

Palace of the prince of Piedmont, 133. The table Isiaque, 135. Chapel of St. Suaire, 137. Church of St. Philip de Neri, 139. Cabinet of inscriptions and antiques, 140. Church of St. Christine, 141. Church of St. Charles Baromee, *ibid.* Church of St. Therese, 142. The arsenal, 143. Uniformity of the town, 146. The environs, 147. Galley-slaves, 148. The palace La Venerie, 150. The opera, 193. Foreign ministers, 194. The ladies, 196. Spies, 197. Police, 198. Restrictions on the theatre, 200. Regulations for improving the town, 208. The roads about, why so good, 209. Restrictions on the press, 210. Duelling, *ibid.* Precautions at the post-office, 215. The Inquisition, 216. The punishment of breaking on the wheel, lately introduced there, 217.

Tuscany, general remarks on, ii. 175.

Tusculum, ancient, the modern Frascati, historical anecdotes of, iii. 156. Ruins of the ancient town, 164.

V

Valentine at Turin, described, i. 147. The palace, 149. iii. 329.

Vanini, recommendations of their inn at Florence, ii. 74, 182.

Vatican palace at Rome, iii. 56. The library, 70.

Veia, situation of the ancient city of, iii. 170.

Velleia, antiquities found among the ruins of, i. 413.

Venerie, the palace la, at Turin, i. 150. The paintings,

INDEX.

paintings, 152. The chapel, 155. The orangerie and ftables, 156. Gardens, 157. *Venice*, view of, from the Lagunes, iii. 243. The hotel called Palazzo Contarini, *ibid.* Nothing but water-carriage there, 246. Place St. Mark, 247. The Broglio, 248. Manners of the people, 249. The Ducal church, 250. Treafury of, 252. The Ducal palace, 254. The lawyers wigs injurious to the paintings in the courts of juftice, 256. The prifons in the palace, 257. Tradefmen's fhops, 258. Provifions and cookery, 259. The water brackifh, 261. A Venetian wedding, 262. Church of St. Zaccaria, 266. Church of St. Fantino, 267. Scuolo di St. Fantino, *ibid.* Churches of St. Lucca, St. Salvadoro, and I Miraculo, 268. St. Giorgio Maggiore, 269. Church of St. Sebaftiano and St. Maria Maggiore, 271. Palazzo Pifani, 272. Palazzo Barberigo, 273. Palazzo Graffi, *ibid.* General obfervations on the palaces, 274. The caffinos, 277. The Giardini Giudecca, 279. The Arferial and Bucentaur, 280. Charitable inftitutions, *ibid.* Curious female concert, 281. The glafs-houfes, 282. Wooden madonnas and faints, *ibid.* Manners of the ladies of diftinction, 284. The cavalieri ferventi, *ibid.* New regulation in the coffee-houfes there, 287. Loofe women, new law againft, 288. The Rialto, 289. Voyage to Padua, 290.
Venus de Medicis in the gallery at Florence defcribed, ii. 110.
Verona, the amphitheatre there, iii. 300. Is ftill ufed by the inhabitants for public fpectacles,

tacles, 301. Mufeum in the piazza Bra,
ibid. The theatre, 302. General remarks
on the town and its antiquities, 303. Petrified fish, 304. Road from thence to
Milan, 306. Defcription of a natural bridge
in the neighbourhood of, 331.
Veronefe, Paolo, his picture of the Supper at
Cana, with the price he received for it, iii.
270.
Verfoix, the intended town of, i. 16. Is aban-
doned, 19.
Vefuvius mount, profpect of, from Naples, ii.
227. Some account of, 373.
Vicenza, the road from, to Verona, iii. 297.
The town, bridge, and theatre, 298. The
piazze d'Ifola, 299. The church La San-
ta Corona, ibid. The public walk there,
300.
Vigne de la Reine palace near Turin, i. 185.
The gardens, 186.
Virgil's tomb, ii. 336.
Volfcium, ruins of the ancient town of, ii. 188.
Voltagia, in the Genoefe territory, i. 233.
Voltaire, his character of the people of Geneva,
i. 21. His caftle at Ferney, 23. His ac-
count of the battle of Affietta corrected,
221.
Urbano alla Caffarello, church of, at Rome,
iii. 50.

W

Wedding, a Venetian one defcribed, iii. 262.
Woman of Samaria, the fign of, the beft inn at
Milan, iii. 306.

Women,

INDEX.

Women, common, new law againſt, at Venice, iii. 288.

Y

Year, the wiſh of a happy new one, not agreeable to a French woman, ii. 157.

Z

Zaccaria, St. church of, at Venice, iii. 266.
Zambecari palace at Bologna, ii. 24.
Zamperini, the opera ſinger at Turin, i. 193, 201.

F I N I S.

For the following ERRATA, and many other inaccuracies of diftribution, pointing, &c. the Editor's diftance from the Prefs muft apologize to the Reader.

VOL. I.

Page 5 *line penult. after* blackfmith *read* appears
— 12—*ult. for* they are beacons, and are placed, *read* which they do by beacons that are placed
— 39— 3. *from bottom, for* de Cuifine *read* de la Cuifine
— 51— 3. *for* that one do not know *read* that chance may throw in our way
— 62—12. *after* feigneur *add* a comma
— 81— 5. *from bottom, dele* about it is
—100— 8. *from bottom, dele* and
—107—11. *from bottom, for* to the fpectators, *read* turned away from the fpectators
7. *from bottom, for* are more ftrongly expreffed than, *read* as ftrongly expreffed as
—115— 7. *from bottom, for* and, as well as I can remember, *read* and, to my beft remembrance
—124— 9. *for* fuits. As *read* fuits, as
—131—10. *for* actres *read* actors
—304— 9. *from bottom, for* Barrie *read* Barré
—305—11. *after* each *add* of
—324— 3. *for* fight *read* fight
11. *dele* he
—328— 3. *after* fay *add* you
—342—10. *for* combatants *read* combatant
13. *for* culpa *read* culpo
—348— 5. *from bottom, for* per year *read* yearly
—349— 6. *from bottom, after* only *add* a comma]
—350—*penult. for* Here muft quit *read* Here I muft quit
—353— 9. *from bottom, for* is a felucca arrived with two Englifh *read* here is a felucca with two Englifh
—362—*ult. for* one *read* you
—363—*ult. dele* that
—364— 8. *for* there is too great a diftance between *read* too great a diftance is obfervable between
8. *from bottom, for* which feems as if he was about to put it to the ground, appears lame and hurt, by the fearful manner it feems to defcend ; *read* which he is about to put to the ground, appears lame and hurt, by the timorous manner in which it feems to defcend ;
—367— 4. *from bottom, for* filled *read* fed
—381—*penult. for* Protegie's *read* Protege's
—387— 9. *for* it is not therefore furprifing *read* is it not therefore furprifing
12. *for* fort. *read* fort ?
—412—*penult. dele* here
—416—*penult. dele* into

VOL.

ERRATA.

VOL. II.

Page 61 line 1. for la Marchionefe read la Marchefe.
—— 78 Note. for ifolée read lonely
——122——7. from bottom, for agrees to read equale
————5. for exactly parallel with read a duplicate of
————5. for coffre read coffer
——134——4. dele is
————5. dele is
——183——4. for five pofts read fix pofts.
——197——6. for appellation (as in France) to every, read appellation in France of every
——236——7. from bottom, dele the
——255——7. from bottom, for painted purple read painted of a purple colour
——256——penult. dele grains
——259——8. from bottom, for Licinium, Fauftinum, Vatium, read Licinius, Fauftinus, Vatius
——264——7. for in read of
——269——13. for fardonyfe read fardonyx
——352——5. for it is fo filled up with earth, which prevents your penetrating it farther than about twenty paces with eafe, read and is fo filled up with earth, as to prevent your penetrating farther than about twenty paces without difficulty.
——415——11. from bottom, for Carpegni read Carpegnia

VOL. III.

—— 89——8. for merit read merits
——252——3. from bottom, for relic read relics